COMING
OF AGE
IN THE
WAR ON
TERROR

RANDA ABDEL-FATTAH is a well-known writer and scholar who is currently a postdoctoral research fellow in the Department of Sociology at Macquarie University, Sydney. Her books include *Islamophobia and Everyday Multiculturalism* and she serves on the editorial boards of *Journal of the Contemporary Study of Islam* and *Continuum: Journal of Media & Cultural Studies*.

Randa is also a prominent Palestinian and anti-racism advocate, and the multi-award-winning author of 11 novels published in over 20 countries. She is co-editor of the anthology *Arab, Australian, Other* and is currently adapting her bestselling novel *Does My Head Look Big in This?* into a feature film.

COMING OF AGE IN THE WAR ON TERROR

RANDA ABDEL-FATTAH

NEWSOUTH

A NewSouth book

Published by
NewSouth Publishing
University of New South Wales Press Ltd
University of New South Wales
Sydney NSW 2052
AUSTRALIA
newsouthpublishing.com

© Randa Abdel-Fattah 2021
First published 2021

10 9 8 7 6 5 4 3 2 1

A catalogue record for this
book is available from the
National Library of Australia

ISBN   9781742236865 (paperback)
          9781742244938 (ebook)
          9781742249476 (ePDF)

Internal design Josephine Pajor-Markus
Cover design Design by Committee
Printer Griffin Press

Some names have been changed to protect the privacy of individuals.

This book is printed on paper using fibre supplied from plantation or
sustainably managed forests.

CONTENTS

TRACING RACE

How did this terrorist stay in the shadows,
hiding among us in plain sight?

—*Prime Minister Scott Morrison*

It was balmy winter weather during the Queen's Birthday long weekend in 2019. We were spending the public holiday in a popular seaside town on the New South Wales Central Coast. My sister-in-law, a veiled woman, went to the small fair set up in the waterfront area to buy showbags for her children. When she returned, she told me that as she had made her purchase, the vendor had leaned in close to her and quipped: 'I'll have the Lebs back any day'.

My sister-in-law wasn't sure what he meant but had instinctively corrected him: 'I'm Palestinian'.

The vendor had motioned to her hijab. 'I mean *you guys*. You guys come here, and you spend; you're generous with your kids. The Indians and Asians are tight-arses.'

Later that day, as we were walking through the fairground, my sister-in-law pointed out the vendor to me. He looked about as quintessentially 'Aussie battler' as you could get. I took a closer look as we walked past and recognised him as one of the people I'd

1

interviewed six years prior, when I'd been conducting my doctoral fieldwork in the town. My interviews with residents explored their feelings about the demographic shift that occurred in the town during peak season. A shift from an unmistakably Anglo-majority population to multicultural – mainly Western Sydney and obviously Lebanese Muslim – crowds. The vendor's words had been a familiar refrain from the people I'd spoken to back in 2013: 'At least the Lebanese Muslims spend money, the Lebanese Christians don't. So that's a good thing at least.' Others had more strident views: 'It feels different in those periods. Like you're being taken over by the wogs from Western Sydney'; 'The Arab race. It's a different race to the Anglo race. Islam's different.' 'I say shoot the bloody lot of them! Drop a bomb on Beirut and another one in Iraq! There's your war on terror done.'

When I'd interviewed the vendor, 'Paul', he'd said:

> The Lebs are family people and they spend on their families which is good for us. We put up with them because they're good for tourism. It feels like a takeover in those months, they take up a lot of space. But the majority are okay. It's only a minority who are bad and, like, the terrorists you see on the news.

'Race', critical race scholar David Theo Goldberg argues, has the 'conceptual capacity to morph in meaning and significance in response to prevailing social and economic conditions'. It's for this reason that Paul's words to my sister-in-law didn't shock me. On the contrary, I was both repelled and somewhat impressed. Impressed again by racism's shameless, chameleon-like capacity to 'morph' and adapt whenever it sets its gaze on a new object of resentment. In one equal-opportunity racist moment, all brown bodies were collapsed as undesirable, under the label 'wog'. In another moment, Muslims fluctuated between 'Leb' and 'Arab', and 'the Arab race' became 'Islam'. Muslims were 'okay' or 'terrorists'. And now? Now, 'you guys' (a mish-mash of Muslim, 'Leb', Palestinian, Western Sydney, the Middle East ...?) were acceptable, while 'Indians' and 'Asians' were not.

Paul's words reminded me of the slogans and signs that marked the Cronulla race riots in Sydney in 2005. If one were to momentarily forget the deadly intent and terror they unleashed on a minority community, one can almost admire racism's remarkable shape-shifting talents. The chants happily subsumed religion, culture and ethnicity into one amorphous target: 'Fuck the wogs', 'Fuck off, Lebs', 'Get Lebs off the beach', 'Kill the Leb'. There were T-shirts with offensive slogans about Lebs, wogs, Allah and Prophet Mohammed. Slogans painted on people's bare backs: 'We grew here, you flew here'; 'If you don't love it, leave it'; 'Ethnic cleansing unit'. To add to the confusion about whom the rioters were targeting, two Bangladeshi men and an Afghan man were attacked because 'Leb' was also a signal for any person of colour. Like the rioters at Cronulla, Paul was simply availing himself of a whatever-synonym-turns-you-on smorgasbord of inspiration for racism's 'Aussie Aussie Aussie, oi oi oi' fantasy.

In his book *Is Racism an Environmental Threat?* anthropologist Ghassan Hage writes about racism's fluidity and how racists happily move from one vague form of racism to another with little care for logical contradictions or inconsistencies. But he goes further to criticise the tendency for anti-racist academics to take these vague statements seriously, spending time judging them on terms racists could not care less about. As somebody involved in anti-racism activism, I return to Hage's analysis often, and it came to my mind as I was processing the vendor's words. Hage writes that racists have always managed to be exceptionally efficient *specifically by being vague.*

Nobody encapsulates how efficiently and shamelessly all-over-the-place racism can be better than Australian politician Pauline Hanson. When she first entered Australia's political space in 1996, leading her new party One Nation, she rallied against 'Aboriginals, multiculturalists and Asians'. I remember Hanson's emergence vividly. I was a 19-year-old Melbourne University Arts/Law student when I was called on a few weeks from the 1998 federal election to stand as a candidate for the newly formed party Unity – Say No to Hanson. Back then I was a Muslim defending Indigenous people and 'Asians'. In 2016, Hanson opportunistically reinvented herself on a platform that switched to Australia being 'in danger of being swamped by Muslims', not, as she had campaigned in 1996, 'Asians'. Now 'Asians' and Indigenous people were defending us.

It's the vagueness, the unabashedly scattered quality to how racism is expressed and practised in everyday life that makes the fight so exhausting. The terms on which you, as a minority in a settler-colonial multicultural society, are judged, included, excluded and negotiated keep changing. You are instrumentalised – tolerated as being good for business in a seaside town is really just a cruder form of Australia's national immigration policy, which celebrates or punishes migrants in relation to their economic value. You are pitted against other 'multicultural minorities' in a hierarchy of good and bad people of colour – here, the Muslims/Lebs are preferred to 'Indians' and 'Asians'.

What endures, no matter how casual, crude, vague or deadly the racism expressed can be, is this one fact: race is never one experience, one policy, one media headline, one deprivation. What enables an Anglo showbag vendor to lean into a power dynamic that empowers him to casually tolerate, casually insult, casually racialise entire communities is not a question about Paul as an individual; his personality or psychology is irrelevant. It's the cumulative history behind this power dynamic that matters. The weight of words, policies, media headlines, repeated and sustained political rhetoric, ahistorical debates, laws and institutions have produced a deeply ingrained identity among White* Australia of playing owner and host of the nation space. Of constructing people into categories of good and bad, less equal and more equal. That this nation space has been created on stolen land makes this posture of entitlement even more insidious.

When I returned to Sydney, I looked up the transcript of my interview with Paul and the notes I'd made at the time. One statement Paul made stood out for me: 'you just notice the Muslims more'.

To notice, and to be noticed, is deeply political.

To be ignored, and to therefore be enabled, is equally political. And dangerous.

Within days of the live-streamed massacre of 51 Muslim worshippers in New Zealand by 28-year-old Australian Brenton Tarrant in March 2019 came a spate of articles and interviews by politicians, white commentators, journalists and academics suddenly concerned about 'far-right extremists'. Some of these commentators had built careers on marginalising and gaslighting those people of colour and Muslims speaking up about the threat posed by the mainstreaming of White supremacist voices and movements. In fact, just days before the attack, the Australian government succumbed to pressure from conservative members of parliament, media commentators and the former human rights commissioner

---

* In this book, I capitalise White whenever I am referring to Whiteness as a political position and identity.

5

Tim Wilson and revoked its initial decision to block a visa to British far-right, Islamophobic provocateur Milo Yiannopoulos. It was only after the Christchurch attack, and Yiannopoulos's social media comments describing Islam as a 'barbaric and 'alien' religion, that the government reinstated its initial decision and banned him from entering the country.

Some of Australia's 'fringe' politicians, such as former independent senator Fraser Anning, who had the year before stood up in the federal Senate and called for a 'Final Solution' to the 'problem' of Muslim immigration, blamed the attack on New Zealand's 'immigration program which allowed Muslim fanatics to migrate to New Zealand in the first place'. Anning was swiftly and widely condemned, and the Australian Senate subsequently passed a motion of censure against him. This was the same Senate that, in October 2018, had *almost* passed a motion (28 votes to 31) put forward by Senator Pauline Hanson that 'it's OK to be white' – a bill initially supported by the ruling Liberal–National coalition and several senior ministers, including a former federal Assistant Minister for Multicultural Affairs, who had just the year before spoken at a Ramadan community iftar in Sydney.

Then came the tortured exercises of public soul-searching by institutions and public figures debating whether Australia is racist and whether far-right extremism in Australia is on the rise. Among these public discussions was a proposed debate, organised before the Christchurch massacre, to the topic 'Does Australia still have a problem with racism?' The debate was to be between Tim Soutphommasane, an Asian-Australian academic and previous Race Discrimination Commissioner for Australia whose parents fled Laos as refugees, and Tom Switzer, a White political adviser and executive director of the Centre for Independent Studies. An open letter to La Trobe University signed by approximately 170 academics called out the insensitive and unethical premise of approaching racism in Australia 'as an idea, a proposition, or a concept to be debated' and requested that the debate be cancelled or reframed as a dialogue on the nature of racism and anti-racist strategies, with participants to include Indigenous and Muslim speakers.

La Trobe University therefore changed the topic to the still-flawed 'Has racism in contemporary Australia entered the political mainstream?' and invited one of Australia's leading public intellectuals, Indigenous academic Chelsea Bond, and a Muslim woman activist, Tasneem Chopra. As reported by social-media platform IndigenousX, Bond delivered a 'masterclass' critique of the entire debate as 'fundamentally flawed because it's premised on the idea that racism is an artefact of a bygone era and as something that is external to Australian political life. Australian history has more than a racial dimension. Race has been foundational to this country, it arrived on the ships in 1788.'

To treat race in Australia as a question to be *debated* is to disavow and disappear Indigenous sovereignty. That is the only way the public conversation can remain fixated on the false idea that White supremacy is an ugly, violent anomaly to Australia's 'we are better than that' attitude. As Indigenous professor Aileen Moreton-Robinson argues, race is the organising grammar of Australian society, rooted in patriarchal White sovereignty, in a politics of White anxiety over dispossession shaped by a refusal of Indigenous sovereignty.

This patriarchal White sovereignty that refuses Indigenous sovereignty shaped the logic of a young white man who carried out a murderous rampage against Muslims in Australia's settler-colony neighbour on the basis of his anxiety over 'invasion'. When, in his manifesto, Tarrant described immigrants as invaders in the midst of a 'White genocide', and referred to Muslims as 'the most despised group of invaders in the West', his anxiety over genocide, over dispossession, was a projection of his fears of white people being attacked and killed in the same way that they have (and still do) attacked and killed Indigenous populations and brown people globally in the war on terror. In the words of Moreton-Robinson: 'The unfinished business of Indigenous sovereignty continues to psychically disturb patriarchal white sovereignty'.

One notable shift occurred in public conversations around Christchurch. After years of the war on terror systematically constructing terrorist as a signifier for 'Muslim' only, there was now, among some politicians and media elites, a self-congratulatory pronouncement that Tarrant was a terrorist. And yet, the label 'terrorism', offered now, in fact served to shield the state from its role in making such violence possible. In seeking to relegate Tarrant to the lone wolf, deviant, 'not one of us' margins, White Australia was denying its past and present violence, which has intensified in (and been justified by) the global war on terror.

On the afternoon of the attack, I mingled with other parents at school pick-up time as we waited for the bell to ring. We were extremely distressed. Our children were attending an Islamic school and our fears about it being a target were now even more heightened. There was a weird sense of déjà vu for me. I attended an Islamic school in Melbourne in the 1990s and remember well how the Gulf War spilt into our school: graffiti on the walls and school bus – 'terrorists', 'Saddam'; a bloodied pig's head thrown in the office window; an arson attack.

Not one Muslim I spoke to in that school carpark was surprised by what had happened in Christchurch. After almost 20 years of the global 'war on terror', the shock and horror was not, *How could this happen?* but, rather, *We knew this was coming.*

We weren't surprised because when Australia became a member of the Coalition of the Willing in the US-led global war on terror, it was signing up to extend the Western empire through

US foreign policy in Afghanistan and the Middle East. And true to imperial form, that meant a war prosecuted on two fronts, the global and the domestic. Moreton-Robinson explains Australia's binding itself to the US, and enacting its particular anxiety over borders and security, as once more reinforcing the existence, protection and maintenance of patriarchal White sovereignty tied to the unfinished business of Indigenous sovereignty.

We also weren't surprised because to understand violent White supremacy on the domestic front means acknowledging that such violence is business as usual for Australia, not an aberration: martial law in the Northern Territory Intervention, Indigenous deaths in custody, the carceral system that imprisons black bodies at home and imprisons and tortures brown bodies in offshore detention centres.

Finally, we weren't surprised because to understand violent White supremacy on the domestic front – killing Muslims – means understanding how violent state policy on the global front – killing Muslims – has emboldened those domestic White supremacists. Put another way, a 28-year-old White Australian male has grown up watching the decimation of Iraq and Afghanistan, proxy wars in Yemen, Syria and Libya, drone warfare against Afghans and Pakistanis, the massacres of Palestinians in Gaza with the support and blessing of Western, including Australian, governments. He has grown up witnessing Guantanamo Bay, Abu Ghraib and Bagram, Australia's complicity in torture by rendition, and the punishment and demonisation of refugees fleeing countries destroyed by wars we participate in. He has grown up witnessing Australian military exports to states accused of war crimes in Yemen (such as Saudi Arabia and the United Arab Emirates), and Australia providing military cooperation and training to the Myanmar military, accused of ethnic cleansing of Rohingya.

White Australia has largely ignored the slaughter of Muslims around the world in the name of the war on terror, because it has always been desensitised to violence against its Indigenous population. White supremacists at home see that wilful disregard as a permission slip for dealing with the 'enemy within'.

The idea that the 'enemy within' is the floating signifier for 'Muslim' has been created by millions of dollars of federal government funding since the mid-2000s mainly targeting Muslim communities, years of law reform, political discourse, policy frameworks, policing practices, media rhetoric and community partnerships, which have all normalised the perception that Muslims are a suspect community and the natural targets of counter-terrorism's gaze and practice. Yet after all these years, following Christchurch, questions were suddenly being asked, including by Australia's Prime Minister, Scott Morrison: 'How did this terrorist stay in the shadows, hiding among us in plain sight?'

Morrison probably didn't realise how incisive his question was. He had effectively defined Whiteness as ideology, structure and resource. Whiteness has always hidden in plain sight, rendered invisible because it's everywhere, a taken-for-granted universal. Whiteness is what stole, cleared, prepared and secured the land over which Australia was then built. Whiteness was poured into the concrete slab. It erected the frames and walls. It's in every nook and cranny of the running of this nation. To say that Whiteness is invisible is not to name Whiteness, but to name what Whiteness does. It actively works to conceal itself. Tarrant was able to 'hide in plain sight' because White Australia does not see itself; it does not see or acknowledge its violence. As 'national security' in Western nations has remained fixated on violent imperial policies against Muslim-majority nations on the one hand, and Muslim minority populations at home on the other, the far-right community, especially in the online frontier, has worked steadily and unimpeded to mainstream White nationalist ideologies.

In his speech, Morrison went on to ask: 'What laws need to change, what additional actions and precautions need to be taken?' A true reckoning with the organising grammar of patriarchal White sovereignty in this nation, by facing up to our settler-colonial origins and the state violence that continues unabated within our borders, outside our borders and against other nations' borders, would be a good place to start.

But if I must start somewhere, I might as well start with 9/11. To be more precise, sitting in a packed theatre in Toronto, Canada, in 2018, beside my 12-year-old daughter watching a musical, *Come from Away*. Based on the true story of the thousands of passengers stranded in Canadian towns on diverted planes on 11 September 2001, the production juxtaposes the horror of the attacks with the everyday lives of the disoriented and terrified passengers, and the residents of a town tasked with hosting them. In this way, 9/11 becomes the tragic backdrop to an otherwise uproarious, exuberant musical, which approaches themes around racism, homophobia and Islamophobia from multiple perspectives. My aunt had purchased the tickets for us, and I was not sure what to expect. As the scenes built up to news of the first attack, a wave of unexpected emotion came over me. Everybody around me was laughing at the lyrics, offering deafening rounds of applause and enthusiastic cheers at the end of each big scene. My body was tense, my throat closing up. When a Muslim passenger, 'Ali', emerged on the stage, I let out a quiet sob. I was mortified. My daughter didn't notice as I tried to cover up the tears now flowing down my face, coughing and blowing my nose under cover of the applause. For the entire first act, I was on edge, fighting back tears, trying to ignore my quickening heart rate and sweaty palms. I was utterly confused. After almost 20 years of the war on terror, it had taken a rollicking, upbeat musical about 9/11 to trigger a torrent of pent-up emotions.

I hesitate to mark 9/11 as the beginning of a new epoch. Race, Islamophobia, terrorism didn't start on 11 September 2001. Anybody who thinks that has not been paying attention to history. To privilege 9/11 in an analysis of race and Islamophobia is to erase the experiences of black and brown Muslims, who have *always* been 'visible' in a White society.

Further, to write a book about the war on terror is not to freeze my analysis into two decades. The global war on terror may have begun on 11 September 2001, ushering in a new 'crisis' for which Muslims were collectively held responsible, but its Islamophobic logics, intellectual justifications, racial blueprints and precedents borrow from a world-historical repertoire of key events, practices and racial thinking. From the crusades, to the 1492 expulsion of Arab Muslims from Andalucía, to the kidnapping and enslavement of Africans in the Americas, to the colonisation of Africa and Asia, to the attempts to crush anti-colonial resistance movements in the 18th to 20th centuries, to state surveillance and security structures implemented against Iranian, Palestinian and Libyan populations in the 1980s, to backlashes against state policies of multiculturalism, to wars in the Middle East, to the global war on terror. Referencing this historical trajectory feels like a bit of a stretch and reading it probably does too. In the 'we're running out of time' soundbites of every tweet, Instagram story and Facebook post, history is yesterday, not the course of centuries.

But contained in my body's visceral reaction to a play about 9/11 was the weight of hundreds of years of history. Unpacking race, Islamophobia and the war on terror means peeling away the onion layers. One can't understand national security without understanding the origins of the nation state. One can't understand border protection without understanding imperial cartography, how nation-state borders were established. One can't understand non-state terrorism unless one understands state terrorism.

When Ali stood on that Toronto stage in front of an audience of hundreds, playing the Muslim character shunned by other passengers on the plane, I felt both validated and exposed. When he was the only passenger to be subjected to a humiliating body search, I held my breath. The moment Islamophobia was acknowledged I felt an unbearable paradox, one that follows you as a Muslim navigating a world at war on terror, indeed as a person of colour in a white man's world: you want racism to be acknowledged, but you know that as soon as it is, you are necessarily characterised as victim. The complex, relentless work of claiming agency, of denying victimhood but seeking justice, of trying to rewind beyond 2001 to address the causes and structures not symptoms, seems impossible to articulate. And I think that was why my body revolted the way it did. I was reminded of how much my life had been – and continues to be – affected by the events of 9/11.

I was 22 when the twin towers were attacked. Like many Muslims of my generation, 9/11 is a formative reference point in my political consciousness. For some, the beginning; for others, a rupture; for me, the point at which my political subjectivity escalated and intensified. For it was the first Gulf War that served as the crucible for my politicisation as a teenager. To be a Palestinian/Egyptian Muslim in the 1990s was to be 'of Middle Eastern Appearance', collapsing exotic, inferior, Saddam loyalist, incomplete citizen all under one crude misnomer. To be Palestinian in Australia pre-9/11 was to be subjected to a system of state surveillance that simply intensified and recalibrated after 9/11. In the 1990s, my father helped to run a 'Palestinian club' in Melbourne, a community organisation made up of Palestinian families who met up for picnics and weekend feasts in local community halls. One day, out of the blue, my father received a telephone call. It was an ASIO officer, requesting an interview with my father. ASIO was aware of the club. It wanted to know the club's purpose. Was it 'political'? Being Palestinian in the West has always been an accusation rather than an identity.

My father's family, denied the right to return to live in their village in occupied Palestine since 1967, were living in Kuwait when Saddam Hussein invaded it. They were forced to flee to Jordan and went from a relatively comfortable life in Kuwait to a one-bedroom apartment in the poor suburb of Zarqa. Intergenerational unemployment and poverty followed. The ongoing trauma, loss and struggle of dispossession haunts those in the Palestinian diaspora. We oscillate between different states of consciousness and being: Australian citizens (and even then contested, conditional) and dispossessed Palestinians.

After 9/11, the plot thickened. A war was explicitly waged against 'terror' – and 'terror' signalled 'Muslim' and 'Islam'. In the words of George W Bush, 'you're either with us or against us'. I was now an italicised *Muslim*.

It's easy to forget that as I and other Muslims of my generation in Western countries faced collective culpability and were propelled into a cycle of guilt-by-association, defence and forced condemnations, a new generation was being born into this world at war on terror. A generation born into a purported 'clash of civilisations' between 'Islam' and 'the West', into the global circulation of fears and moral panics about the 'Muslim Other', into unparalleled security measures around their bodies and lives.

Those babies are now coming of age.

They are coming of age bookmarked between US President Barack Obama and President Donald Trump. That's not to imply a comparison between 'good' and 'bad', between a 'post-racial' society and a racial one. To come of age in the war on terror is to have grown up in a world where the triumph of America electing its first black president diverted attention from the fact that a liberal, black president expanded the war on terror with an unprecedented increase in drone-based assassination campaigns. To grow up in these times is to face the fact that Barack Obama's successor, Donald Trump, has emboldened White supremacist and Neo-Nazi movements, is ideologically committed to White supremacy as a matter of rhetoric and policy, is accused of rape and sexual misconduct by more than two dozen women, has been investigated for colluding with the Russian government, uses his Twitter feed to mock, ridicule and defame other world leaders and, since taking office, has been found to have made more than 20 000 false or misleading claims (and counting). But it's also to come of age at a time when the US Congress has its youngest ever congresswoman in Alexandria Ocasio-Cortez, or its first Muslim representatives in Ilhan Omar and Rashida Tlaib, or its first black vice president in Kamala Harris.

In Europe, those born around 9/11 are coming of age in the context of Brexit and the emergence of Britain's own version of Trump, Boris Johnson. Young people are learning about the Holocaust at school while witnessing the rising electoral success of right and far-right 'populist' parties across the region. They are coming of age witnessing the war-on-terror narrative used to render the Mediterranean Sea the 'largest graveyard in modern history', as one analyst describes it. Refugees drowned, pushed back, in the name of security and cultural purity. In Australia, they are growing up watching refugees be cruelly interned in offshore detention centres in the name of national security and deterrence, prevented from even being transferred to countries which have offered them asylum.

Muslim youth around the world, whether living under Muslim-majority despotic, totalitarian regimes or their allies in Western governments, have witnessed their leaders use the war-on-terror narrative to justify all manner of heinous crimes against humanity, from bombing and starving Yemenis, to proxy wars in Syria, to supporting China's interning more than a million Uyghur (Muslims of Turkic ethnicity) in concentration camps. Muslim leaders have leveraged the war on terror to justify their dictator-ships, brutally repress dissent under the guise of 'fighting terrorists' and defeat any gains made in the Arab Spring. Their efforts have been praised by Western leaders, including Tony Abbott when he was Australia's Prime Minister, who package such repression as an exemplar of promoting a 'reformed', 'moderate' Islam in the battle for hearts and minds in the global war on terror. In Australia, those born after 9/11 are coming of age in the context of governments, law enforcement and communities turning a systematic blind eye to the mobilisation and organisation of alt-right groups over the last two decades, and the rise of anti-Muslim, anti-immigrant and anti-refugee policies, hostility and rhetoric.

Nobody can deny that 9/11 was a watershed, but it's too easy to speak in verities about what it meant and means, particularly to the generation born after it. *Coming of Age in the War on Terror* is based on face-to-face, in-depth interviews and writing work-shops I conducted with Muslim and non-Muslim high school and university students in Sydney, Australia. I was interested in understanding how young people born around 2001 have expe-rienced a world they've only ever known to be 'at war on terror'.

For this generation there was never, as one 16-year-old non-Muslim boy I interviewed put it, 'a "pre" and "post" 9/11' difference'. For a 16-year-old Muslim boy, 'the war on terror is just everywhere, I don't know any different'.

I wanted to explore the impact of growing up in this political environment on their experiences at school – do they feel their school offers them a safe space to express themselves? Does the war on terror affect their trust relationships with their peers and teachers? Does it impact on their political consciousness, participation and expression? Various scholars have interrogated the assumption that widespread fear grips majority-Western countries. A 2017 major study by UK think-tank *Demos*, involving six European states, found the emergence of an age of anxiety and 'acute fear' among the general population. I wanted to know if this resonated with young people. Are they scared? If so, about what? And about whom? Are there differences between Muslim and non-Muslim students in this regard?

Since 2005 I've been in schools around Australia, as a guest author delivering talks about my young adult novels or running writing workshops or individual classes in specific subjects such as History, Society and Culture, or Studies of Religion. The idea for this research project was inspired by what a year 10 student, Bilal, at a school in South Western Sydney (with an Arab-majority student body) told me during an author visit in 2015: 'School used to be the one place I felt safe'. Bilal explained that he was worried that what he said about 'stuff in the Middle East' might be 'taken the wrong way'. This was in the aftermath of the murder of New South Wales (NSW) police employee Curtis Cheng by a 15-year-old boy in October 2015, a tragedy that prompted government-led 'countering violent extremism' initiatives in schools (although they were worded more euphemistically, which I'll address later on).

Bilal's words – 'taken the wrong way'– lingered with me. If this is how he felt, it opened up so many questions. After all, fear threads through relationships of trust (fear of your teachers' or friends' suspicions, for example), and through political participation (fear of expressing your opinion, fear of being seen as 'too angry' and so on). I was curious to understand from young people themselves what scared them; what and who made them feel safe and empowered. Most importantly, I wanted to *compare* the generational impact of the war on terror's political climate on Muslim and non-Muslim youth born into a post-9/11 world.

Ironically, in a study that sought to explore whether young people feel that school is a safe space to navigate questions of religious and political identity and expression, I didn't receive ethics approval from the NSW Department of Education to conduct my interviews and writing workshops in public schools. My ethics application was first approved by my university after a rigorous process. I was granted permission to carry out my project in private, independent and public schools, although doing so in public schools was subject to the additional approval of the Department of Education. The Department of Education rejected my ethics application on the grounds that 'the nature of the research topic, the proposed writing prompts and the comparative nature of the research objectives' posed a 'risk to the psychological and social wellbeing of participating students and their schools'.

The irony was not lost on me. Not only was I already in these same public schools, by invitation, running writing workshops with no issue of me posing any 'risk', my project was specifically about whether students feel they can freely talk about their identities, politics and experiences at their schools. I chose to conduct this research via face-to-face, in-depth, semi-structured interviews and writing workshops, because I wanted young people to have the freedom to express themselves on their own terms, without constraint, to 'name their reality' as critical race theorists advocate.

I appealed the decision, providing a copy of my writing prompts and workshop materials, as well as letters from schools in support of my project. The appeal was rejected.

I was bitterly disappointed, not least because I know so many non-Muslim researchers have been given access to research Muslim students for many years now. Taking this project into public schools was important to me, particularly given the excellent research on race and everyday multiculturalism conducted in schools, which I sought to build on. For example, recent research by Australian academic Christina Ho explored self-segregation and gentrification in Sydney's public and selective school systems. Ho found that everyday multiculturalism is 'unevenly distributed' in Sydney's schools, with cultural diversity varying dramatically between public and independent high schools. According to Ho's study, in all regions of Sydney, public schools have the highest levels of cultural diversity, and independent schools the lowest, with Catholic schools falling in between. Some elite private schools are, Ho argues, 'nothing less than pockets of cultural and socioeconomic exclusivity', and there is evidence to suggest white and middle-class flight from comprehensive public schools in the most disadvantaged suburbs in Sydney. It's essential that we learn more about how racial and class demographics in schools, intersecting with the specific context of coming of age in this political climate, affect students' experiences of their schools as 'safe spaces' to explore their identities.

Despite being denied the opportunity to explore this question in public schools, I was still able to access public school students through word of mouth, interviewing students outside of school. I also conducted a writing workshop at a public library in Blacktown in Greater Western Sydney. The workshop was attended by students from a mix of surrounding public and Catholic schools.

The names of students I interviewed, the schools they attended and the teachers they mentioned have been changed to protect their anonymity. I attended two co-educational Islamic schools, which fall under the independent school system. The first, which I've called 'Inner West Islamic School', is located in Strathfield in the inner west of Sydney, approximately 12 kilometres from the CBD, where the most common ancestries are Chinese, Indian, Korean, English and Australian. Almost every student I interviewed at the Inner West Islamic School lived *outside* of Strathfield, travelling to school from suburbs such as Lakemba, Greenacre, Punchbowl, Auburn – all suburbs with sizable Muslim populations.

The second Islamic school I attended is located in the Hills Shire, and I've called this school 'Hills Islamic School'. I also attended a nearby private school in the Hills Shire, which I've called 'Grammar College'. The Hills Shire is located in North Western Sydney, about 30 kilometres from the CBD. The three largest ancestries in the Hills Shire are English, Australian and Chinese, with the dominant single language spoken at home being English (65.2 per cent of the population, compared with 58.4 per cent for Greater Sydney), and the largest religious group being Western (Roman) Catholic. Unlike the rest of Western Sydney, Muslims are a minority within a minority in the Hills Shire, with the Muslim population at around 2.6 per cent compared with 5.3 per cent in Greater Sydney. It's important to understand the class and race variations of suburbs within 'Western Sydney', especially as they have significant impacts on the responses of students I interviewed.

Western Sydney contains about 9 per cent of Australia's population, and 44 per cent of Sydney's population. It has the largest single Indigenous community in the country and is the most multicultural region in Australia, with 35 per cent of its population born overseas and 60 per cent of new immigrants to Australia settling in the region, making it the epicentre of Australian migration. Over the past decade, 50 per cent of these arrivals were from Iraq and Sudan. Western Sydney is an overall lower income area than the rest of Sydney, but advantage and disadvantage vary significantly across the region. This is a region that covers both the suburb of Fairfield, which has Sydney's highest rate of unemployment – almost double the Sydney average – and the Hills Shire, where the median weekly income for residents is approximately 150 per cent higher than the national average. The Hills Shire is also the home of students I interviewed at Hills Islamic School and Grammar College.

In my interviews with Muslim students, it became fairly obvious to me that Muslim youth don't rate being 'groomed by ISIS' as a concern in their lives. Abdu (17), who attends a public school in South Western Sydney with a sizable Muslim population, told me:

> Forefront of our minds is whether we're going to submit our assignments on time or not. Whether or not we can afford housing … The guys at my school are interested in soccer, wrestling, boxing, gaming. There was this boxing match between two Youtubers and it's all they've been talking about today. The latest birthday party, or who's going out with who. That's what we care about.

But no matter how many Muslim students spoke to me about their typically adolescent hobbies and interests, all were affected in some degree by the racialising impact of the war on terror and moral panics around their 'radicalisation'. Fadi, a 17-year-old devout Muslim boy at Inner West Islamic School, put it this way: 'I'm not afraid of terrorism. I'm afraid of being *accused* of being a terrorist.'

Almost all the non-Muslim students I interviewed and worked with in writing workshops said that they were largely unaffected in any direct way by the war on terror. Charlotte, (17, Anglo-Australian, Grammar College), said: 'It's never personally impacted my family at all, so it's just a background thing that we feel sorry for, but there's no real immediate impact on us'. Many of the non-Muslim students admitted that when they thought of a 'terrorist', the first image that 'popped into their head' (more than one student used this phrase) was 'a Muslim'.

There was a common-sense, taken-for-granted quality to the ideas, thoughts and feelings relayed to me about radicalisation and terrorism by both Muslim and non-Muslim students. For a 17-year-old Muslim student to understand how he is positioned in the wider cultural imagination as potentially 'accused' is devastating, but not surprising. When the image of a Muslim 'pops' into non-Muslim students' heads if they think of a terrorist, we need to ask what work has been done to allow this to happen. 'Popping in' suggests a brief visit, the image arriving uninvited, because it's familiar. Yet the image of the Muslim terrorist 'popping in', in fact, suggests it's anything but a brief association; it means that on countless earlier occasions it arrived unnoticed, lingering a little longer each time, building up its familiarity.

It's not possible to point to any one policy document, political speech, counter-terrorism raid or media headline and say *that* is when the familiarity was born, *that* is when a racialised image assumed the freedom to pop in, *that* is when a teenage boy knew his existence was an accusation, *that* is when a girl realised that her presence unsettled others. This book is not a chronology of political flashpoints in the years since 9/11. Rather, it's an attempt to unpack the social history, the structure and assemblage of common-sense ideas, myths, values, beliefs, maxims and assumptions about the war on terror that the students I interviewed have grown into and with. I am interested in the *practical ideologies*, to borrow from the late cultural-studies scholar Stuart Hall, the 'level at which ideologies become real, enter experience, shape behavior, alter conduct, structure our perception of the world – the level of ideas as a "material force"' in the lives of the young people I have interviewed.

The analytical frame I use in this book is very much influenced by the work of Australian legal scholar Victoria Sentas in her exceptional book *Traces of Terror*. Arguing that counterterrorism is an ideological system that reproduces race as social power, Sentas traces processes of racialisation and race in counterterrorism law and policing practices. She does so by drawing on critical race theory and Italian Marxist philosopher and politician Antonio Gramsci's concepts of hegemony and common sense, 'as an everyday practical trace of ideology' which is 'observable in the form of its fragments'. I found Sentas's approach incredibly powerful, and it inspired me to think about how these 'fragments', 'traces' and 'practical ideologies' touch young people's lives.

And so, in the first part of the book, I introduce you to some of the young people I met – the issues that matter to them, the questions that engage them, their fears, dreams and hopes. The practical ideologies of the war on terror – and more – are apparent in the young people's voices and speak to the particular context in which they have come of age.

I then go on to consider why *these* issues matter to the young people I interviewed. What work has been done by the media, politicians, policymakers to shape these students' particular politics? To do this means unpacking the intellectual, theorised framework that informs the practical ideologies in young people's lives. I therefore offer a close and critical reading of certain 'countering violent extremism' policies, political practices and moments of media coverage, to set up my analysis, in the third and fourth parts of the book, of how such 'ideological work' leaves its traces on students as they come of age.

In the war on terror, ideology is, as Gramsci wrote, 'an infinity of traces gathered together without the advantage of an inventory'. Gramsci went on to say that it's 'imperative at the outset to compile such an inventory'. This book is therefore my attempt to compile an inventory of the traces – the fragments of race and Islamophobia – left on Muslim and non-Muslim youth growing up in a post-9/11 world.

CHAPTER 1

THIS IS AUSTRALIA

This is Australia.
Low key racist.
Should be a republic.
Political memes
Great Barrier Reef is basically dead.

—*Sara (16, Anglo-Australian, Christian)*

I was scrolling my Twitter feed, sitting in my car in the carpark of a co-ed Islamic school in North Western Sydney where I was soon to conduct a writing workshop. 'This is America', rapper Childish Gambino's new video clip, had dropped. I opened the link, watched the music video. It was electrifying. I must have watched it five or six times on loop.

It gave me an idea.

I started the workshop with the year 11 students by showing them the clip. None of them had seen it yet. I watched them watch the clip. Every single one of the 15 students didn't look away from the screen. When the clip finished, I wrote the title of the song, 'This is America', on the whiteboard. I invited the class to share their thoughts about the clip. What followed was a discussion about the power of point of view in storytelling, in narrating histories. We spoke about how nation, safety, security, identity were experienced differently. We considered why the artist hadn't qualified the song title with, say, 'This is *my* America'. Was this just a black man's interpretation and experience, or was he making a statement, exposing what America really is? I then wrote 'This is Australia' on the board and asked the students to write their own song lyrics. What did Australia mean to them? How did they imagine it, experience it? What were its enduring myths and narratives? What did they love about Australia? What did they reject and want to change? How would their own class, gender, race, religious 'identities' inform their song lyrics?

Before I asked students to write their poems, I asked them if they thought of themselves as 'political' and what they understood the 'political' to mean. These were questions I also asked in one-to-one interviews. The vast majority of students – Muslim and non-Muslim – didn't consider themselves 'political'. Politics was commonly understood as 'parliament', 'voting', 'Labor and Liberal', 'politicians'. Their answers accorded with research showing that young people tend to narrow the domain of citizenship and politics to formal political and electoral processes, rather than issues that concern their everyday lives.

And yet, as is instantly obvious in the poems below (and almost all the poems written throughout the course of the project), these 'not political' young people were, in fact, deeply invested in the political.

The poems I've selected to publish here were written by students across Sydney: from Grammar College, Inner West Islamic School, Hills Islamic School and students from the various Catholic and public schools who attended the writing workshop at a library in Blacktown. The poems drew on particular events that were happening at the time. I visited one school just after the Liberal Party's leadership spill, which saw Scott Morrison replace Malcolm Turnbull as Prime Minister of Australia. Former

Prime Minister Tony Abbott had also recently been appointed as the government's Minister for Indigenous Affairs, and the same-sex marriage plebiscite had just passed. I visited another school at the time that the introduction of a ban on plastic bags in one of Australia's largest supermarket chains, Coles, resulted in a public backlash and decision by Coles to delay the ban.

One of my tasks as a researcher is to identify patterns and themes and group data into those themes. What was so delightful about so many of the poems was that they refused categorisation. There was rarely a 'one-issue' poem.

> This is Australia
> A land of the flannies and thongs
> We're getting too many 'chongs'
> But that's not racist because – 'Asian friends'
> Sinking tinnies every day
> Keeping refugees away
> This is Australia
> White dude looks after Indigenous affairs
> As if he fucking cares.
>
> —*Nate (17, Anglo-Australian, no religion)*

> This is Australia.
> We're not really nice to Aboriginals
> The Queen is our God
> We really enjoy alcohol.
> Unjustifiably patriotic
> Tony Abbott ate a raw onion
>
> —*Nick (17, Anglo-Australian, Anglican)*

This is Australia.
Lots of guns in my area.
I love it, snags.
Our politicians put us in tags.
It forms a part of my identity,
But in today's age no one connects with me.
We call it the land under the heavens,
But we didn't give Aboriginals their rights to 1967.
This is Australia,
Don't catch you slipping up,
Don't catch you slipping up.
See the lies they're whipping up.
This is Australia.
No love in my area.
Inequality is now our strap.

—*Mark (17, Lebanese-Australian, agnostic)*

This is Australia.
Bunnings snags and meat pies.
Ice addicts and druggies.
Homelessness is there, but no one really cares.
Just stereotypes at the perfect Aussie.
Domestic violence is high.
Women die.
What are we doing about it?
Another hotline.
This is Australia.
Natives invaded. Yeah.
People clear the streets as the unprivileged start to sleep.
     Yeah.

Gang violence is high. Yeah
Everyone is in disguise.
This is Australia.
Healthy Harold's abandoned.
Taxes are high. Where does it fly?
30 million cut from NDIS funding to go to corporate
    companies.
Farmers are struggling.
Coles is rumbling. Plastic bag ban.
Save our turtles or die trying.
This is Australia.
Coward punches are tearing us.
Yeah.

—*Fatma (16, Lebanese-Australian, Muslim)*

This is Australia
Literally prison BLACKout
But plastic bags we be pissed about
Don't like actual change just let people shout
This is Australia
If you don't like Vegemite
You become an Aussie-lite
People think we ride kangaroos
Our national culture's based on booze

—*Warda (17, Palestinian-Australian, Muslim)*

This is Australia,
home of the lucky ones.
Grew up in Parramatta,
Bogans be scared. Yeah.
This is Australia,
land of the red rock.
Trying not to be knocked
or the boys will stop you having fun
in my area, which way to Cabramatta? (Yeah, yeah.)
I'm gonna get this car. (Yeah, yeah.)
Just got a job
Parra Maccas
Got my accent
Know my place

—*Marcel (17, Lebanese-Australian, Catholic)*

This is Australia
Cities are heating up
Then they are cooling down
Rainfall for weeks on end
Then droughts follow them
This is Australia
Refugees are pushed away
Or locked up and hidden away
This is Australia
Indigenous: who are they?

—*Tia (16, Anglo-Australian, Christian)*

This is Australia.
Racism that's gone out.
Multiculturalism in the house.
It's here, just look around,
This is Australia,
It's almost summer
But the weather's weird
Because climate change action is so feared
This is Australia
Land of the Commonwealth,
Medicare for your health
Can't buy a house in Sydney with all your wealth.

—*Stephen (17, South Sudanese–Australian, Christian)*

This is Australia.
A place of suffering and loneliness.
A place of different cultures.
One ring to bind them all.
I try to fit in but I can't change.
I have to talk to myself or who will hear me?
This is Australia.
But will Australia see me?

—*Jordan (17, Chinese-Australian, Buddhist)*

Notice that justice for Indigenous people matters to young people. 'We're not really nice to Aboriginals' is part of Nick's opening, while Nate closes with a scathing dig at Tony Abbott's appointment as Minister for Indigenous Affairs ('As if he fucking cares'). 'But we didn't give Aboriginals their rights to 1967', writes Mark.

'This is Australia/Natives invaded', says Fatma, an explicit defining of Australia by its settler-colonial foundations. 'This is Australia/Literally prison BLACKout' writes Warda, offering a clever wordplay on Australia's shocking rates of incarceration of Indigenous people *and* national concealment ('BlackOut'). As for Tia, she ends her poem on climate change and refugees being locked up by asking, 'This is Australia/Indigenous: who are they?' For Tia, this is the question that everything else must be held accountable to.

These poems are also narrations of class and race. Marcel in Merrylands zooms in on his local world of Parramatta, Cabramatta. It's the local that defines young people's everyday lives. Western Sydney is where Marcel sees himself having some power: 'Bogans be scared.' He writes about his material aspirations: 'I'm gonna get this car,' on getting a job at 'Parra Maccas'. In the city of Parramatta, McDonald's is well-known as a central hangout for young people, mainly boys. There is cheekiness here – nobody's buying 'this car' on a 'Parra Maccas' income. And then this: 'Got my accent/Know my place'. This is intersectionality as lived experience, stripped bare of jargon. In six words, Marcel captures how class and race overlap to keep people in their place. Mark, from Guildford, writes, 'No love in my area./Inequality is now our strap.' Stephen, from Mount Druitt, is in high school and already thinking, 'Can't buy a house in Sydney with all your wealth.'

These poems are unsentimental meditations on the personal effects of racism too. Jordan, Chinese-Australian, experiences Australia as 'A place of suffering and loneliness'. 'A place of different cultures.' He then invokes *Lord of the Rings* when he writes, 'One ring to bind them all'. It's a powerful image that captures what Whiteness demands of and does to minorities. As we will see later on among some of the Muslim students I interviewed,

Jordan's attempts to fit in have backfired. He ends his poem by recognising Australia, waiting for Australia to recognise him.

Then there are the poems taking on the grand myths and lies Australia tells about itself.

> This is Australia.
> Pack, piss, Winnie Blues
> I'm in love with Alex
> I'm scared of microwaves
> I'm not talking to Mrs Robertson
> I'm not a white supremacist
> We don't call it shrimp. It's just a prawn.
> We don't really have culture just snakes and the barbie.
> Cash rate 1.5%
> Bunnings is a monopoly.
>
> —*Harry (17, Anglo-Australian, agnostic)*

> This is Australia.
> A good time, g'day mate
> Sticky fingers, racist banter, Pauline Hanson
> Shannon Noll was robbed in Australian Idol.
> Maccas, Woolies mud cakes, abbreviate everything
> Thongs, The Wiggles, The Irwins, White Australia,
>   not easily offended
> Slang. Pay gap. Good gun control.
> Nobody really cares about anything.
>
> —*Jacinta (16, Anglo-Australian, Christian)*

This is Australia.
Low key racist.
Should be a republic.
Political memes
Great Barrier Reef is basically dead.
Good living standards.
Excellent place to live.
Low cash rate, good education, good hospitals
Abbott ate an onion
Racist banter.

—*Sara (16, Anglo-Australian, Christian)*

This is Australia.
Refugees on islands
An apology that came so many years later

—*Lisa (17, African-Australian, Christian)*

This is Australia
This is where we live
All we want is to have fun
We don't care about anything
The only thing is about having fun

—*John (17, Anglo-Australian, atheist)*

This is Australia.
VBs, we're chugging down.
Meat pies we're giving out.
Akubras. A-K-U-B-R-A-S we wearing out.
This is Australia.
Gay people married now.
Lots of cultures we seeing around
but need water for the dry ground.

—*Natalie (17, Anglo-Australian, agnostic)*

This is Australia.
It is a home for some
A dream for others
Impossible to reach
Impossible to appreciate.

—*Mostafa (16, Turkish-Australian, Muslim)*

This is Australia
Like all, there's good and bad, no in between
Just like every other place
Snakes, spiders, vicious animals
Every stereotype certainly exists
The seas that divide us from the rest of the world
Are the seas that divide us from communism
The seas that separate us from guns and violence
These seas, also, are places that people die trying to
    pursue freedom.

A luxury that Australians can afford.
As we watch on television
As the horror proceeds on the screen
We can turn off the television
Forget what's happened
And move on.
Because this is Australia.

    —Ahmad (17, Lebanese-Australian, Muslim)

This is Australia
People think all Muslims are the same
That we're all terrorists or girls in scarves without a
    brain
They hear it all in the news
I was born on 11 September 2002
First anniversary of 9/11
No one in my family forgets my birthday
because no one in my family forgets 9/11

    —Aisha (17, Afghan-Australian, Muslim)

This is Australia.
'For those across the sea, with boundless plains to share'
BAN THE BOATS: Australian government.

    —Sahar (15, Pakistani-Australian, Muslim)

This is Australia
home of the rich and the poor
Tourist come and go to see the various shows
Collection of people from all over the globe
They give me hope.
This is Australia.
Police in my area
They don't like what I do
I don't have a choice
'cause I've lost my job
Australia, where is my chance?

—Ray (17, Australian, Jewish)

This is Australia.
The local park is where we go.
Heavy drinking is what we know.
Cooking the snag is how we show.
But giving a shit is what we don't.

—Dan (16, Anglo-Australian, atheist)

These students are acutely aware of the stereotype of the easy-going, laid-back Aussie larrikin: 'flannies and thongs', 'A good time, g'day mate', 'Nobody really cares about anything', 'All we want is to have fun', 'We don't care about anything', 'The only thing is about having fun', 'Giving a shit is what we don't'. This idea of Australia as an easygoing people and place is juxtaposed against its underbelly of violence: 'refugees on islands', 'locked up and hidden away', '"boundless plains to share"/Ban The Boats', 'people die trying to pursue freedom'. Warm and fuzzy images of 'Bunnings snags and meat pies' are undercut by 'ice addicts and druggies'. There is contempt, too, for the apathy around homelessness, drug addiction: 'People clear the streets as the unprivileged start to sleep'. Ahmad ends his poem by defining Australia in terms of its capacity to turn away from the 'horror' we are implicated in. We have the 'luxury' of freedom but also the luxury to turn off the television, forget what's happened, move on 'because this is Australia'. When Fatma asks 'what are we doing about' domestic violence, about women dying, her sarcasm is palpable: 'Another hotline'. The casual inclusion of 'White Australia' in Jacinta's list of iconic Australian ('thongs, The Wiggles, The Irwins, White Australia, not easily offended') brilliantly captures the banal centrality of race and Whiteness in Australia.

The political is in every line of these poems, in every one of these young people's lives. When I asked students to write these poems, I framed my request in terms of my project exploring growing up in the war on terror. The only person to directly reference 9/11 was Aisha, and in the wider collection, less than a handful mentioned the war on terror directly. Even if the students didn't use the language of the 'war on terror', they were expressing their own political literacies, drawing on their own repertoires of meaning, to describe an inventory of 'wars' that have been launched since, or extended by, the war on terror. Some students questioned why their climate strikes provoke fear and hostility among the powerful and elite. Others mentioned the flows of refugees out of countries destabilised and destroyed by conflicts Australia is directly involved in. In the class discussions that flowed after the writing workshops, I opened up a conversation about how students who felt 'unaffected by the war on terror', who expressed 'distance' and felt it didn't apply to them because they 'weren't Muslim' or felt protected because of their 'class', might start to think about the connections between the war on terror as explicitly targeting 'Muslim terrorists/extremists' and the other 'wars' fought since 9/11 that have shaped the society they're growing up in, and which their poems clearly show us they are cognisant of.

EVERYDAY POLITICS

Some of the poems produced in the writing workshops focused on family life, local worlds (weekend netball or soccer games, for example), favourite foods. There were poems and narratives that were critical of 'focusing on race' and 'political correctness'. One poem contained the following lines: 'This is Australia. Where we focus always on politics and racism. I don't care.' Another poem: 'I don't really care about the war on terror. It's never affected me. I like to mind my own business and let the world sort itself out'. And another: 'We care too much about the news from the rest of the world. Why do we have to bring up the past all the time? Australia is a peaceful country. Too much political correctness. I'm not into politics.'

What does disinterest or even apathy do? Doesn't it sometimes mask power and privilege? Apathy and disinterest are still political acts that have an effect. If you enjoy White privilege, neutrality reinforces the status quo, of enjoying the material benefits of Whiteness. If you are male and 'neutral', you benefit from a patriarchal system. Disinterest and apathy are not a divestment from the status quo. They are an investment.

On the other hand, I am wary of reducing all retreats from politics among young people to a story of deficit, of what they should be or do. A political identity is performative. Anybody who's spent five minutes on Twitter can attest to that. The causes you champion, the demands and claims you make, the risks you take, the wrongs you call out, the reasons behind your visibility or withdrawal. So for some young people, disengagement can be a refusal to perform. It must be understood within the context of the performative and the costs that can come with it, like being labelled, judged, co-opted as 'a feminist', a 'nerd', 'identity politics' etc. Sometimes disinterest is a defence mechanism. Sometimes it's also reflective of how young people are trying to figure out what to care *about*. Jess (17, Anglo-Chinese-Australian) wrote: 'I think anger is productive. It's what changes society. But growing up in today's day and age I still don't know what I'm angry about. I'm still figuring it out.'

Then there are the young people I interviewed who were in their senior high school years and 'put their politics on hold' to focus on their studies. They had a firm plan in place: do well in their HSC, go to university and then go out and 'change the world'. Abear, a first-year university student of Syrian/Lebanese background, closed all her social media accounts when she started year 12 and focused on her studies. Haroon, 20, an Afghan-Australian student at the private Catholic University of Notre Dame, reduced his gaming and social media time and 'hit the books' intensively. They cared, but for the short term, they didn't have time to perform their care.

In some cases, this strategy was subtly infused with the political. Remy (16, Indian-Australian, Blacktown) told me, 'When I think about my place in the world, I think change comes in the form of power. Without me succeeding by myself, getting my degree, good job, putting myself in a position to make change, I'll be forgotten. I will have failed.' Remy was 'focused on getting the marks'. Remy considered himself interested in politics. His statement reminded me of Australian youth-studies scholar Anita Harris's work on the neoliberal model of youth citizenship. Although Harris was writing about girlhood specifically, there was here a similar theme of understanding empowerment and agency as being contingent on taking personal responsibility for one's future economic success. Those who make a difference and effect change must first accrue economic power.

Alternatively, there were those who didn't want to 'think about things in day-to-day life because it's depressing'. Emma (17, Grammar College) wasn't born in Australia, migrating to Sydney from China when she was ten years old. In our interview she recounted to me, in a quiet, affected tone, the pain of being racially abused on the street. She avoided thinking about politics for this reason. She was subject to racial abuse, so she was not switching off as a matter of privilege. She 'cared' but didn't like to 'think about that stuff'. This resonated with me. For example, when I picked up my children from school on the day of the Christchurch attack, I asked them if they had any questions, how they were feeling. My eldest, 13, and my second-eldest, 10, both promptly shut me down. They refused to talk about it. My eldest turned on the radio. They bickered over the choice of song. It was business as usual. I have to admit a part of me was horrified at what I thought was gross insensitivity. But it was also quickly apparent that they were shutting out 'politics' in order to maintain normalcy. A week later the topic came up, and my daughter snapped, 'I don't want to think about it or talk about it. It's too sad, okay?' And that was the end of it. Despite my public activism on the topic, they remained in a cocoon until a month later, when my daughter had a doctor's appointment before school. The hijab is part of her school uniform, but she refused to wear it to the doctor and decided to put it on in the school carpark when I dropped her off. I asked her why and she told me, somewhat defensively, 'I'm scared'.

Occasionally my daughter will send me a meme via Instagram, something about Islamophobia, or an empowering quote about anti-racism or Palestine. This is her way of 'doing politics':

gently cultivating her worldview, easing herself into a world that can be utterly confusing and terrifying in its violence. From the outside, she may appear disinterested or apathetic, but that kind of judgment denies young people the chance to find their voice at their own pace and in a register that makes sense and feels safe and comfortable to them.

'DOING LITTLE THINGS'

In a research project with 970 young Australians, Anita Harris found that while young people are interested in social and political issues and seek recognition from the political system, they tend to discount their own political involvement and activities. Their participatory practices 'are not oriented towards spectacular anti-state activism or cultural politics', Harris notes, 'but take the form of informal, individualised and everyday activities'. Harris also documents 'new modes of participation', new subcultural activism in virtual communities, for example. But Harris also draws our attention to 'ordinary' young people who fall between these two loose groups: 'those who are neither deeply apathetic about participation nor unconventionally engaged' and who opt for 'modest and mundane acts'. I would say most of the young people I met in my research were involved in what I think is fair to describe as quiet and informal acts of protest and activism in their everyday lives, even if they didn't see it that way, or have the language, or desire, to describe their acts as 'politics'. Recognising their efforts and political gestures matters, because their politics challenges common-sense understandings of what counts as politics and what doesn't.

Rokaya is a 21-year-old Lebanese-Australian university student. When she started at a large public school in Penrith in year 11, one of a handful of Muslim students, she experienced 'a

42

massive jump from "no politics", to being questioned about everything to do with politics and Islam'. As Rokaya began a process of self-education, she says she started 'doing little things that people saw as too much'. She put decal stickers on her laptop: a cartoon portrait of Edward Said, 'Seeking Asylum is a Human Right', 'Stop the Forced Closure of Aboriginal Communities. #SOS Black Australia. #NoConsent.' Her laptop case took 'hashtag activism' to another level. Every time she opened her laptop, her 'politics', the causes that mattered to her, were proudly on display.

On a few occasions Rokaya wore a 'Free Palestine' shirt (there was no school uniform). Some of her teachers pulled her aside and told her she couldn't wear 'slogan shirts', despite other students wearing 'cringe-worthy slogan hipster kind of shirts. You could largely brand them as non-political stuff.' In the end, it was because of her deputy principal's support that Rokaya was allowed to wear the shirt: 'She told me, "I like your shirt. Leave it."' Rokaya recalls this being one of the most validating and redeeming experiences of her high school years. To other students, however, Rokaya was seen as 'overdoing it. They said I shouldn't bring that platform to school. That politics isn't important, the Palestine thing can stay at home, what does that have to do with our school? And so on.'

Rokaya might say wearing a Free Palestine T-shirt is a 'little thing', but given the objections raised by some teachers and students, we can see how there is no measure for the political. And of course, Rokaya knows this. A T-shirt has the capacity to evoke a strong reaction; it is scaled up as 'overdoing it', 'too much'. The demand that 'the Palestine thing can stay at home' recites the kind of public/private binary that has often been used to silence those (usually women) who seek to trouble the status quo and step out of the spaces assigned to them. Further, for students (and possibly teachers) to also ask what Palestine has 'to do with our school?'

demonstrates how a T-shirt is interpreted as trespass. 'Our school' is also Rokaya's school, and yet students are policing what properly belongs in the school with reference to a majority-white student body. What matters – what stays out and what is allowed in – at school does not include what mattered to Rokaya, as a minority Muslim and Arab student. In wearing the T-shirt, Rokaya was doing so much: claiming space, establishing new norms, refusing Palestine's invisibility.

Daniella (17-year-old Greek-Australian, Castle Hill) moved from a Catholic school to Grammar College, where she experienced a political awakening. Daniella told me she's now

> extremely passionate. I started doing the 40-hour famines, started going for Relay for Life, which is raising money for cancer. Honestly, I just feel, as a citizen, we all need to take responsibility for what's going on in the world and I feel like people aren't. They're just pushing it on other people and they expect, 'Oh, the politicians will do things'. If we don't tell the politicians what we want to happen and we just keep with the majority and we say, 'Oh, we want national security', nothing's going to change.

Daniella joked with me that her teachers were encouraging her to 'go into politics', but she wants to be a speech therapist and was adamant that 'you can still make a difference without being in politics'.

Another individualised strategy adopted by students included modifying their own behaviour when it came to their news media consumption. Mark, a year 11 student at Grammar College, for example, was skeptical about certain media. 'Growing up in the internet age,' he told me, tabloidy sort of headlines are something my generation are very aware of, like the idea of clickbait. So I feel like my generation definitely does sort of pick up on how misleading those headlines and just tabloidy articles can be. There are certain news outlets which you can tell are trying to make big statements, whether for political motivations or just because it makes more money.

Mark said he 'refused' to read the tabloids. 'I try to be selective about where my news comes from.' The word refusal is important. It's intentional. There is conviction and principle behind Mark's personal decision. Mark is interested in doing something, no matter how mundane and small-scale, to effect social change.

Caley (17, Anglo-Australian, Grammar College) is on Instagram and 'likes make-up'. She uses her account 'to consume more than post' and follows various feminism accounts, because she finds them 'inspiring'. Caley told me 'the beauty community ... is starting to be, I guess, more vocalised about shade ranges in foundations and even just, I guess, supporting brands by women of colour or by Latino women. I guess just empowering the people who have previously been, I guess, oppressed in society.' In becoming aware of this, Caley tries to 'follow women of colour' online, support them 'so they have a bigger audience'. The 'follow' button here becomes a political strategy, a decision guided by Caley's values. Caley also followed accounts on 'school shootings, politics, like a mixture of things. Some of them are kind of memes. Some of them are just photos from protest rallies and the like. Some of them are ... stories and news stories of people.' She told me she did so because

with the digital world it is so easy to get consumed in, I guess, the artificial side of it so I think it's good to have something there that, I guess, makes you more aware of the world around you and actually, I guess, take advantage of, I guess, what global connection can do.

How Caley curates the accounts she follows says something about the kind of political identity she is learning to cultivate. She is trying not to be superficial, trying to bring a social conscience to her use of the internet so that it's more than just socialising or a platform for consumer culture.

Robbin (16, Filipino Catholic, Wentworthville) was skeptical about online politics, about the performativity of sympathy and solidarity. In a workshop he wrote this poignant, angry reflection:

> We're merely bandwagoners that don't put the effort into swiping and searching for news at the bottom of a melting iceberg, and only scrape the surface of irrelevant celebrity news. We only care about politics, and society's problems when it's too late to hear the warnings and they have already affected our society, or the society that WE live in because our generation today says, 'It's all about me'. Do we really care when we're posting apologetic pictures about terror and social and political trauma, or is it about merely for likes and the compliments, and validations? We continue afterwards scrolling through pictures of puppies, memes, food posts, and never speak of our social and political problems again, until it happens again.

Robbin captures so much in this short piece. The way sympathy and concern are distributed unequally; the way social problems only matter when they impact on 'the society that WE live in'; the way the act of posting on social media can serve as a masquerade, a cynical exercise in accruing 'likes'. For Robbin, there's not enough 'effort' put into learning more, paying attention in the time between crises.

ON RETHINKING WORLDVIEWS

Asking questions, rethinking assumptions and developing critical narratives were some of the most impressive moments of 'doing politics' that I encountered among some of the students.

Mark was upfront and honest about his 'leg-up' in life. 'I'm white, middle class, male'. Mark was interested in 'art and films' and was keen to pursue filmmaking. 'All art is political in some respect', he told me. After watching *Black Panther* ('brilliant movie'), he told me that he started thinking about people's reactions. 'People were saying, "This is such a big deal", but it's like, this is the first out of, like, 20 Marvel movies where they've decided to have a black director and a cast of African Americans. And it's like, is that our benchmark now?' Mark felt that 'all the debates around race and identity politics has made me think about how people can get celebrated like in tokenistic ways. It kind of shouldn't be a big deal, having a black director and cast. It should be normalised.'

In thinking through his aspirations as a filmmaker, Mark was already attuned to questions around voice, authenticity and power:

Sort of white privilege is a difficult thing to navigate because I want to like push causes that I believe in forward. But sometimes it's like, *Am I the right voice to even be saying this?* There are lots of minority directors or actors who I like who just do not get roles or projects ... I feel like [on] the corporation side of films, they can be just adding token ideas in, when we need to just normalise it so that we can have a proper representation of our society in films – because at the moment it's relegated to a lot of smaller budget stuff and smaller release stuff, which just doesn't reach an audience outside of the intended audience.

Raising these questions, thinking through the complexities of power, privilege and the arts, demonstrated remarkable maturity on Mark's part.

Caley was also quietly thinking through her White privilege when she told me:

> It's extremely unfair that some people are being oppressed because they aren't necessarily the same. And I guess that's one thing that I've always found hard to come to in being a white person is that ... I guess I feel bad for ... the idea of white supremacy and the fact that that is, I guess, my race and that there are other races and other backgrounds who are being oppressed. I guess, one thing that is motivating about our generation is that people are becoming more vocal about it.

Caley was thinking through what she knows and how she knows, questioning her Eurocentric, 'West and the Rest' education:

> I guess my understanding of terrorism would, yeah, mainly revolve around, I guess, the bombings of different kind of places. So obviously 9/11, the Pentagon, and obviously we had the more kind of recent things, so Sydney [Lindt Café] Siege and the like. But there's definitely a lot that is happening overseas that we aren't necessarily exposed to or learning about as much as we are, I guess on the Western front.

Cynicism about the war on terror and the state of public discussion was something many students brought up with me in interviews or workshop discussions. Sometimes this was expressed in sweeping and passionate terms. Other times it was a casual, offhand comment. Both were examples to me of young people paying attention, pausing through all the propaganda and political slogans to think critically about the narratives presented to them.

Take Ray (17, Australian, Jewish, North Western Sydney), who spoke to me about his expectation that 'some form of an attack' would occur in Australia in his lifetime. He believed 'we live in a world of fear, but I don't think it's necessarily a conscious fear'. I asked him what he meant. 'We carry it at the back of our minds in our day-to-day lives', he said. 'Climate change, Islam/ISIS, Donald Trump. These kinds of headlines are what us millennials see on a day-to-day basis. But it's corporations in the end. They manufacture our fears.' Ray is processing the media, making connections between the local and the global, thinking through his emotions and seeing how they fit a wider context. Others, like Fatma (16, Lebanese-Australian, Muslim) were questioning why so much attention was 'put on terrorism when you've got so many other issues that are, I guess, more pertinent in society such as domestic abuse, which as far as I'm aware is causing more deaths than terrorism is, compared to national security'. Daniella was upset about Australia's mandatory detention policies. 'Australia's meant to be, like, this simple place, multiculturalism, yet we're the ones wanting to kick everyone out'. Daniella was upfront about her politics:

> I don't think you need to be a politician to be involved in politics … I'm really passionate about domestic violence and issues surrounding that. So many women die each year. I'm

thinking, *What is Australia doing about it?* It really upsets me because all these women, they don't have anywhere to turn to. Australia should be providing support.'

Some students felt the war on terror was 'distant' to their lives, but their saying so seemed to be a principled refusal of a narrative, rather than them expressing 'distance' as a benefit of their race, gender or class privilege. Nick (16, Anglo-Australian, Grammar College), for example, told me,

> there are much, much, much bigger issues than terrorism. And it sounds really cold to say, but if you think of the amount of people that are affected by terrorism, that pales in comparison to the eight billion people that are on the planet that potentially are in danger because of global warming. I think that's a much bigger issue but governments won't focus on climate change because there are votes in keeping people scared.

Mark was also cynical:

> The war on terror just becomes a talking point. If you can make them out to be this massive scary entity, and then you just say, 'Oh, and Labor wants to let them all into the country', then that's an easy way to just manipulate people by using their fear to continue to support you because they're like, 'Oh, sure all this stuff is happening, but if I go with this other team, then they're going to let this terrifying sort of evil into the country', or whatever, that doesn't even have like a corporal form. You know?'

This is Australia – from the perspective of a specific generation. Almost twenty years since 9/11, it's crucial that we take stock of the policies, practices, debates and agendas that have defined Australia for young people born in a post-9/11 world. The constellation of fears, hopes, values and investments expressed by these young people, the very way they apprehend the world they're growing up in, has been framed by a particular culture and ideology, by sustained ideological and political work. It's to this that I now turn.

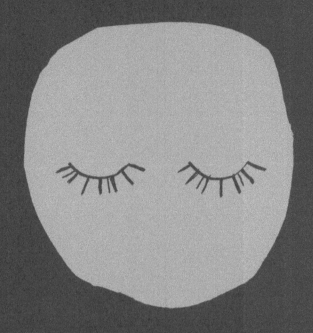

AN INVENTORY OF 'COMMON SENSE'

CHAPTER 2

CREATING A SUSPECT COMMUNITY

The reality is it's not like Muslims are lining up in their masses to become radicalised. I mean, I work with Muslims every single day, with the youth every single day, and I can tell you that the problems do not revolve around radicalisation and so, at the end of the day, what we've sort of framed is this narrative that you have young Muslim angry men – young Muslim angry men – ready to tear down Australian values and that's just not the case.

—*Sheikh Wesam Charkawi*

In May 2018, during an interfaith Ramadan iftar in Sydney, Australia's recently appointed most senior Muslim Sunni cleric, the late Mufti Sheikh Abdel Aziem Al-Afifi, outlined what he believed were the 'key' issues facing young Muslims. He cited 'the threat of extremism, the dangers surrounding social media, and drugs'. His priority was to 'do something to save our kids, and to keep them away from any bad idea, and to teach them how to be good Australians and to represent their country, and to serve our nation'. 'Our duty', he added, is 'to work hard and to stop any harm and to keep Australia safe and secure'.

Also attending the evening was Liberal senator Concetta Fierravanti-Wells, former Assistant Minister for Multicultural Affairs. (The same senator who would, later that year, cross the Senate floor to shake hands with Fraser Anning after his 'Final Solution' maiden speech.) Senator Fierravanti-Wells took the microphone and delivered the stock-standard script of politicians at Muslim community events: 'In a country like Australia where we pride ourselves on religious freedom, but with religious freedom also comes tolerance and understanding and respect within the law and of the law'. Invoking 'Australian values' and the rule of law was entirely consistent with how successive Australian governments, federal and state, have used their public engagements with Muslims as opportunities to school Muslims on what they supposedly 'lack' ('Australian values'), an instance of how the war on terror repackages the old colonial civilising mission.

SBS News covered the iftar under the headline 'New Grand Mufti hopes to save young Muslims at risk of being radicalised'. The iftar was a non-event, really. Just one of countless examples of how the idea of Muslim youth as vulnerable to extremism endures as 'common sense' knowledge in both public consciousness and the vernacular codes exchanged between Muslim community organisations and government. The figure of the vulnerable Muslim youth pops up time and time again, from moral panics around Muslim teens and children being seduced online by ISIS, to Australia's 'jihadi watch' schemes in schools. As I was reading about opposition to a proposed mosque in the Sydney suburb of South Hurstville, I came across a petition on Change.org in which a Muslim local resident supported the mosque as a space to 'reach out to youth' and teach them Islam is a religion of peace before 'the current political radicalisation narrative negatively affects them'. In another example of the humdrum way in which the war on terror is linked to Muslim youth, I learnt of a professional development program for teachers titled 'Understanding Islam and Muslim students'. The one-day course is run out of Auburn Gallipoli Mosque and endorsed by the NSW Department of Education. It advertises itself as offering teachers, senior executive and school counsellors a 'better understand[ing] of Islam in the Australian context and Muslim students in NSW schools ... help[ing] teachers to differentiate (critically evaluate) between religion and culture and more importantly be able to better understand Muslim students from diverse backgrounds'. The program's testimonials report participants feeling better equipped to understand Islamic teachings and the religious beliefs and needs of Muslim students. So far, so good. And yet, the session's agenda is listed as: 'Central teachings of Islam, culture and history; morning tea and lunch; contemporary issues: Jihad & extremism'. There is only one way to interpret this: jihad and extremism are among the most important issues linked to Australian Muslim students.

Before I asked the Muslim students I interviewed what it means to them to be a young Muslim today, I needed to first understand how and what being a young Muslim in the Western world today is *made to mean*. What quickly became apparent is that young Muslims are measured against two ideologically loaded and fluid categories: their 'Muslimness' and their 'youth'.

Scholars in the broad field of childhood and youth studies in the Western cultural context take up different positions about how to even define childhood, youth and adulthood. Politicians, researchers, policymakers, media, educators and professionals rely on different theories and conceptual frameworks. Are childhood, youth and adulthood distinct developmental stages, or, as youth scholars Anoop Nayak and Mary Jane Kehily ask, are the boundaries between them slippery? Can we talk about emerging adulthood, young adulthood? Does age matter? When politicians talk about 'young Muslim men' or 'Muslim youth' at risk of radicalisation, how do they define 'young'? Primary-school aged, early tweens, mid-teens, late teens, early twenties, mid-twenties? When a control order is applied to a 14-year-old, is it being applied to a child, a youth, a young adult or an emerging adult? How 'youth' as a category is constructed in relation to Muslims, and how it collapses a wide age range that would normally be approached with more nuance, affects law and policy. Youth researchers Johanna Wyn and Helen Cahill make the point that conceptual frameworks around youth and childhood 'create truths and naturalise particular ways of thinking' about young people, which in turn frames how 'children and young people are understood, managed, and administered'. Framing Muslim youth as at-risk fuses certain assumptions and tropes about 'Muslimness' with certain assumptions and tropes about youth. What 'truths' become naturalised influences how moral panics are imagined.

Moral panics differ across time and place. In her excellent book *The 9/11 Generation*, Sunaina Marr Maira argues that youths, straddling childhood and adulthood, are imagined as 'dangerously outside of normative social structures and always teetering on the brink of revolt', seen to threaten the status quo and arouse moral panics. Whereas childhood is generally imagined as a time of innocence, adolescence is viewed as a time of rebellion, and young people become the symbol of what is wrong with the neighbourhood or the country more generally, as scholars have put it. Young people are viewed as emerging citizens, on an 'apprenticeship for adulthood'. The 'danger' Muslim youth poses in the context of the war on terror relates to their potential radicalisation, which is linked to suspicions that they are 'improper' emerging citizens who must be guided away from 'extremism'.

Casual discourses about Muslim youth as at-risk assume the authority of 'truth', because of how 'knowledge' about Muslim youth is entangled in relations of power. Sitting between highly publicised counter-terrorism raids, arrests and trials are what French philosopher Michel Foucault called 'meticulous rituals' or the 'micro-physics of power' – the stuff that happens at the everyday level, like speeches at an iftar, or support for a mosque, or a professional development day for teachers where young Muslims are so casually spoken about as at-risk of radicalisation. A regime of truth about Muslim youth is disseminated and enacted as 'true' through cumulative, repetitive, seemingly innocuous practices between the state, wider society and some Muslim community organisations and leaders, who over time, and through their 'unwitting buying in', as Australian academic Mohamad Tabbaa writes, have created Muslim youth as the natural target of counter-radicalisation's focus and work.

If there is no evidence that the paramount threat to Muslim youth is extremism, why does such a dangerous and damaging construction of Muslim youth persist? A declaration by the most senior Muslim cleric in the country at an iftar, or a professional development day run by Muslims, lends truth and authority to this fear. But these statements must be understood in a wider context. The cumulative weight of years of policies, grants programs, and political and public debates have created unspoken 'rules' about young Muslims, constraining the way many Muslim leaders speak about them such that the discourse about Muslim youth as threatened (by terrorist recruiters/'bad ideas') ends up imagining and therefore producing the potentially threaten*ing* Muslim youth (the at-risk Muslim child/teenager/young adult).

Suspicion doesn't create an actual community. It creates an imagined one. I can't emphasise this enough. Irish researcher Marie Breen-Smyth writes that the 'suspect community' isn't just a product of law or security practices but becomes folded into a society's culture. Because it's an imagined community, the boundaries are 'permeable and shifting and in the eye of the beholder'. Sustained ideological and political work has been done to stimulate this cultural imagination when it comes to young Muslims, creating maps of meaning, ideas, feelings and social images about young Muslims as a common-sense social category of at-risk youth. So let's go back to where it all started, to trace how Muslim youth became a suspect community after 9/11.

FIGHTING THE BECOMING TERRORIST

Australia's response to the 9/11 terrorist attacks and 2002 Bali bombings has often been analysed as combining 'hard-power' and 'soft-power' measures in its war on terror. Its hard-power responses included ignoring hundreds of thousands of protesters in Australia to join the US-led military campaign in Afghanistan and the invasion of Iraq. It also included a massive increase in funding and powers to intelligence, security and law enforcement agencies, and the introduction of an unprecedented wave of new counter-terrorism laws. Before 2002, terrorism was not even an offence under the Commonwealth *Criminal Code*. Since 9/11, Australia has passed more counter-terrorism laws than the UK, Canada and even the US.

After the 2004 Madrid and 2005 London bombings, Australia, following the UK, focused domestic counter-terrorism policy and efforts on the threat of 'homegrown terrorism'. This marked the beginning of a soft-power approach in Western nations, the 'battle for hearts and minds', leading to the highly contested concepts of 'radicalisation' and 'violent extremism'. Counter-terrorism shifted from fighting terrorists to fighting the *becoming terrorist*.

For racialised black and brown communities, especially Muslim ones in Western countries, this shift changed everything. It's been a fight against a cultural imaginary, which means that the lines as to what counts as *terrorist* are forever changing.

In Europe, the concern with countering violent extremism (CVE) translated into various policy regimes: the UK's *Prevent* strategy introduced in 2003, and various European Union policy measures such as the *2004 EU Declaration on Combating Terrorism*, the *2004 EU Plan of Action on Combating Terrorism*, and the European Commission's Expert Group on Violent Radicalization, established in 2006. In the US context, 'preventing violent extremism' became part of counter-terrorism strategy in 2011. In 2011, Obama formally instituted counter-radicalisation as his administration's signature CVE program. According to American legal academic Khaled Beydoun, 'in five years, Obama built a counter-radicalisation infrastructure and institutionalised the presumption that radicalisation is a purely Muslim phenomenon'.

In Australia, the shift towards CVE as official policy (taking the UK model as an explicit reference point) took place in 2007, based on a model of 'community resilience', which continued the 'social cohesion' model developed by Prime Minister John Howard's government. This CVE approach was formalised in 2010 with the release of the *Counter-Terrorism White Paper (Securing Australia: Protecting our Future)* as a response to concerns of an increased home-grown threat. The focus was now counter-terrorism ideology because of the risk of 'homegrown terrorism' and the need to 'build a strong and resilient community to resist violent extremism and terrorism'. Building 'strong, resilient and cohesive communities' remains the core strategic outcome of Australia's national CVE policy regime.

Australia's *National Counter-Terrorism Plan 2017* states that the aim of CVE is to 'stop people becoming terrorists'. To stop people 'becoming terrorists' you have to work backwards, picking off who you think is *likely* to become one. There's a pre-emptive logic to the process, and that logic is a racialised one. It's the logic that explains why, for example, one of the teenage Muslim boys I interviewed, Amjad (17, South Western Sydney), told me, 'the beard, it can be seen as, you know, hey, he's extreme, especially after something big in the media … so I shave my beard, just to not be out there, you know?'

This logic of 'becoming terrorist' can explain why a Muslim imam I spoke to told me that he monitors who enters his mosque and pays special attention to males who 'look like Salafis with the big beards and thobe'. Or why an eight-year-old Sydney schoolboy, wearing his backpack across his chest, was sent to the principal's office after being accused of telling a classmate he was carrying a bomb. The boy denied saying this, and the school's investigation found no evidence that he had. These are lived experiences produced as effects of a legal and policy regime.

The war on terror waged explicitly against Muslim terrorists since 9/11 has framed CVE discourse and, as counter-radicalisation expert Anne Azza Aly notes, the 'meaning-making practice of counter-terrorism' has covered the full spectrum of Muslim bodies: offensively, in wars fought in Iraq and Afghanistan against Muslims outside our borders; defensively, in laws and policing or security operations targeting Muslim threats inside our borders; and pre-emptively, in counter-radicalisation 'soft' programs for 'the Muslim community', with a focus on Muslim youth, since this is where 'future danger' lurks.

After 9/11, Western governments were faced with the problem of how to narrow the pool of Muslims who may 'become terrorist'. As international-relations academic Nadya Ali writes in her analysis of a similar governmentality towards British Muslims, the absence of a 'homogeneous Muslim community as imagined by policy makers' meant that 'one had to be created'. No Muslim population offers a homogenous 'pool'. It's preposterous to assume Muslims can be contained into a defined 'community'. Populations are rich with diversity, fragmented on multiple lines – sectarian, ethnic, geographic, gender, generational, to take just a few. How would Western governments contain and discipline diverse and complex minority populations? UK race academics David Tyrer and Salman Sayyid eloquently describe the process of producing a contained population as 'fixing the content of the label "Muslim"'. This resonates deeply. To be, look, act, perform and practise Muslimness is never one fixed, stable identity or way of being. It's constantly in flux, dynamic, *in* practice, in context. This is why, in 2003, Western governments around the world reached back into their colonial toolboxes and did what had been tried and tested for hundreds of years: divide and conquer, classify and categorise: 'fix the content' of a colonial label. And that's how the war on terror created the latest version of 'good Muslim, bad Muslim': 'extremists' and 'moderates'.

EXTREMISTS AND MODERATES

Using humour to subvert tropes about the war on terror has been a key feature of the post-9/11 Muslim comedy scene, what US academic Zara Zimbardo refers to as the 'comic undoing of Muslim otherness'. One of my favourite early comedy sketches was on the TV program *Salam Cafe*. The skit, featuring internationally renowned Australian Muslim comedians Nazeem Hussain and Aamer Rahman, starts by introducing four 'makeover' experts in the areas of 'fashion, haircare and armoury'. They're on a mission: to help 'extremist' Hamoudeh. 'Graduating as 'the top recruit from the terrorist academy', Hamoudeh has since 'let himself go'.

Hamoudeh steps out of his front door to greet the makeover team, sporting an angry scowl and massive beard. The team get to work: '20 years ago the beard was scary', but now it's 'tacky', very 'Cold War'; the Kalashnikov is a fashion disaster; the weaponry needs downsizing. Hamoudeh emerges after his makeover clean-shaven, with a Palestinian keffiyeh tied in a fashion knot around his neck, a beret and no sign of a Kalashnikov. He's no longer an 'embarrassment to militants around the world'. Hamoudeh tells us he's now confident he can 'go out in style'. It's group-hug time as the team proudly declare: 'You're *extremely* worth it'.

The sketch cleverly played on the typical visual signifiers of an 'extremist', but also mocked the artificial and contrived project of rehabilitating and 'taming' the extremist, something that has been at the heart of CVE programs from the start. From the US$1.3 billion dollars put to 'reform' Islam by the US National Security Council in 2003, to the highly influential Rand Corporation's 2007 monograph *Building Moderate Muslim Networks*, to Australia's government-funded tertiary National Centre for Excellence in Islamic Studies, to the establishment of the Australian National Imams Council, governing Muslim populations in the war on terror has relied on promoting and grooming the 'moderate' Muslim by excising and taming the 'extremist' Muslim.

In the aftermath of 9/11, I was horrified by my religion's association with these attacks and naively bought into this extremist/moderate dichotomy. I say naively because so many of us who emerged as Muslim 'activists' at the time did so from a deep and urgent sense of religious duty to rehabilitate the image of Islam. When 9/11 happened, I was 22 years old, in my final year of an Arts/Law degree at Melbourne University and also working as the first media liaison officer at the Islamic Council of Victoria, the first such position in an Australian Muslim organisation. I had been trained to respond to Islamophobia as if Islam needed a public relations campaign to correct the widespread ignorance and misconceptions. I cut my 'Muslim activist' teeth on challenging the Islamophobia and racism that shamelessly and effortlessly saturated local and national media and Hollywood films (I remember well our local campaigns against *The Siege* (1998) and *Rules of Engagement* (2000)). My role also involved liaising between establishment media (this was pre–social media days) and Muslim community members and organisations to create counter-narratives. This was generally the activism of mythbusting, of taking a racist proposition and then offering a 'rebuttal'. A kind of, I'll raise this fact or statistic to yours, by, say, countering 'bad' Muslim examples with 'good' Muslim examples, or responding to a racist generalisation with information and statistics. The logic was badly flawed: Western society has a problem with Muslims, therefore let's prove why we're not a problem. So many of us involved in activism after 9/11 were seduced by the myth that a settler-colonial multicultural nation would 'accept' us if only people were armed with the proper definition of jihad or shariah law!

This nascent response was reactionary, certainly not strategic. With 9/11 and then the Bali bombings, hate crimes and everyday racial violence on Muslims were intensifying, and the instinctive – and presumed correct – response was disassociating the Muslim 'majority' from Muslim 'terrorists'. Defending Islam against gross interpretative theological claims was motivated by a sense of correcting the record by dispelling myths about Islam, creating distance from its terrorist adherents. Such dissent didn't adequately call out the politics of empire and imperialism underpinning the war on terror, or challenge the ideological structures of Islamophobia, especially in a settler-colonial nation, or sufficiently destabilise and refuse the racist conditions that seductively defined the 'Muslim moderate majority' as *not* terrorist, *not* extremist, *not* oppressed. This was a failure to understand that the Muslim was permitted to speak only as a disclaimer. The sense of religious duty to condemn and explain was deeply entangled with a fear that to not defend Islam would leave a void in which Islamophobia would fester. It was a flawed understanding of Islamophobia as misinformation and ignorance, which didn't see that 'extremist' and 'moderate' were not religious categories, but political ones.

These political categories have a longer history than 9/11, of course, but they emerged as authoritative distinctions in the war on terror and were explicitly coded into Australian policy documents in 2004 with the Howard government's release of two publications: *Protecting Australia Against Terrorism* (PAAT) and its *White Paper on Terrorism – Transnational Terrorism: The Threat to Australia* (White Paper). The PAAT charged 'Muslim extremist terrorism' with being the 'principal force driving transnational terrorism', asserting that such terrorism was 'inspired by an extreme and militant distortion of Islamic doctrine that opposes the values of the West and modernity'.

Here Muslim extremism was defined in terms of violence (militant), perversion (distortion of religious doctrine), and civilisational opposition. The White Paper emphasised that it used the phrase 'extremist-Muslim terrorism' to emphasise 'Muslims' deeds and actions, which can fall short of the Islamic ideal'. Thus, 'extremist-Muslim terrorism' is driven by 'extremist ideology' and 'perpetrated in the name of a Muslim extremist cause'. Its perpetrators were described as 'a radical but tiny minority of Muslims [who] have twisted Islamic teachings to further their revolutionary ideals'. The White Paper claimed that Australia's focus was not Islam but an 'extremist interpretation of Islam', 'far removed from mainstream Muslims' tolerance of other faiths' and 'flout[ing] what the overwhelming majority of Muslims accept as fundamental precepts of their religion'. The war on terror was all about a clash of values and civilisations, a contest between good and bad Muslims. At the time of the White Paper, the enemy was the fabulous tongue-twister 'transnational extremist-Muslim terrorist', rather than what was to become the new threat after 2005; namely, the 'homegrown terrorist'.

The 'radical extremist-Muslim terrorist' was juxtaposed against a majority 'peaceful and law-abiding', 'moderate and tolerant' Australian Muslim population, who were valued for making 'a significant contribution to the struggle against terrorism', contributing to Australia's 'political, economic and social life' and 'embracing opportunities to participate in a tolerant, inclusive and culturally diverse Australia'. The White Paper framed the threat of terrorism as 'a battle of ideas', engaging 'not only reason but religious faith' and set out the values threatened by 'extremist-Muslim terrorists' as 'tolerance, openness, freedom and equality'. It contained a short primer on 'Salafism', noting that while it's 'not of itself a doctrine of extremism, groups like Al Qaida draw on extremist interpretations of it'. In other words, if it looks and sounds like a Salafi, it probably is a terrorist.

What these documents did very early on was stitch up Muslims into a moderate/extremist dichotomy, so that terrorist motives could more naturally be assumed among those who were 'extreme'. Extreme was moored in opposition to legitimate, 'mainstream', depoliticised 'majority' Islamic teachings. Extremists were 'intolerant', 'not contributing to counterterrorist efforts', 'politically, economically and socially disengaged'.

This is a division and classification which endures as a hegemonic truth in the war on terror to date. In 2017, former Prime Minister Tony Abbott referred to extremists as 'Islam's "death to the infidel" strain', as 'crazy death cult' Muslims. On the other hand are 'moderate' Muslims, 'peace-loving and law-abiding Muslims', 'live and let live Muslims'.

Consider, for example, that the chief of Australia's Security and Intelligence Organisation, Duncan Lewis, came under pressure from One Nation leader Pauline Hanson in a 2017 Senate estimates hearing for rejecting her claim of a connection between terrorism and refugees. Lewis's response, widely considered authoritative given his position as the head of Australia's spy agency, was that 'people become terrorists because they adhere to a violent interpretation of Sunni Islam'. This is just one of numerous examples of the casual, offhand way terrorism has become synonymous with 'radical Sunni Islam' in public discourse.

Soon after, Liberal MP and former SAS commander Andrew Hastie appeared on the ABC's *Lateline* program to discuss Duncan Lewis's comments. He referred to a 'warped radical version' of Sunni Islam and declared it 'the primary cause and driver of modern-day terrorism'. Also appearing on *Lateline*, then Attorney-General George Brandis referred to the 'plainly ... inherent link between that extremist version of Sunni Islam, what is sometimes called the Wahhabist interpretation of Islam, which inspires ISIL and which ISIL uses to justify its violent acts'.

That so many politicians, journalists, public servants and academics feign fluency in the sectarian nuances (Sunni, Salafi, Wahhabi, etc.) that Islamic theologians spend their entire lives studying is a staggering example of the depth of their arrogance and entitlement. Not to mention the astonishing disregard for the impact of this totalising language on actual communities. The interchangeability of terrorism with 'radical Sunni Islam' hasn't assumed its common-sense status overnight. It's accumulated legitimacy since the first policy steps in the war on terror. This is how you build a language that contains Muslims into enduring categories. This is how you reinforce the social reproduction of race and mystify the deeper political and historical causes of terrorism. 'The war on terror is about politics', Uzma Jamil (and other scholars) have long argued, which 'requires an analysis of political contexts'. When the political is suppressed, a 'reformist' agenda steps in, moving into the wider project of using terrorism as a means to 'reform' Islam.

Over the course of 2017, ABC *Lateline* anchor Emma Alberici conducted several interviews on the subject of terrorism. In the May interview with Andrew Hastie, Alberici asked Hastie 'Is there something, do you think, fundamentally at the heart of Islam that creates this violent reaction?' and why he thought it was important to 'articulate the link between a religion and terrorism'. The line of questions then led to the slam dunk any Muslim watching would have sensed Alberici was trying to land: 'But what is the point of articulating that? Is it because … you want to see some sort of revolution within Islam, a kind of reformation and enlightenment?' In her interview with then Attorney-General George Brandis on the same day, Alberici insisted on drawing him 'back to the question … [of] whether you think there is some sort of an inherent link between Islam and violence'. The following month, Alberici interviewed Richard Barrett, former director of global counter-terrorism operations at the UK's MI6 and current director of the Global Strategy Network, in the aftermath of the London attacks. She asked, 'Do you think we need a broader conversation about Islam and … whether there is something inherent in the religion that promotes violence?' Barrett was quick to discern how such a question and narrative led to looking at 'Islam should reform'.

This is a stunning example of how the colonial logic of the Western civilising mission has become casually embedded in public commentary. Casual calls for a Christian-centric model of reform are made about a religion that boasts a complex and rich corpus of jurisprudence developed and contested over centuries by scholars from every part of the world. Whether it's the tabloids or our national ABC, the agenda is the same: Islam is a problem to be fixed. The distinction between 'moderate' and 'extremist' is how this fix is achieved. The extremist is the disease to be removed from the healthy core of the Muslim body. It's crucial to understand how this 'civilising' mission unfolds, not least because it clearly reveals itself among the young people I interviewed.

CVE AND POWER

It's easy to think about power as top-down, a relationship of domination and coercion. But the war on terror, especially the CVE strand of it, could never work if it relied on state coercion and repression alone. There's no state office handing out 'moderate' and 'extremist' ID cards and, anyway, how many undercover ASIO officers are you going to embed in Australia's mosques and prayer halls? How many lines in sermons are you going to scrutinise with your 'moderate' and 'extremist' highlighters?

Common-sense understandings about radicalisation, vulnerability, religiosity, race and Muslim youth are more efficiently diffused in society when Muslims are both regulated by the state, its institutions and its discourses *and* 'educated', guided and directed to monitor and regulate their own behaviour. This is what French philosopher Michel Foucault theorised through his concept of governmentality, turning our attention to how state power is internalised rather than always being imposed from outside.

Australian academic Mohamad Tabbaa, applying Foucault, writes about how, in the war on terror, Muslims are under intense pressure 'to declare that they are good, "moderate" Muslims who denounce violence and extremism'. Muslims who participate in 'clarifications, rebuttals, demystifications, condemnations and the like' have been incited to speak, provoked to 'come forward and "clarify" their truth'. He cautions Muslims to understand how power is therefore 'less … an obtrusive, crushing force, and more … an accommodating, smooth driver that directs our gaze upon a particular path, utilising us as its vehicle while convincing us all along that we are in fact resisting'. For example, an imam of a Sydney mosque told me that it's not unusual for him to receive a telephone call from an AFP officer after a sermon delivered at the Friday prayer has steered into political, more 'firebrand' territory. The call is the 'top-down' exercise of power signalling: 'We are watching, we are listening'. The imam also told me that because of the threat of these calls, he made sure that the sermons delivered (by him or visiting *khaatibs*) were not controversial. This is the self-governance, self-disciplinary exercise of power.

Another example is Mehmet, a 15-year-old boy of Turkish background from Inner West Islamic School. Soccer obsessed, Mehmet spoke to me about how he goes to the local park in Auburn near his home almost every day after school and on weekends to kick a ball 'with anybody who will play with me'. He told me that if he meets somebody new, he will often try

> very hard to show I'm not the kind of Muslim they see on
> TV because their parents might not let them play with me
> so I try to give a good image and show, like, I'm Muslim, I'm
> not one of those extremists, and like, they can be comfortable
> around me.

There is no government official standing in the park to make sure Mehmet is 'being a moderate'. At only 15, Mehmet has already internalised a community expectation that he project an image of himself 'as moderate' to reassure others of his safeness. This is unlikely to be on his mind in *every* encounter at the park, nor is it likely that his efforts are contrived. The point is that the idea of Muslims as suspicious has entered Mehmet's consciousness as a material force, subtly shaping his conduct and behaviour. Mohamad Tabbaa writes that in the war on terror, to 'speak back' (to reassure, to condemn, to explain) 'accords so cleanly with the demand [by Western societies] to speak'. This defensiveness, Tabbaa argues, is 'one of the key tactics of Islamophobia'. We are used to thinking and talking about Islamophobia as someone shouting 'go back to where you came from' on public transport or ripping a hijab off a woman's head as she walks in the street. But less attention is paid to Islamophobia as a 'strategy for keeping Muslims in the dock': the Islamophobia that has subtly worked itself on a 15-year-old boy such that he must 'speak back' to the imagined suspicions of other kids in his local park.

Later in our interview, Mehmet told me about a talk given at his school by 'some religious guy in the community, maybe a sheikh I'm not sure', who 'spoke about Islam is a religion of peace and moderation and we should, like, be careful about what we read and watch, and it's not good to look at pictures of dead kids in like Syria and stuff – it can affect you in a bad way'. Mehmet then smiled. 'I remember he then goes, 'cause his English ... or maybe because he's not online, he goes on "the Facebook" and we died laughing, and then we got in trouble because we weren't taking it serious.' Mehmet went on to explain to me how he and his friends just 'switched off' at these 'kinds of lectures': 'I understand why they're saying it, but it's like, why mention it to us? We're not dumb. And it's far away from our life.'

But is it? Mehmet does not have the luxury of completely 'switching off'. In the banal spaces of a suburban park, he feels the need to work strategically to prove himself against a default negative assumption. The tentacles of suspicion, no matter how slight, reach into his school, reach into his park.

Yasin, 17, who attended a boys' public high school in South Western Sydney that has a large Arab and Muslim student body, spoke to me about some of the sermons delivered at the prayers held at the school each Friday. 'The regular topic was respect the teachers,' he said, rolling his eyes, 'but after any big event, we'd get a talk about, "Well the Prophet tended to go away from extremes, you should follow his suit. Not go into the extremes." Then we'd pray and go to lunch and play soccer.' Noura, 17, was another student I interviewed, who attended a girls' public school in South Western Sydney with a large percentage of Muslim students. She recalled a

> guy came to the school, to give some kind of religious talk, like a lecture. I was in year 11. He was trying to be supportive about how we should have strong faith with all the stuff about our religion in the media and then he went on a tangent about not being brainwashed by extreme ideas. It was weird. Obviously, these days you can't even go to Friday prayer or listen to a *khutbah* without hearing some kind of policy.

These opportunities to remind students about the moderate path are not random; they don't emerge out of thin air. They are fragments in an inventory of common-sense ideas about Muslim youth as at-risk.

Moreover, they demonstrate how CVE operates as a form of governmentality producing Muslims (in this case, teachers and imams) who guide and shape the conduct of their own communities by regulating the flow of ideas, values and religious learning within Muslim community spaces. All of this operates within the logic of pre-emptively denying the threat of extremism – or being seen to. One of the dominant ways in which this threat is denied is by linking vulnerability and riskiness to questions of young Muslims' identity, values and belonging, and by Muslim communities fostering a *not* extreme, *not* radical Australian Muslim youth identity.

A HOME AMONG THE GUM TREES

Writing in the UK but with equal application to Australia, race academics David Tyrer and Salman Sayyid describe the figure of the young Muslim as 'an awkward presence, interrupting the closure of the nation because of an assumed lack of shared symbolic grounds between Muslims and the "host" nation'. This has been the common-sense current that runs through CVE policies targeting Muslim youth. But even in the absence of any explicit school policies, the practical ideologies of the war on terror maintain a hyper-attention to Muslim students, who are imagined as incomplete and improper national subjects, lacking civic education, 'Australian values' and, most notably, loyalty and commitment to an ideological narrative of Australia that can brook no dissent. We have seen changes to citizenship tests to include questions on 'Australian values', ministerial directives to Islamic schools as recently as 2017 to 'sign a register pledging their support for Australian values' and calls for revoking the citizenship of those who 'don't share' these values.

The political lineage of this can be firmly traced back to the Howard government's weaponisation of 'Australian values' against Muslim communities, particularly Muslim youth. In August 2005, Howard convened the highly publicised 'Muslim leaders summit' to 'seek advice on ways to ensure that terrorism was denounced and repudiated in Islamic schools', resulting in an agreement with Muslim leaders 'that schools and mosques must not encourage terrorism'. Pronouncing that the government didn't intend 'to interfere in any way with the freedom and practice of religion', Howard cautioned that Australians 'had a right to know whether there is, within any section of the Islamic community, a preaching of the virtues of terrorism'. The government was 'willing to go inside mosques, prayer halls and Islamic schools to ensure they are not preaching terrorism'. The message was unambiguous: Muslim schools, educators, religious leaders were promoting terrorism.

The signification of Muslim schools as sites of crisis was reinforced just one day after the summit, when then Minister for Education Brendan Nelson relaunched the *National Framework for Values Education* (first launched in May that year), Australia's first official values education policy. Values such as 'doing your best', 'a fair go' and 'freedom' were listed on a poster issued to schools, featuring an iconic World War I image of Private Simpson and his donkey. Nelson warned Islamic schools that they must teach Australian values and announced that he would be meeting the Australian Federation of Islamic Councils to discuss programs to ensure those in Islamic schools and all other children fully understood Australian history and values. 'If you want to be in Australia,' he warned,

> if you want to raise your children in Australia, we fully expect
> those children to be taught and to accept Australian values
> and beliefs. We want them to understand our history and
> our culture, the extent to which we believe in mateship and
> giving another person a hand up and a fair go. And basically,
> if people don't want to be Australians and they don't want to
> live by Australian values and understand them, well basically
> they can clear off.

I can never forget attending a local Islamic school for an assembly around that time, and the primary school students performing 'Give me a home among the gum trees' to an audience of parents and teachers. Girls in hijabs, boys and girls with non-Anglo faces, stood on the stage enthusiastically singing about the white colonial-settlers' dream of a semi-rural property. We were in a suburb in South Western Sydney. The juxtaposition was ridiculous. We all smiled, because the students were utterly endearing, but the entire spectacle bothered me deeply. It felt unnecessary, a contrived patriotism. There was nothing cynical about it – the students and teachers were obviously having great fun – but in the context of the political pressure being exerted on Islamic schools, I felt the weight of wider culture wars bearing down on that stage. I could see how Muslim schools were being induced to prove they were 'integrated' Australian Muslims.

As a result of the Muslim leaders summit and with input from a national Muslim Community Reference Group, the Howard government introduced its *National Action Plan to Build Social Cohesion, Harmony and Security* (NAP), which explicitly linked national security/countering terrorism with social harmony and cohesion, aiming to 'reinforce social cohesion, harmony and support the national security imperative in Australia by addressing extremism, the promotion of violence and intolerance, in response to the increased threat of global religious and political terrorism'.

The Howard government's linking of terrorism to questions of Muslim integration, identity, values and belonging mirrored what was happening in the UK; namely, the promotion of an assimilationist social agenda which deployed 'Western/Judaeo-Christian' values as a discourse of power. The message was clear: national security had pivoted to Muslims proving they were *not becoming terrorist*; proving their loyalty and commitment to 'common, shared values', where 'common' was particularised as Judaeo-Christian.

The NAP was the genesis of the 'social cohesion' agenda that persists in Australian national and state policies today.

The NAP was introduced seven months after the Cronulla riots in which a throng of about 5000 mostly Anglo-background young men descended on Cronulla beach in Sydney and attacked anyone 'of Middle Eastern appearance'. Following this violence, there were no crisis summits with Anglo 'leaders', no calls for White blokes bashing brown men to 'clear off', no programs and policies to rehabilitate and educate White Australians. In fact, John Howard cynically announced the details of a proposed citizenship test on the first anniversary of the Cronulla riots, a move which gave purchase to the claim that the riots were 'provoked' by the pathologically sexist and anti-social 'un-Australian' behaviour of 'Middle Eastern' men on the beach. The invocation of Australian values via the incarnation of the citizenship test functioned to 'remind' and 'school' such men about their need for citizenship rehabilitation in a war-on-terror context.

At every opportunity from the very beginning of the war on terror, governments have signalled loudly and clearly that Muslim youth are the problem.

And so, today, Mehmet must prove himself in the park, and Yasin and Noura must be reminded at school to take the moderate path.

CHAPTER 3

REINFORCING A SUSPECT COMMUNITY

If you spend your career working with young Muslim
men, then you are absolutely essential to what we are
trying to achieve because what we are trying to achieve
is to prevent young Muslim men being enticed and
ensnared into the false allure of ISIL ...

—*Then Attorney-General George Brandis*

I've always had this almost pre-conceived
guilt attached to who I was.

—*Jeena (18, Lebanese-Australian, South West Sydney)*

The first sort of image that comes to my
mind when I think of a terrorist is a Muslim.

—*Steven (16, Anglo-Australian, Grammar College)*

The website's homepage had three women in hijab, among other 'multicultural faces'. Under the heading 'Celebrate our shared values' were more hijabi women, at what looked like a citizenship ceremony. The image accompanying the link to 'What can your community do?' contained an image of a little girl in hijab. The website's 'Partners–Communities' page stated that 'Australian community groups and leaders from diverse backgrounds have a strong interest and responsibility in addressing violent extremism'. 'Diverse' here was a misnomer. The countering violent extremism (CVE) security gaze was clearly fixed on Muslims.

The federal government's Living Safe Together website, launched in 2014, is the government's main online presence addressing CVE narratives and showcasing how communities and the government are 'building resilient communities'. Up until 2018, the website was a good example of how meaningless the discursive shift from Islam to targeting 'all forms' of extremism is, when one considers that the images used on the pages of the Living Safe Together website over several years reinforced the centrality of Muslims and non-Anglo Australians to the CVE agenda.

The page referred, as its sole example, to a statement from the Mufti of Australia, Dr Ibrahim Abu Mohamed, about the need to stop radicalisation, stating that 'we must collectively pool our efforts and resources to build a more resilient community'. Links were then provided to the Mufti's statement in both English and Arabic. A prominently positioned 'related links' panel bar on the side of the webpage again provided the links to the Mufti's statement. No other links were provided. Despite referring to 'leaders from diverse backgrounds', it was only the Mufti's statement which was splashed across the page.

Images matter.

These images and 'partnerships' are a prime example of how the hegemonic 'truth' about Muslims, particularly Muslim youth,

as the common-sense focus of CVE policy is produced and reproduced in the politics of everyday life. Politicians, the police and
security services repeat the mantra that 'the Muslim community
is our necessary partner in the battle against violent extremism';
that the wider community and government must work with 'the
Muslim community to ensure that we can take on this scourge'.
CVE grants and policies are announced by politicians on the
steps of mosques, CVE operations target geographic and demographic populations deemed 'at risk' (in other words, suburbs
with large Muslim populations), consultations and round tables
between 'the Muslim community' and government over national
security laws are highly publicised, Islamophobic attacks are condemned by politicians and the police because of how it might
undermine relationships of 'cooperation' between 'intelligence
and law enforcement' and 'the Muslim community'. The public
is routinely reassured that the government is tackling the problem of young Muslim Australians being 'radicalised and misled',
'with strong, deradicalisation programs, working with Muslim
communities'.

Millions of federal and state dollars have been poured into
government grant schemes targeting Muslim youth since 9/11.
The programs and academic projects funded by research grants
have been wide-ranging, from a large-scale arts-based interfaith
comparative project among children as young as preschool age in
Australia and the UK, to sports programs and leadership programs
with teens. Over a decade on, the message endures, from changes
to citizenship tests to include questions on 'Australian values', to
ministerial directives in 2017 to Islamic schools to 'sign a register
pledging their support for Australian values', to calls for revoking the citizenship of those who 'don't share Australian values'.
This has arguably been the premise underlying millions of dollars'
worth of government grant schemes targeting Muslim youth.

Only a fraction of young Australian Muslims would have participated in these programs, and many of the programs took place when the students I interviewed were in primary school or starting out at high school. And yet, these programs, as material practices in the war on terror, generate specific effects that can't be ignored. What interests me is what Australian legal scholar Victoria Sentas eloquently describes as the 'fragments of practices' and the common-sense 'traces of race and social power' these policies and grants programs have produced about Muslim youth, which endure and trickle down into young people's lives, especially in their schools. There is a coherence of effects in the way CVE programs, even as they pose as race-neutral, contribute to entrenching in the public's imagination the figure of the at-risk Muslim youth.

CVE AND GRANTS REGIMES

If I am to create an inventory of the traces of race and construction of Muslims as a 'suspect community', then Australia's CVE grants regime belongs in it. When we talk about CVE we are, as a 2019 US-based report stated, talking about 'a field of youth practice'. And CVE is ultimately, as Arun Kundnani has shown in his body of work analysing the globalisation of CVE policies, 'a master signifier of the late "war on terror"' and a 'lens through which to view Muslim minorities'.

Australia's CVE grants regimes have had various iterations. The *National Action Plan* grants (2005–10) were based on a social harmony and cohesion agenda linked with national security and countering terrorism. The 2010–14 *Building Community Resilience* grants were based on a community resilience model. Both regimes were led by the Attorney-General's Department. The *Living Safe Together Grants Programme* (2014–15) fell under the 'diversion and deradicalisation' arm of Australia's national counter-terrorism strategy and was led by the Department of Social Services. The current federal *Strong and Resilient Communities* program (2018–21) is led by the Department of Social Services.

The shift to programs now being led by the Department of Social Services also includes the removal of any explicit reference to violent extremism or radicalisation. Yet, arguably, the grants no longer need to use such language, for efforts have been made over years to ensure that 'social cohesion', 'resilience' and 'harmony' are signifiers for CVE work. I will focus on the *Building Community Resilience* grants scheme to show how such language was first entrenched.

While the 2010 White Paper continued to emphasise a 'distorted and militant interpretation of Islam' as the primary terrorist threat, it took a discursive shift from Islamic extremism to 'violent extremism' and introduced 'resilience' into its strategic focus, defined as 'building a strong and resilient Australian community to resist the development of any form of violent extremism and terrorism on the home front'. The White Paper and *Building Community Resilience* scheme set out a resilience model which assumed that 'marginalisation and radicalisation' could be mitigated through 'social inclusion' and a multi-causal approach to combating radicalisation that included 'hostil[ity] to liberal democratic norms and values and the broader political environment' as a factor in the radicalisation process.

It's important to take this in. A government policy is explicitly listing hostility to liberal democracy as a warning sign. This is a striking example of what race and Islamophobia scholar Salman Sayyid sees as 'the heart of Islamophobia', namely, 'the disciplining of Muslims by reference to an antagonistic western horizon'.

While some project descriptions specifically referred to addressing violent extremism, many others avoided the term and were presented as positive, empowering and educative initiatives, despite coming under the specific remit of the government's CVE strategy. These included school-based activities such as group discussions, assignments and creative team projects to promote 'mentoring' and 'opportunities for young Muslims to achieve a number of aims, including to voice their opinions, critically analyse situations and increase participation in democratic decision making and conflict resolution'. They also included sports-based youth mentoring programs, 'critical peace-building skills' focused on Islamic schools, leadership and mentoring workshops, media training, and cross-cultural and interfaith community activities. Projects also involved Muslim youth learning how to use sound design, sound editing and audio mixing to create soundtracks and movies, to 'encourage young people to participate in development projects that supported them to express their views creatively and positively'. One of the most popular programs was the AFL's Muslim star player Bachar Houli's football competition for Islamic schools, which required that participants be engaged in mainstream community clubs and participate in education and leadership sessions.

These projects constitute a small sample of the many programs funded over the years. From their descriptions, the initiatives seem harmless and their objectives laudable. However, the CVE imperative at the heart of the projects is one of the reasons these grants schemes are so controversial in Muslim communities. One of the most critical assessments of how counter-terrorism policy targets the Muslim community is contained in the seminal 2013 report *Government Intervention in the Muslim Community*, produced by the Australian wing of the global Muslim political organisation Hizb ut-Tahrir. The report provides a meticulously comprehensive survey and analysis of key political speeches, policies and programs from 2001 to 2013, brilliantly documenting how the Muslim community is recruited, manipulated and used to implement CVE strategies, particularly with those 'deemed "moderate" promoted and funded to challenge those deemed "radical"'. One of the report's key recommendations is that Muslim organisations should refuse to participate in CVE programs and initiatives, because of how such participation legitimises the government's agenda and narratives.

To secure funding under the *Building Community Resilience* program, all project proposals were required to explicitly address one or more specific 'issues' listed, including violent extremism, radicalisation or 'factors that may contribute to susceptibility to radicalisation', such as 'subscribing to intolerant beliefs, rejection of mainstream society, disconnection from family, friends and the broader community'. 'Susceptibility to radicalisation' is another way of saying that a Muslim who is not 'radicalised' is by default at risk of being radicalised. This puts them in the domain of pre-suspects. Simply being a young Muslim, often a teenage male, qualifies you as susceptible to radicalisation. Abdul-Rahman, a 16-year-old student at Hills Islamic School, felt this acutely. 'You kind of feel that you start off guilty. Especially somebody like me with the beard and being religious. Like, they think you're so weak and any minute you can turn, you have to be kept on the right path.'

Framed in the context of a security agenda, the education, training, mentorship and guidance offered in these CVE projects firmly constructed a racialised category of Muslim youth as at-risk and therefore the natural site of crisis management. As CVE interventions, the projects were inscribed with the state's agendas and narratives. They may have appeared mundane, but regardless of intent, they reinforced racist ideas about young Muslims, a criticism levelled at CVE initiatives in the UK and US too.

The narrative presented by the government about these grants is equally important in tracing the fragments of explanations and ideas that sustain the racialisation of young Muslims in this way. For example, take the 2010 press release issued by former Attorney-General Robert McClelland, entitled 'Youth Mentoring Grants Program to counter violent extremism'. Even kicking a football or learning how to use digital and sound technology encloses the young Muslim into a security agenda. According to the press release, the grants provided 'mentoring to individuals that are *identified as vulnerable* to extremist views' and invited applications from 'experienced community organisations interested in conducting projects to mentor *at-risk youth*' (emphasis added). There is a clear line of implication between these statements and the constitution of every participant in the programs as 'at-risk'. The press release claimed that the program sought to 'help young people develop skills to deal with these issues in a positive way, while at the same time *reducing the appeal* of extremist or radical ideologies' (emphasis added). Again, traces and fragments, suggestions and signals that produce a regime of truth: reducing the appeal of extremist ideologies implies that the children and youth participants were inherently predisposed to be attracted to such ideologies.

Consider, as another example, the Bachar Houli football competition. This has been a highly successful ongoing program, providing pathway opportunities for young Muslims to play AFL football as well as engage in 'football, leadership and religious and cultural development'. And yet, despite its successes, it remains tainted as a CVE intervention, with then Attorney-General George Brandis attending the program's award ceremonies and the program being showcased on the Living Safe Together website.

Sports programs have, in fact, been a large part of CVE interventions. They are an excellent example of how CVE can be tacked on to youth activities, scaling up sports to a wider agenda. Australian academics writing about one particular sports-focused project funded under the *Building Community Resilience* scheme, the 'More Than a Game' program in Melbourne, state that participation in sports programs in the domain of CVE is said to 'contribute to community resilience, enhance civic participation of socially marginalised youth, and weaken the likelihood of young people becoming involved in groups engaged in violent extremism'. The idea is to increase 'forms of civic participation and attachment to community, thereby enhancing resilience toward narratives and ideologies that promote violence'. Unsurprisingly, the 'More Than a Game' program involved young Muslim men in Melbourne's western suburbs through a local Islamic society. According to the academics evaluating the program, the 'obvious benefits of sport participation' for participants and the broader community are 'relevant to strategies aimed at countering violent extremism'. It seems to me that just about any activity involving Muslim youth and community, personal well-being and so on is capable of being scaled up to 'the domain of CVE'. What is remarkable is that such claims are made even though the researchers themselves acknowledge the 'methodological problem of trying to establish a link between sport-based mentoring programs and the prevention of violent extremism' and report stakeholders involved in the project also raising this problem.

The way around this problem is to note it as a 'limitation' rather than as clear evidence of the racialised logics underpinning such programs. The programs are deeply racialised because CVE practitioners rationalise such programs 'despite these limitations' on the grounds that the positive outcomes – for example confidence, self-esteem, intercultural communication – create 'alternative pathways' for young people (read: Muslims) 'at risk of becoming involved in forms of violent extremism'. There is only one logical way to interpret this: Muslims are on a conveyer belt towards violent extremism. We must divert them before they encounter violent narratives and ideologies, because if they do, they will, intrinsically, be attracted to such narratives and ideologies. The racism inherent in this structuring logic is devastating and reveals the dehumanising lens through which Muslim youth are viewed. And there are young Muslims savvy enough to understand this. Take Iram, a 17-year-old Fijian-Australian university student and spoken-word artist. She told me that she had made it her

> mission to move away from anything involving
> deradicalisation. A part of me automatically gets angry.
> So we're going to punish people for being Muslim?
> Because they got closer to their deen? It's another excuse
> for politicians to integrate themselves into our community
> with police and laws that are detrimental to us.

CVE AND COMMUNITY RECRUITMENT

Since the beginning of the war on terror, the message from governments has been clear about terrorism being a phenomenon Muslims need to 'solve', and enormous pressure has been placed on Muslim organisations by governments to prove they are 'tackling the problem' of radicalisation. As early as 2006 at the Conference of Australian Imams, then education minister Andrew Robb told the conference, 'Because it is your faith that is being invoked as justification for these evil acts, it is your problem'. After the Manchester bombings in 2017, then foreign affairs minister Julie Bishop urged 'community leaders, school leaders, religious leaders, family members to ensure that young people in particular hear the voices of moderation and not the voice of hate and bigotry and savagery that we have seen in recent times'. Acknowledging 'there are community leaders who are very, very forceful in their condemnation of these terrorist attacks', she added, 'but it has to be across the community ... We need to be continually condemning this, condemning these acts and also ensuring that other members of the community who are at risk of radicalisation hear that the voice of moderation is the powerful voice'.

There is no end to these kinds of top-down demands made on the Muslim community, particularly after a terrorist attack in a Western country. One of the most recent such demands was made by Prime Minister Scott Morrison following the 2018 Bourke Street attack by Hassan Khalif Shire Ali. Appearing on Sky News, he declared: 'If you're an imam or a leader in one of those communities, you need to know who those people are in your community that might be doing that'. His comments were echoed by the home affairs minister, Peter Dutton, who said, 'Let's be real, we need people to do more and certainly that's what we would expect from the Islamic community.'

This kind of heavy-handed government rhetoric exposes the conditions in which CVE strategies, promoted as social inclusion, empowerment and self-determination, recruit (or compel) Muslim communities into counter-terrorism work via community 'partnerships'.

Another important point is the impact of intensifying neoliberal policies, which contract state funding of grassroots social justice and welfare work in favour of privatisation and marketisation. Critical race scholar David Theo Goldberg's seminal work on racial neoliberalism resonates deeply with how CVE is an expression of neoliberal logic. 'Far from dismantling the state, or drowning it', Goldberg argues, neoliberalism makes it 'more robust, more intrusive, more repressive'. The neoliberal ideology that emphasises individual responsibility places community organisations under enormous pressure to carry out their social work via CVE funding. In many cases, the only funding available has been through CVE-based grants. In her book *Young Migrant Identities*, Australian youth studies academic Sherene Idriss refers to government funding for arts programs and projects in Western Sydney having either decreased in some sectors or shifted in focus to include the language of 'deradicalisation'. During the course of her research among artists of Arab-Australian backgrounds, she found they 'have much better chances of securing funding if they feed into the current concerns over "countering violent extremism"'. In one case, the director of a prominent South Western Sydney community arts centre told her that government funding was swiftly secured when he simply changed the language in his funding proposal to 'state that such projects will reduce potential Islamic radicalisation'. Without such a change, the projects he had been producing for the past ten years would have received no funding.

Having worked with Muslim community organisations, mosques and youth organisations, I understand first-hand how CVE-funded projects can appear completely removed from an underlying 'CVE agenda', and why so many Muslim academics and activists – myself included – have at some point been implicated in the deliberately convoluted CVE apparatus. The seduction of these projects, particularly when the grants first emerged and Muslims were desperate to do any work for their community, especially for young people, is undeniable. The programs were potentially transformative for individual young people, opening up opportunities to them and leading them to think that they could control their own narratives. Projects could run at arms-length from government to the extent that their funding as CVE projects wasn't clear (unless one was politically savvy enough to ask). Working with Muslims (as liaison officers in government institutions or Muslim community organisations) can provide a veneer of safety and legitimacy to projects that form part of a wider CVE agenda.

The ultimate cooption of these projects to the government's CVE agenda undercuts any 'positives' yielded, and certainly undermines any supposed potential of such projects to subvert and destabilise Islamophobia. Many Muslims, including Muslim organisations who once took CVE money, now understand that the fragments and traces of race and Islamophobia are too deeply embedded in community CVE projects – even those that appear as innocuous and laudable as youth groups creating their own films or playing sports.

This is how governing Muslims in the war on terror works, and it's a strategic part of the story here in Australia, as well as in the US and the UK. For example, Nadya Ali, writing in the UK context, argues that governance of Muslims in the war on terror is 'not the imposition of a way of life onto subjects ... but a relational exchange between Muslims and government on the very idea of what it means to be a Muslim'. Governance works from a distance to 'govern the conduct' of Muslims. Khaled Beydoun, writing in the US context, speaks of CVE surveillance relying on Muslim coop-eration, and so 'dividing Muslim communities, turning classmates against classmates, imams against their mosque's congregants, and family members against their loved ones'. CVE strategies rely on policing, security, law *and* the diffusion of governmental power onto Australian Muslims, represented through peak organisations, youth and community groups, professionals, leaders and Muslim educators who are 'educated' into taking responsibility for disci-plining and taming their 'extremists', or 'building the resilience' of their young Muslim 'moderates' through the veneer of creative, sporting and artistic endeavours. Iram, the spoken-word artist we met above, told me about a youth forum she had been invited to perform at a few years ago. Iram was 'filling out their Google form' when she came across a question: 'how do you think we should target radicalised Muslim youth?' Iram was furious. 'I immediately felt like I was there to educate as a Muslim. Like I was being used to reach Muslim youth because they'd accept it coming from me. I withdrew. I will not align myself with that.'

These kinds of grants programs and CVE-affiliated events, combined with the language used to discipline Muslims into embracing Australian values for almost two decades now, have had several effects. The programs have helped to normalise CVE strategies as being for and about Australian Muslim youth. CVE programs differentiate Muslims from the national community, rendering them as outsiders and, as Victoria Sentas argues, locating their alienation in their inherent difference and supposed self-segregation, rather than in Islamophobia and race. Despite many project descriptions clearly not envisaging their targeted participants as 'at-risk', it remains the case that official government policy about the programs firmly described the grants as targeting 'at risk' or 'vulnerable' individuals. Were the young people who participated, or their families, even aware that their participation ascribed to them the label of 'at risk'? The framing of Muslim youth through a security agenda has racialising effects, no matter the lengths to which governments go to disavow race and racism in CVE work.

Even if we were to ignore the explicit framing of the grants as being for 'at-risk youth' as mere rhetoric, we are left with another troubling effect: as preventative, diversionary work, such grants targeted the not-extremist, the not-terrorist, the not-radical-*yet*. As work structured around identifying, monitoring, disrupting potential vulnerabilities and threats, young Muslims were constituted as predisposed to extremism. The CVE agenda purports to distinguish between the extremist Muslim (suspect category) and the moderate Muslim (pre-suspect). The only difference between subject positions is their degree of temporal removal from terrorist act. In marking the pre-suspect Muslim as needing specific inclusion, education and discipline, under these programs every Muslim is effectively subsumed into a default stage of 'could become terrorist'.

To be pre-suspect means one is never *not* suspect. As race scholar Arun Kundnani writes, so long as violent extremism is constituted as a pathway from Muslim to violent Muslim, *every* Muslim remains pre-suspect, infected with the dormant extremism virus. There is nothing facetious about using the word virus. Critics of CVE strategies have traced how the language of contagion informs CVE's idea of vulnerability. Australian academic Cameron Smith notes, for example, that many CVE 'instruments and policies' 'read like public health interventions', 'pathologising what is essentially a political phenomenon'. In her analysis of the language used in CVE interventions in the UK, education philosopher Aislinn O'Donnell draws attention to the 'histories and associations of terms associated with vulnerability, for example, contagion, therapy, immunisation, susceptibility, purity, colonialism, and autonomy'. Other critics of CVE regimes, particularly in the UK context, have also drawn attention to how 'radicalisation' evokes epidemiological concerns and approaches.

Muslim youth are imagined as vulnerable to infection. They are at risk, they must be immunised before they catch extremism germs. Despite the clear rise of far-right White supremacist violent narratives and ideologies, spreading online and offline, glorifying White supremacist violence including as it's live-streamed, white youth are not racialised as an at-risk collective, predisposed to be attracted to such ideologies, in need of sports mentoring/resilience building/cross-cultural awareness programs. 'Could-become terrorist' is reserved only for Muslims.

In 2014, the *Building Community Resilience* grants regime was replaced with a new CVE approach, *Living Safe Together*, based on the promotion of government and community counter-narratives and a directive that Australia's 'broader social cohesion and social policy programmes, led by the Department of Social Services (DSS), should be more actively tailored to support CVE objectives'. CVE projects would continue to prioritise working with 'at-risk communities' through the 'geographical prioritisation of programmes'. Programs that were run and are still running under the DSS, rather than the Attorney-General's Department, remain focused on the strategic outcomes of 'strong, resilient and cohesive communities', despite the government's own admission that 'activities designed to build cohesive and resilient communities have not of themselves proven to be sufficient to stop all individuals heading down a pathway of radicalisation'.

No matter which department leads CVE programs, the fact remains that issues of national security and community relations have been conflated under the CVE umbrella. If, as Victoria Sentas argues, we see racial regulation not as a predictable or intentional act by 'panoptic architects', but as a series of practices with effects and consequences on the construction of race and the operation of power, we can better understand the way in which Australia's CVE regime so effectively racialises Muslim youth as a common-sense problem to be 'solved' in the war on terror – and how this common-sense knowledge then follows Muslim and non-Muslim young people in their everyday lives.

Lebanese-Australian Jeena, whom I interviewed in her first year of university, told me she regrets participating in a CVE program when she was a high-school student:

> I was naive then. I think our community was too. They didn't see it as, like, *CVE, CVE*. It was never even mentioned in

that way. They wanted to give us any chance to help us out they could get their hands on, but I've read up a lot since then. I feel like now I'm at uni and reading about racism, I understand things more. I feel used.

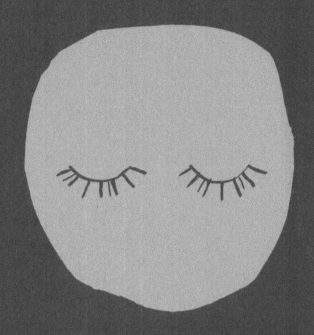

AN
INVENTORY OF
IDEOLOGICAL
WORK

CHAPTER 4

THE 'SCIENCE' OF EXTREMISM

As a teacher, how do you spot an extremist in your school?

—*Australian Multicultural Foundation*

When we talk about countering violent extremism, or counter-radicalisation, we're talking about a contested, controversial *concept* that has been transformed into an expansive global *industry* made up of governments, corporations, advisers, academics, educators, law enforcement agencies, entrepreneurs, community organisations and even artists. We're talking about a concept that originates in government policy and national security agencies, not in evidence-based, peer-reviewed scholarship. We're talking about an industry based on the shared intelligence, research, policy and funding among the 'Five Eyes' intelligence alliance (Australia, Canada, the US, the UK and New Zealand). Not surprisingly, the banner of countering violent extremism (CVE) work covers a hotchpotch of programs and studies. It's a field structured around preventing something that has not happened, working with people who are predicted to *maybe* pose a threat. It's a field which cites the need for evidence-based policies and outcomes in a space where such evidence is impossible to produce.

How do you measure a causal link between your efforts (arts workshops with preschoolers or sports programs, for example) and the prevention of a hypothetical future event? CVE efforts are designed to target the space before intention or motive exists: the 'pre-criminal space' as it has been described by academics in the UK context. The space *before* acts occur or threats are made. CVE operates under the logic of predicting and disrupting motive in anticipation of it becoming intent and ultimately action.

This logic should raise alarm bells for anybody interested in human rights.

You don't have to apply a specific policy or be involved in a CVE program to participate in enacting this risk reversal. To be attuned to the culture of CVE is to pick up hints about how to spot an extremist, to internalise signs as to what arouses suspicion not only about the 'pre-terrorist', but also about those vulnerable to extremism. Who has the dormant virus? Who is at risk of infection and must be treated?

A psychologist in Melbourne told me about a year 6 Muslim student who had been referred to a Department of Education school counsellor because of concerns raised by her classroom teacher and school principal. The concerns? She was on a path to extremism because she had started to wear black tights under her school uniform instead of green tights.

MUSLIMS, RUBRICS AND 'SCIENCE'

The CVE 'expert field' and policies that draw from it are important to understand. They define the terms and establish the archive of knowledge, expertise and authority. CVE training developed by researchers at Monash University has been rolled out to social workers, psychologists, teachers, council workers, university staff and the general public across Australia. The research, described on the project's website as 'the most significant and detailed examination of radicalisation in Australia', was produced under an Australian Government–funded 'Monash Radicalisation Project' at Monash University's Global Terrorism Research Centre in partnership with Victoria Police, the Victorian Department of Premier and Cabinet, Corrections Victoria and the Australian Federal Police.

The project explicitly focused on 'self-styled "jihadist" terrorism from Al Qaeda and associated or inspired groups' (citing the 2010 *Counter-Terrorism White Paper: Securing Australia, Protecting Our Future*), and the bulk of peer-reviewed publications, media articles and conference presentations developed relate to 'radicalisation' and terrorism involving Muslims.

Monash University's research has informed key policy documents in Australia's CVE space: the 2015 federal government's *Preventing Violent Extremism and Radicalisation in Australia* kit; the Australian Multicultural Foundation's *Community Awareness Training Manual*, which is used in the national frontline policing training program and been adapted for community use online and as a train-the-trainer course; and the Australian Association of Social Workers' (AASW) *Building Resilience and Preventing Radicalisation to Violent Extremism* guide, which has formed the basis for training over 700 social workers nationwide. The AASW's embrace of CVE policy and training has been vehemently opposed and resisted by many social work experts and Muslim community organisations, who have criticised it as 'social work collusion' with Islamophobia.

RADAR Solutions, a private consultancy (whose director is a former researcher at Monash University), provides CVE training and advice to senior government and law enforcement personnel, agencies and organisations. RADAR's partners include the

Australian Multicultural Foundation and the federal Department of Education, Skills and Employment. At the time of writing this book, this department had contracted RADAR to provide CVE training to school leadership staff, engaging academics and researchers to facilitate and deliver such training.

Because CVE efforts are so clearly exposed as self-fulfilling prophecies, experts and policymakers have attempted to respond to criticisms of the legitimacy of CVE by 'operationalising' it. The policy documents I analyse below use a 'rubric', a set of 'risk indicators', to help identify 'behaviours which can indicate that a person may be at risk of radicalisation'. The policies attempt to standardise CVE, to apply so-called scientifically based methodologies and frameworks – which pose as race-neutral and even anti-racist – to help 'detect' the signs of extremism. This is despite the fact that no risk profile that stands up to scholarly scrutiny has ever been discovered, as race scholar Arun Kundnani notes.

Removing race does not remove the racialised logics underpinning the risk indicators. UK sociologist Katy Sian has critiqued the methodology underpinning the UK's *Prevent* policy on the basis that it shares the logics of 19th-century positivist criminology, which relied on racial science, eugenics, psychiatry, biology and social Darwinism to make the case that criminality was inherent and biological. Criminals could be classified and behaviour objectively predicted based on an individual's physical traits, such as the colour of their skin, the size of their skull, facial features, how tall they were. Sian convincingly shows how *Prevent* similarly pursues 'objectivity' with its typologies, predictions and evaluations of extremist behavior. CAGE, an independent advocacy organisation in the UK, is a leading critic of the 'science' underpinning *Prevent*, exposing how the evidence base relied on is not only unproven, but extends far beyond the original remit set by the psychologists who developed the framework.

This positivist impulse has similarly shaped the scientific veneer that attaches to the risk indicators formulated in Australian CVE work. In the UK, *Prevent* is based on the formulation of various indicators based on the Extremism Risk Guidance 22+ (ERG 22+), a framework developed by psychologists Christopher Dean and Monica Lloyd that assesses an individual against 22 factors.

Australian intervention programs have used the Violent Extremism Risk Assessment (VERA-2) tool and RADAR assessment tool to assist in the early identification of risk indicators for violent extremism. A 'standardised research measure' has even been developed to measure young people's resilience to violent extremism at community level ('BRAVE-14').

Policymakers insist that CVE criminalises violence, not radical beliefs or speech. But CVE's preventative, presumptive, disruptive mandate looks for potential danger, not actual danger. In fact, we need not go so far as 'danger'. We need only examine how the entire conceptual framework of CVE is to follow *potential vulnerability*. What do governments and the policymakers they engage imagine signifies vulnerability? Potentiality?

In the UK, the *Prevent* duty guidance defines extremism as 'vocal or active opposition to fundamental British values, including democracy, the rule of law, individual liberty and mutual respect and tolerance of different faiths and beliefs'. Australia also locates 'potentiality' in suspected or actual disassociation from so-called normative Australian values and identity. The invocation of 'Australian values' maintains the linking of vulnerability to questions of integration and assimilation. The *Community Awareness Training Manual* (CATM) is a resource that shows how this plays out.

THE SCRIPT FOR SOCIAL COHESION

Media coverage about the rolling out of the CATM in *The Educator*, Australia's only magazine and news website for senior educational professionals and decision-makers, opened with the following questions: 'As a teacher, how do you spot an extremist in your school? Is it what they believe? Is it how passionate they are about that belief? Is such a thing even possible to spot?' According to the article, the CATM 'helps communities answer these questions', as well as dispelling misconceptions about what constitutes radicalisation.

The questions raised in the article go to the heart of what instinctively feels so fraught, subjective and dangerous about the 'countering' part of CVE work in schools. Indeed, the idea of training teachers to 'recognise signs of radicalisation in their students' in the context of another, related intervention into schools, the federal government's 2015 'jihadi watch' strategy, was met with criticism by the Queensland Teachers' Union, who considered it an 'extraordinary' and 'abhorrent' expectation on teachers given 'the generally nurturing and caring role' teachers perform for students.

During the initial phase of the CATM in 2013, trainers were drawn from the Australian Multicultural Foundations's Muslim Youth Leadership and Peer-to-Peer Program alumni, the Australian National Imams Council and the 'general community', once again clearly centring Muslims, in particular young Muslims, as the natural objects of counter-radicalisation regulation, despite assertions by those involved in formulating the CATM that the program 'is not specific to any one particular national, political, religious or ideological group'.

The CATM uses the 'scientific' Behavioural Indicators Model developed by Monash University as its rubric for 'increasing awareness and understanding of warning signs of anti-social behaviours that can lead to forms of criminal activity including violent extremism'. It adopts the resilience, social inclusion and harmony models underpinning Australia's CVE regime. The logic of these models is that marginalisation and social disadvantage make individuals – indeed, entire communities – vulnerable to extremist ideologies, while the promotion of social inclusion makes individuals and communities resilient.

The first part of the training emphasises the importance of social cohesion in building community resilience. The CATM asserts that 'cultivating and nurturing' social cohesion is 'extremely important', to protect against the breakdown of social harmony and to build community resilience against anti-social behaviours. Participants are presented with statistics about Australia's policy of multiculturalism, and social cohesion is conceptualised as being about belonging, respecting diversity and fostering engagement with Australian values, identity and citizenship.

The reference to social cohesion, to Australian values, is built on the foundation of a wider policy landscape developed over many years. For example, the Australian Government's 2010 *Counter-Terrorism White Paper (Securing Australia, Protecting Our Community)* includes as part of the 'factors' in the process of radicalisation: 'identity politics ... the search for individual identity among sometimes apparently conflicting cultural reference points ... identification with, and adoption of, particular ideologies and belief systems that are hostile to liberal democratic norms and values and the broader political environment'. The CATM can be read as a civilising mission against a young population which must be directed to appropriate identities, political participation, beliefs and values rooted in a Western liberal framework. Words like 'values', 'identity', 'citizenship', 'norms' and 'cultural reference points' are ideologically loaded.

The CATM offers a disclaimer that 'radical thoughts' are not inherently bad. It reassures readers that radical thoughts 'may mean you want to see big changes to society and may think there are things wrong with how things are now. Being radical can mean positive changes. Radical thinking becomes a threat when individuals or groups engage in violence.' A line between radical thinking and violent action is supposedly drawn here. But that line is blurred in the pre-emptive reality of CVE work, which is focused on radical thinking that *could turn* to violent action. Individuals or groups who actually engage in violence are not the business of CVE.

In every Western society, including Australia, the CVE agenda has sought to anticipate the 'becoming radical' by categorising 'extreme' Islam as illegitimate and suspect, and moderate, de-politicised Islam as legitimate. As CVE critics have argued, radical thoughts and speech by non-Muslims don't mark them as *becoming extremist*. It's the Muslim – who is on the ideological margins, who expresses dissent, who challenges Australian and Western 'values' and culture and foreign policies – who is, at the very *least*, problematised, identified as needing direction or discipline.

The claim in the CATM quoted above therefore raises several questions given the various policy iterations analysed thus far, including the 2010 White Paper's explicit definition of the radicalisation process as including 'hostility' to 'liberal democratic norms and values'. Is a Muslim really free to 'be radical'? Can they convert their radical thinking into radical speech without fear of repercussions? Can they agitate for 'big changes to society' without arousing concern and suspicion? Can they expose what is 'wrong with how things are now' without consequence? Does wanting to change society, to change 'how things are now', not sit in fundamental tension with the discourse of social cohesion and Australian values, both of which rely on conceptual notions of unity, uniformity and loyalty?

The CATM emphasises the 'challenge for all Australians of accepting difference while also promoting social cohesion'. But what level of difference is envisaged here? A narrowly imagined cosmetic difference in culture and ethnicity? What about differences in competing ideologies? Fundamental disagreements as to how societies should be arranged? Indeed, opposition to Australia's CVE operations?

There are countless examples of how the Muslim who speaks of 'big changes to society', who speaks 'off-script', is attacked. The discourse of counter-radicalisation 'rules in' certain ways of talking about terrorism, foreign policy (for example, moderate Muslim condemnations) and Islamophobia, and 'rules out' other ways of constructing knowledge about terrorism (for example, discussing the relationship between state terrorism, Western foreign policy and individual acts of terrorism).

Mehreen Faruqi, a Pakistani-Australian civil and environmental engineer who, in 2013, became the first Muslim woman to be a member of an Australian parliament, knows this all too well. A federal senator for New South Wales, Faruqi is one of the most fearless and principled politicians in the country. But her identity as a Muslim woman is what rallies the most hate, and she receives particularly vitriolic attacks questioning her loyalties, her right to speak, her right to even be in parliament. When Faruqi has spoken in defence of Palestinians, she has been the victim of media smear campaigns, accusing her of being 'mates with radicals'. When she called out White supremacy after the Christchurch massacre, the home affairs minister, Peter Dutton, claimed Faruqi was 'just as bad' as Fraser Anning. To challenge Islamophobia and race as a Muslim woman, and hold politicians to account for stoking hatred, is to be equated with a fascist. As Faruqi said at the time, such a false equivalence is 'vile'. It is also typical of how calling out racism in this country, especially as a woman of colour, attracts the most vicious takedowns by White elites.

The sustained media witch hunt and political backlash unleashed on the Mufti of Australia Dr Ibrahim Abu Mohammed, in the context of his initial response to the terrorist attacks in Paris in November 2015, is another case in point. Following the terrorist attacks, the Mufti issued a press release expressing sorrow for the deaths of the victims, extending his condolences to the families and friends of the deceased, reiterating that the sanctity of human life is guaranteed in Islam and referring to 'causative factors' in terrorism, including racism, foreign policy, military intervention and increased powers for police and intelligence services. A former head of Britain's security agency MI5 had made similar comments in 2010 in Britian's public 'Iraq Inquiry' regarding the UK's role in the Iraq war, and even more 'controversial' statements and analysis had been made by white commentators in the media without consequence. Indeed, British historian and terrorism scholar Mark Sedgwick has criticised the 'radicalisation discourse' for its emphasis on 'the individual' and de-emphasis of the wider circumstances, the 'root causes': 'So long as the circumstances that produce Islamist radicals' declared grievances are not taken into account', he has argued, 'it's inevitable that the Islamist radical will often appear as a "rebel without a cause"'. And yet the Mufti was accused of justifying, or at the very least failing to clearly condemn, the attacks. He was subjected to a front-page spread in *The Daily Telegraph* depicting him as three 'unwise' monkeys, covering his ears, eyes and mouth next to the words 'Sees no problems, hears no concerns, speaks no English' (the Mufti subsequently sued *The Daily Telegraph* for defamation and the case settled). The backlash at the time against the Mufti was relentless and included a chorus of criticism from politicians including the Prime Minister and Minister for Foreign Affairs at the time. The Mufti was compelled to issue a further press release clarifying his earlier statement.

Another highly publicised episode of disciplining a Muslim for going off-script involved an interview in 2015 on the ABC national TV program *Lateline* between journalist Emma Alberici and Wassim Doureihi, a member of political activist organisation Hizb ut-Tahrir. The interview played out like a cross-examination, with Alberici demanding Doureihi answer whether he 'support[ed] the murderous campaign being waged by Islamic State fighters in Iraq'. Doureihi refused to answer the 'offensive' question, seeking to shift the terms of discussion and address the context in which ISIS had emerged. For this, Doureihi – described in the media and by no less than the Prime Minister at the time, Tony Abbott, as a 'hate preacher' – was widely condemned for *not condemning ISIS*. There were even calls by a prominent media commentator to consider whether Doureihi could be held to account under proposed laws that would make it illegal to advocate terrorism.

In 2014, I appeared on the ABC's national *Q&A* program, a live panel discussion hosted by journalist Tony Jones, with the panel – made up of politicians, media personalities, academics, activists and celebrities – taking questions posted online and from a studio audience. I appeared alongside Dr Anne Azza Aly, academic and expert in counter-radicalisation (who would soon become the first female Australian Muslim federal member of parliament); Michael Keenan, Minister for Justice under the Abbott government; Mark Dreyfus, then shadow Attorney-General; and Scott Ludlum, then a Greens senator. The main topics for discussion were terrorism, radicalisation and the counter-terrorism raids conducted the week before across Western and North Western Sydney, the largest ever conducted in Australia's history. In the early hours of the morning, the NSW police had tweeted that dawn raids were 'underway', supplying television news stations with footage filmed by the police and sending photos to newspapers. Unfolding across television screens like an episode of *Homeland*, the media offered wall-to-wall coverage of what major newspapers' front pages dubbed 'Terror Australis'. As a result of the raids, involving 800 police officers, 15 men were arrested but only two were charged. Media coverage reported an alleged beheading plot, featuring a sword seized by the Australian Federal Police at one of the homes raided. The sword was later revealed to be plastic and was in fact a Dhu al-Fiqar, a common decorative item in Shia homes.

During the panel discussion, Dr Aly and I expressed many views. In short, my position was to contextualise Islamophobia; to demand radicalisation be addressed via a conversation that examined the role of Western intervention in the Middle East as both participating in terrorism, and creating and nurturing the conditions that allow terrorism to emerge; and, finally, to question the timing, motives and strategy underlying the government's counter-terrorism operations and rhetoric. Many of the statements I made had been expressed without serious contestation by that privileged breed of media commentators in our society: White middle-class males. According to Liberal MP Craig Kelly, the views Dr Aly and I expressed 'encourage[d] radicalisation' and had 'the potential to encourage the radicalisation of young people'.

Shortly after the program, I received an email newsletter from Alex Hawke, who happens to be my local federal MP. He informed his constituents (presumably not realising I was one of them): 'Following last week's Q&A program I raised with my colleagues my concern about the lack of balance and the airing of anti-Western and anti-Australian conspiracy theories. The program did us a big disservice and provided a platform for "extreme" views.' He described our views as 'a half-baked conspiracy theory about our Government and also security services and Police' and criticised *Q&A* for framing our comments as 'the dominant view of Islamic Australia'. The newsletter provided links to articles quoting Hawke delivering his message in a speech to the Coalition joint party room: 'This can only needlessly inflame tensions at a time when the Government and the media have a grave responsibility to ensure moderate Islamic views are heard'. The media reported that this 'impassioned speech' was 'praised as the finest contribution of the meeting' by then Attorney-General George Brandis.

The circulation of this newsletter reporting Hawke's disciplining of Aly and me was clearly playing right into his constituency (a safe Liberal seat). What was more insidious and far more interesting is what followed. The grand claims of free speech made in policy documents like the CATM can be taken seriously only if you insist that we live in a so-called post-racial society. To believe that Muslims can freely challenge government narratives and offer 'radical thinking' about the war on terror without being constituted as a threat is ludicrous. The Islamic school my children attend is in Hawke's electorate, where we also live. Because schools rely so heavily on the support of their local and federal representatives, a fortnight following the *Q&A* episode, the school, as a matter of protocol, invited Hawke to attend the opening of a new building. The school agonised over this decision, especially as I had been pre-booked to speak at the opening. In consultation with the school, I decided to withdraw as a speaker and not attend. I didn't want to prejudice the school via its relationship with me. And so Hawke attended the opening at my children's school and delivered a nice speech about multiculturalism and local schools, followed by some friendly chitchat with staff and students over finger food. I stayed home with my 'conspiracy theories' and 'extreme views'.

By all accounts the opening was the perfect example of the CATM's vision of 'social cohesion' and 'harmony'.

ASSESSING RADICALISATION

The CATM's Behavioural Indicators Model is used to help assess whether anti-social behaviour can lead to violent extremism. The model consists of three key 'behavioural categories': social relations, ideologies and criminal/action orientation.

Radicalisation is defined as involving 'the coalescing of all three components and an escalation in intensity across all sectors'. *Social relations* are defined as changes in behaviour such as isolation or involvement with 'radical groups'. *Ideologies* are defined as 'whole of life philosophies that impose a pattern and interpretation on how we see everything, including political events, and what we think we ought to do about them'. A shift in ideology is defined as relating to 'a change in personal beliefs, in general, embracing *narratives, views* and *beliefs* that *diverge significantly from the cultural mainstream*' (my emphasis).

In the context of a document that starts by celebrating Australia's 'diversity' and 'multicultural character', this is as close as one can get to an admission that multiculturalism is structured around a normative, Anglo centre. The wording has clear resonances with the Monash Radicalisation Project, which defines radicalisation as 'a process in which individuals develop, adopt and embrace *political attitudes* and modes of behaviour that *diverge substantially* from the *norms* and laws of *mainstream* society' (my emphasis).

Think of these as the 'symptoms' of the radicalisation virus. Disassociation from the mainstream (that is, White, Western/European) centre can be symptomatic of radicalisation. Like what running a fever, sneezing or having body aches is to a cold and flu, to hold a political attitude (a belief) that sits in tension with the Anglo majority's represents vulnerability, risk.

The CATM asserts that *violent extremism* emerges only when radical ideas are paired with violence or support for violence.

Violent extremism is therefore action *or belief* (*support* for violence). In including as its target those who *support* the use of violence, the definition of violent extremism conflates belief with action.

And so the thinking is that while extremism does not necessarily lead to violence, extremism (not just violent extremism) is still a security concern, because this is where the 'pool' of individuals for recruitment into terrorism or extremist violence exists. In a CVE space, 'extremist' ideas, thoughts and beliefs that are considered non-mainstream (in other words, non-White) are inherently constructed as risk indicators. And so, the Muslim who believes in violence but has no intention to act on such a belief still becomes the *potential* extremist, which, in effect, is treated as the potential *violent* extremist.

The Behavioural Indicators Model rubric for 'warning signs' gives an example of behaviour under the category of 'ideology', which sits at the highest end of intensity requiring intervention. The behaviour is described as 'refusing to recognise the legitimacy of the Australian government and a commitment to an alternative system'. Without a corresponding change in the other categories, the CATM cautions that this behaviour does not necessarily equate to that of a violent extremist.

But CVE is not interested in violent extremists. Violent extremists are at the end of the continuum. CVE is aimed at anticipating points of 'escalation' across the three sectors proposed by the model. Following her interviews with police involved in CVE work in the community, lawyer and academic Victoria Sentas found 'a relationship ... between belief and behaviour in understanding points along the continuum and the basis on which police select persons of interest'. Sentas argued that this relationship between belief and behaviour didn't simply rely on police making discretionary decisions over whom and what to monitor. Sentas concluded that 'police generate knowledge about Muslim

111

extremists, the conditions and processes of radicalisation, and make interpretive claims about who is extremist in order to create the 'opportunity' for 'counter-radicalisation'.

So CVE is about reading motive and intention into beliefs and/or behaviour, predicting when those beliefs and/or behaviour will increase in intensity. This is made clear in the case studies presented in the CATM, all of which are based on real-life examples. They reveal how the practical ideologies of radicalisation are legitimised in policy. The case studies contribute to the everyday common-sense thinking about what behaviours could (and therefore signal to people as *should*) arouse suspicion.

EXAMPLES OF SUSPICIOUS BEHAVIOUR

The CATM uses the cases of Mohammad Sidique Khan (one of the July 2005 London bombers), Anders Behring Breivik (Norway terrorist in 2011) and Tamerlan Tsarnaev (one of the 2013 Boston Marathon bombers) as examples of 'violent extremists', which are 'coded' according to the Behavioural Indicators Model rubric. Facilitators running the CATM training take participants through the case studies, pointing out 'warning signs' and behaviours which 'increase in intensity'. The CATM makes it clear that the warning signs highlighted in the case studies are *not conclusive or exhaustive*, and that processes of anti-social behaviour don't happen in a structured manner or necessarily end in violence.

But this is, of course, an exercise based on hindsight, assembling independent actions into a coherent chain, reconstructing a 'warning sign' after the fact. It's a good example of what a group of academics who conducted an extensive global review of CVE literature and studies described as the tendency for research on radicalisation to suffer from 'selection bias', that is, the 'selection on the dependent variable' such that '"successful" cases of terrorists' are selected and patterns identified among the cases despite the fact that no identifying pattern has emerged'. The problem, therefore, 'is that this works backwards from successful cases to prove the outcome'.

Some of the examples of behaviour highlighted and coded in the case studies as 'notable' or 'concerning' (and so within the pre-emptive logic of CVE) are problematic when you consider how easily they could apply to any young person. Coded as 'notable social relations' is that Mohammad Sidique Khan 'used to be quite easy going but became more introverted and intolerant' and 'started having conflict with his family and many others'.

That Khan's 'new religious practices and attitude caused conflict with the family' is coded as 'Ideology: notable'. So clashing with family over religion is *notable* behaviour. His 'social relations' are marked as 'concerning' because Khan's 'life became intensely narrow and confined to the mosques where he prayed, the buildings where he helped run Pakistani youth groups, the bookshop where he gave talks and his brother's house'. One wonders, what's missing in Khan's social calendar that makes this a cause for concern? Or is it the fact that his circle and interests were focused on Islam (and not football, clubbing, music etc)? Also coded is the case study of 'Sam', based on actual events, who 'started to change the way he practised his religion from his family, disengaging from social activities and his friends'. This is also marked as 'Ideology: notable'. Perhaps the most bizarre of them all is the coding of Tamerlan Tsarnaev's behaviour under 'Ideology: notable': 'Tamerlan renounced boxing as an offence against Islam and went from being cocky and wearing leather shoes and white shirts to the gym, to growing a five-inch beard and dressing conservatively. Tamerlan also stopped listening to rap music and playing the piano and violin.'

These 'warning signs' from real-life cases present as knowable variables *now* only because we have the benefit of knowing 'what will happen'. So what to do when confronted with similar behaviours in real time? Should introverted Muslim teenagers who clash with their family, grow beards, dress conservatively and stop boxing arouse suspicion? What does footwear and the colour of somebody's shirt have to do with anything? As for no longer 'being cocky'? This one still stumps me.

That this hindsight-led grouping of specific behaviours masquerades as expertise and is used to train people working with youth is truly confounding. Behavioural significations for 'Islamist extremist' are set out like a connect-the-dots picture. Crucially, these dots are connected before official intelligence efforts commence. They are, in the pre-crime space, just signs, but signs with the power to label a young Muslim (the obvious subject in mind) as potentially at risk. The risk indicators become a way, as Michel Foucault put it, 'of linking together, simply through analogy, a whole series of illegalities below the threshold, of improper acts that are not illegal, and of piling them up in order to make them resemble the crime itself'.

What is at stake in the CATM training program is how to normalise the young Muslim; how to police their 'risk' by orienting them towards authorised meanings, narratives and myths about Australian identity, 'good' politics, beliefs and ways of living. How to reverse engineer the Muslim subject from the highest negative level of *attention* down through *notable* and *concern* to *neutral*.

Not one of the students I interviewed was aware of the CATM. They didn't need to be. The point is it forms part of the cumulative assemblage and repetitive circulation of laws, public debates, media headlines, political discourse, social and education practices that have produced enduring 'common-sense' ideas about Muslim identity, participation and expression – ideas which both Muslim and non-Muslim students have absorbed. When I asked Mostafa, a year 11 student at a Catholic school in South Western Sydney, why he felt the need to 'think twice' before he talked in class, he said: 'I don't know how I know or when I knew … I just know'.

What do handshakes and 'radicalisation' have to do with each other? Nothing, one would reasonably think. Except in the war on terror, where the anticipatory logic of CVE relies on what Australian Muslim academic Mohamad Tabbaa calls the 'hyper-management of almost every aspect of [Muslims'] existence', even handshakes can be infected with the 'extremism' virus.

In 2017 a moral panic erupted around a high school in Sydney's south, Hurstville Boys. Rupert Murdoch's *The Australian* 'broke' a story about a small group of young Muslim male students from the school who had, for religious reasons, declined to shake hands with women presenters at an award ceremony, instead placing their hands across their chest as a mark of respect. They were permitted to do so, the media reported, because the school had adopted such a policy. A blaze of media scrutiny ensued, and the high school was catapulted to national attention. *The Australian* reported: 'Muslim public schoolboys "excused" from shaking hands with women'.

Then NSW education minister Rob Stokes reportedly declared the protocol sexist and sought legal advice as to whether the protocol was at odds with anti-discrimination law. An editorial in *The Australian* criticised the minister's 'defensive, confused response', asserting that he 'should have stated at the outset that public schools exist to reflect and perpetuate mainstream values, which include a belief in gender equity at odds with the assumptions behind the handshake ban'. One Nation's leader Pauline

Hanson and conservative Australian businessman and personality Dick Smith were called to comment on the issue, stating it was 'un-Australian' and it taught the young men not to respect women. On Sky News, Peta Credlin, former chief of staff to former Prime Minister Tony Abbott, said the handshake rule was 'dangerous' and left a 'vacuum for extremism', 'warning Muslim boys may become radicalised if they refuse to shake a woman's hand'. The story was reproduced on popular parenting website Kidspot and, in another example of 'glocalisation', picked up by Fox News and the UK's *Independent*.

A handful of Muslim guys placing their hand on their chest instead of shaking a woman's hand was an expression of religious belief which, in a climate of hypersensitivity to Muslim religious agency, was turned into a political act, dangerous otherness, dissent against 'mainstream values'. The controversy is a good example of how CVE policies can't be read in isolation. They stabilise meanings around risk, suspicion, extremism – around what counts as 'notable', worthy of 'attention'. They feed into the political climate and common-sense ideologies around Muslim religiosity.

And young Muslim kids are taking notice of this. As one student, Fatina (16, Lebanese-Australian, Inner West Islamic School), told me about the controversy:

> I felt sorry for those guys. Like, they're nobodies – not in a bad way, I mean, they're just like following the deen – and then next minute they're all in the media and everybody is on them. Like, those rich white guys rape girls in those colleges, but shaking hands? That's why I think we shouldn't be too expressive, because it does get taken the wrong way. And I think if Muslims want to go about with getting into politics or their religion and things like that, I don't think that should ever be considered radicalised, but that's how it is. I think

that Muslims always have to watch about how much they could say and the best they could say in front of others. They should just be minimal.

Fatina's words are sobering. No disclaimer or qualification in a policy document is going to undo the political and ideological climate that puts young Muslims under a national microscope. No carefully worded 'rubric' is going to protect Muslim kids from being disciplined and demonised for the most banal rituals and trivial behaviour. The message to Muslims is loud and clear. It's safer to *just be minimal.*

CHAPTER 5

FREE SPEECH AND ANGRY YOUTH

What we want is more learning in schools
and less activism in schools.

—*Prime Minister Scott Morrison*

Jihan was a student at a public school in Liverpool that supported my project but was, due to the education department's rejection of my ethics application, unable to participate. I was in touch with a teacher at the school, who told me that she taught a remarkable student, a refugee from Iraq, whom she recommended I speak to for my project. I emailed Jihan and as she was in the thick of year 12 and too busy to meet me, she kindly offered to fit a phone interview into her gruelling study schedule. I 'met' her over the phone as I sat in my car, parked on the side of a busy main road. After some light chitchat, I asked Jihan to talk me through how she felt about her identity. Her response blew me away: 'I think it's been definitely, like, one of fragmentation and disjuncture', she started,

> particularly in Iraq after the overthrow of the Saddam Hussein administration due to the United States–led

coalitions and then obviously emigrating to Australia as a refugee, there's a lot of difficulties in that story: discomfort, guilt, doubt, despairs and so on. And sometimes I find myself stuck between an ethical dichotomy, between my passion and what I want to do, and then the experiences and the rationality that I try to embody, but it's obviously so difficult, because seeking refuge and then fleeing to the West, to the very place where the policies which funded the chemical weapons, the bombs, the new technologies, the new wars that just keep killing us, so it's a bit of an irony, I guess.

I remember how exhilarated I felt, sitting in my car listening to this young woman on my bluetooth speaker, as cars zoomed past me, the banal sounds of passing traffic juxtaposed against Jihan's bold, fierce and passionate voice reverberating in the enclosed space. Jihan's voice was powerful – which is why her subsequent account of feeling managed and censored disturbed me deeply.

Throughout high school, Jihan had been active in the refugee advocacy sector but was frustrated by the taming of her voice, her personhood, her anger:

It's mostly when I do my public speaking or I get asked to speak in conferences, and I get told to sort of not be too, how should I say it, angry in my voice. But I guess that's just my personality and anything I say sort of comes out as, not aggressive, but almost I guess being seen as an attack. I can't tone down my emotions.

Jihan's experience resonates with the tone policing of black women, whether African-American women, who are attacked with the Black Angry Woman trope, or Aboriginal and Torres Strait Islander women, who are similarly attacked for having 'the audacity to be angry', as Indigenous academic Chelsea Bond writes.

At some speaking events, Jihan had been given parameters on what she could say: 'They make it very clear that you can't go on this sort of stream of thought'. For Jihan, the refugee experience 'from young people in particular' is 'not filtered at all, it's very raw and authentic'. She believed this 'authenticity' scared and intimidated people, who interpreted the anger, the raw emotion, as 'an attack on them'. Jihan said:

> Sometimes, even within sort of progressive refugee
> movements, there's a lot of their politics, it's really, like,
> put under serious scrutiny because voices of any difference,
> including mine, can threaten to unravel those fragile
> bounds of solidarity. Some of the supposedly progressive
> groups have particular agendas. They only want to show
> that they're accommodating refugee needs. I felt like I was
> being commodified ... I sort of have to assimilate with the
> subcultures and conform to their standards and their claim
> over what a real suffering agenda is.

Jihan was struggling to be taken seriously on her own terms, while simultaneously challenging how refugee experiences can be coopted to serve other agendas and narratives. Jihan's story reminded me of what youth studies scholar Anita Harris has traced in her studies of girlhood in Australia as the 'self-made girl' as 'ideal citizen', particularly among young refugee women. This triumphalist narrative reinforces neoliberal notions of self-invention and individual responsibility. In Jihan's experience, 'a lot of Australians ...

just want to hear your story ... They don't want to hear my anger, they don't want to hear my concerns, my opinions, my perspective, and I think that's been my message throughout my advocacy work, and it's that I'm more than my story, I'm more than just a statistic, I'm more than just a stereotype, and certainly I'm more than just a refugee and a young person.

Jihan's story is an important one. It provokes us to think about the pressures and expectations placed on young people when they express anger, when they push against celebratory accounts of multiculturalism to demand attention to the geopolitical and imperial frames of the war on terror.

When I think about countering violent extremism policies, such as the *Community Awareness Training Manual* (CATM) I covered in the previous chapter, I think about them as webs spun around young people – people like Jihan. The webs hang discreetly in the background. Very often little explicit attention is given to these webs, but their implicit significance is key: they are a network of fine threads constructed to mark – sometimes going as far as to then trap – certain speech, behaviour and political identities. Perhaps there is no better policy document that demonstrates how far and wide the CVE web spreads than Australia's *Radicalisation Awareness Kit: Preventing Violent Extremism and Radicalisation in Australia* (RAK), published and prepared by the federal Attorney-General's Department in September 2015 as a complement to the CATM. The RAK is an extraordinary document that reveals a deep contempt by the state for young people's political activism. What's made abundantly clear by the RAK is that in the war on terror, the state's practice of demonising Muslim youth set the stage for demonising all youth.

THE POWER OF POLITICAL RHETORIC

The RAK is one of the principal documents setting out Australia's conceptual framework for radicalisation and violent extremism. It's also based on the expertise and research of the Monash Radicalisation Project. At the time of its launch, then Minister Assisting the Prime Minister on Counter-Terrorism Michael Keenan wrote to all state and territory education ministers to 'encourage them to share and promote the kit in their schools', despite the fact that two of the Monash University experts quoted in the report publicly declared that their research was never intended to be released in schools.

There seems to be a lot of uncertainty about where and how the RAK is being used. It remains available as an online resource on the Living Safe Together website, the Australian Government's primary output of CVE resources. On 6 September 2017, Pablo Carpay, First Assistant Secretary of the Countering Violent Extremism Centre in the Attorney-General's Department, addressed the Joint Standing Committee on Migration in its inquiry on migrant settlement outcomes. He told the committee that the RAK is distributed to a range of schools and other front-line workers in the community, that train-the-trainer sessions are offered and that people are trained in the use of those kits, which they can then roll out to a wider audience.

The RAK was condemned by then president of the NSW Teachers Federation Maurie Mulheron. The academic community also responded to the RAK with warnings that reducing the complex process of radicalisation 'to a checklist of behaviours for general consumption' could result in the 'targeting of Muslim students' and run the risk of mistaking 'ordinary teenage defiance' for 'genuine signs of radicalisation'. Such warnings were all the more potent given the RAK was published one week after a 14-year-old

Muslim student was arrested in Texas because his teachers suspected that the homemade clock he was building was a hoax bomb.

Like the CATM, the RAK uses Monash University's Behavioural Indicators Model as a rubric for defining radicalisation: 'When a person's beliefs move from being relatively conventional to being radical, and they want a drastic change in society, this is known as radicalisation. This is not necessarily a bad thing and does not mean these people will become violent.'

However, the document goes on to define the process of radicalisation as one in which a person advocates or uses violence to promote their cause. This process is explained as a series of decisions:

> As a person radicalises, they begin to develop and adopt attitudes and behaviours that seek to substantially transform the nature of society and government. These attitudes differ significantly from how most members of society view social issues and participate politically. In most instances such behaviour does not pose a danger and can even benefit the Australian community. However, when a person radicalises to the point of justifying, promoting or threatening violence for their cause, both the community and governments have a responsibility to act.

These definitions raise a similar set of concerns to those raised by the CATM: how and who defines what is 'relatively conventional'? What *is* the 'nature of society and government' and who decides? Is it evolving or fixed? What constitutes 'drastic change' or 'substantially transforming'? How do we measure how 'most members of society' view 'social issues'? Which social issues? Which members? What is meant by political participation?

As with the CATM, these questions can't be taken at face value given that for Indigenous people and racialised minorities, nonviolent protest, dissent and critique of mainstream White Australia and the state are so often punished in real and symbolic ways. Furthermore, the case studies included in the RAK reveal the traces of a neoliberal ideological agenda, disparaging collectivist democracy while gesturing towards 'acceptable' individualised, contained political participation.

One of the most prominent human-rights lawyers in Australia, former Human Rights Commissioner Gillian Triggs, has noted that the ambit of Australia's counter-terrorism legal regime 'creat[es] a chilling effect on freedom of speech and the press and breach[es] the right to privacy'. She has argued that the offence of 'advocating terrorism', for example, is 'an imprecise crime whose scope may cover, for example, opposing the Assad regime in Syria or supporting Palestinian efforts to gain statehood'.

Government policy on what constitutes 'radicalisation' must be addressed in this kind of political and legal context. The RAK and CVE policies must also be interrogated in the wider context of Australian parliaments passing increasingly draconian laws that erode democratic freedoms of speech, association and movement, the right to a fair trial and the prohibition on arbitrary detention. According to a report by the NSW Ombudsman in 2016, anti-consorting laws in NSW have been misused as a 'disruption and crime prevention tool' to target children, the homeless and Aboriginal people. Similar laws were before the Victorian parliament, applicable to children as young as 14, attracting widespread criticism. For example, the Police Accountability Project argued against the bill given the wider context of racialised moral panics over 'African gangs' and 'decades of intensive, discriminatory and exclusionary policing of young people of African-background in Victoria'. The

Victorian government ultimately allowed the bill to lapse in the upper house.

One of the fictional case studies in the RAK is about a young woman called Erin, who is drawn into an extreme right-wing movement and becomes involved in 'racist vandalism and hate crimes directed at immigrants and Muslims'. Erin is then reformed, at first dissatisfied with the lack of action, the 'drinking, fighting and hating' instead of 'making any changes'. The RAK tells us that this is what leads to Erin beginning to 'wonder if immigrants were really responsible for many of the problems' and her then starting to 'moderate her beliefs' and 'educate herself on issues rather than just accepting what others tell her'. It can't be easy to write these kinds of case studies, to zoom in on one scenario. But it strikes me as odd that a document aimed at young people would frame the impetus for Erin turning away from a group as her frustration with them not turning their rhetoric (hating) into action (changes). 'The white nationalist project is failing and that is why Erin starts to disengage' seems a rather strange way of 'educating' young white people about the dangers of such groups. How would somebody involved in a 'successful' right-wing movement learn to disengage?

It's in the description of Erin's disengagement process (after a period of imprisonment for having carried out hate crimes) that we can start to tease out some government signalling work about what counts as 'good political activism'. The case study explains: 'Erin does not entirely trust the government or police yet – it takes a long time to change some habits of thinking'. This kind of 'trust us!' rhetoric is obviously unsurprising in a government publication, particularly when the latest election study by the Australian National University reveals that trust in government has reached a record low.

The RAK case study then states that 'a community program helped [Erin] to learn how to protest and advocate for change in legitimate ways rather than dissenting by breaking the law or resorting to violence. She is beginning to feel that she really is a part of society and can have a say on things that matter to her.' Erin has 'moderated her beliefs'. What this means for somebody who has been involved in a right-wing movement is not spelt out. But the case study reassures us that Erin now understands she can protest 'in legitimate ways'. Earlier on in the RAK, in a section under 'ideology', readers are reassured that: 'Hateful ideology and anti-social ideas might be disturbing or offensive, but if someone has not committed to using violence or promoted its use, they have not radicalised to violent extremism'.

Reading this instantly conjures up certain images for me: anti-Muslim rallies held by Reclaim Australia across Australian cities in 2015; a far-right mob gathered in 'protest' over 'Africans' at St Kilda Beach, Melbourne, in January 2019, organised by alt-right leaders Blair Cottrell and Neil Erikson, with protesters giving the Nazi salute, and Senator Fraser Anning attending to declare: 'The revolution will eventually start. People have had enough of these people and they have got to be sent back to where they came from.' It also takes me back to the moment, in 2014, when Australia's then Attorney-General, George Brandis, stood up in federal parliament to defend the proposed repeal of legislative protections against hate speech and declared 'people have the right to be bigots'.

The RAK exists in an environment where political and media establishments seek to discipline the speech of people of colour while simultaneously defending the right to be a bigot, to stage violent anti-Muslim or anti-African rallies. The race-neutral language used in the RAK presumes (as all such policies do) that the 'lessons' from Erin's case study can be mapped onto an abstract, raceless young person. Erin has learnt she 'can have a say on things that matter to her'. But can an Indigenous person, a member of an ethnic or racial minority, a Muslim in the context of the war on terror, really have a say on things that matter to them?

Indigenous activist Tarneen Onus-Williams might beg to differ. In 2018, the 24-year-old delivered a speech at an Invasion Day rally that she and other black women had organised in Melbourne. Addressing a crowd of 60 000, Onus-Williams said, 'Fuck Australia, hope it burns to the ground' and called for the abolition of Australia Day. For this, Onus-Williams was subjected to relentless vitriolic attacks, including from the Victorian government and Opposition, and 'dozens of fiery news articles, including some attacking her family'. Former Victorian Premier Jeff Kennett also weighed in, attacking her 'inappropriate language' and suggesting she, an Indigenous woman, 'buy a one-way plane ticket'. There were calls for her removal from her role with the government-funded Koori Youth Council and demands for the council to be defunded.

She was just having a say on things that matter to her.

In 2017, the Islamic Council of Victoria (ICV), Victoria's peak Muslim body, made a submission to the federal Senate inquiry into the human right to freedom of religion or belief seeking 'urgently needed' federal funding to create a safe space for Muslim youth to meet and talk about a range of issues 'which in a public space would sound inflammatory'. Victoria's Premier Daniel Andrews emphatically rejected the idea, describing it as 'proposing to create a space where people can just rant', and calling it 'a hate space'. Insisting 'there is no safe way to rail against the West. There is no safe way to rail against the values that we hold dear', Andrews added, 'the notion you can safely, without being monitored, without being picked up by authorities, be involved in all the radicalisation we're trying to defuse makes no sense to me'. Despite the fact that the ICV was seeking federal, not state, funding for the 'safe space', the proposal prompted the Andrews government to announce it would review the ICV's state government funding. When it comes to the specific request of a 'safe space' for young Muslims to express their political views outside of the surveillance gaze, the state not only flatly repudiates any right to do so, by representing such a request in terms suggesting that it counts as an ideological war of 'us and them', it also flexes its coercive powers with threats over surveillance and funding. To 'rail against' – to criticise, condemn, protest, denounce, attack – the West will be met with consequences.

When writing a book like this, there is hardly a day when checking in on social media does not reveal yet another example of the problem I am trying to describe in this project. And so it goes that in early December 2019, as I was editing my book, I learnt that Australian Muslim artist Abdul Abdullah, whose work specifically draws on his experiences growing up Muslim in suburban Perth, 'coming of age in a post–September 11 world', was the latest Muslim denied the right to 'have a say on things that matter' to him. Abdullah is internationally renowned for his art, which addresses the politicisation of Muslim identity within mainstream Australian culture, exposing the 'prejudices and stereotypes which have demonised and marginalised Muslim youth'. As one of nine notable Australian artists on a national touring exhibition, two of Abdullah's displayed works, entitled *All Let Us Rejoice* and *For We Are Young and Free*, depicted two non-identifiable military figures with an outline of a smiley face over the top (a signature of Abdullah's artistic style) and invited 'the viewer to think about how the Australian military is perceived in Australia and in places where the military is engaged'. The artworks sparked outrage and were removed from a council-run gallery in Mackay, Queensland, with indications other councils would also forbid the works, on the basis that they were a political message attacking Australian soldiers.

Abdullah defended the works and, responding to the barrage of online abuse, is reported as saying,

> It pisses me off that I've had to defend my loyalty to this
> country for my whole adult existence … Looking at the way
> that people have engaged with this topic is really frustrating
> because it so quickly goes down to that 'I should go back
> to where I came from'. It seems to me that I'm not allowed
> to participate because of my name … I wonder if I had a
> different name or a different religion whether this would
> have been news at all.'

There is no shortage of such examples targeting young people of colour, in particular, which underlines my point that the RAK policy can't be read in isolation. Young people see what is defended, enabled, permitted, ignored and legitimised by governments, political leaders and powerful commentators on the one hand, and what is attacked, censored, shut down and punished, on the other. This provides them with their interpretive tools, their maps of meaning as to what counts as 'legitimate', how far the line can be pushed for the expression of 'hateful ideology', what will be monitored, picked up by authorities. What counts as 'freedom of speech'. Who is allowed to engage in political commentary, and in what form. Young people are navigating the boundaries of their political identities in response to highly publicised political rhetoric, demands and action, not the disingenuous ideals contained in a policy document.

GOOD PROTEST, BAD PROTEST

The second case study in the RAK attracted widespread mockery. It introduces us to Karen, who 'grew up in a loving family who never participated in activism of any sort'. Is this a hint that a loving family, a good family, is a non-activist/non-political family? Karen moves out of home, attends university and becomes involved in 'the alternative music scene, student politics and left-wing activism'. The horror. The case study says: 'In hindsight she thinks this was just "typical teenage rebellion" that went further than most'. The implication here is that student politics and left-wing activism push mainstream boundaries or are a mere childish phase. This is troubling when we consider the patronising message the RAK sends to young people about political engagement.

Karen's disengagement includes questioning 'the effectiveness of the protesting methods [illegal direct-action] used by the group she has joined. It seemed they might make short-term gains but that there was no sustainable change unless it was translated into wider community support and government policies.' Things are going well for Karen who ends up taking 'a paid job with a mainstream environmentalist organisation', working 'broadly in the environmental field', adopting a 'more moderate eco-philosophy' and 'developing a sustainable solution using the legal system'. The publication adds a disclaimer, noting that drawing attention to 'anti-government, anti-globalisation or anti-capitalist' causes through disruptive forms of activism is a legitimate expression of freedom of belief and free speech. It's the use or support of violence, threatening behaviour and/or criminal damage which steps over the line.

On the face of the case study, the undesirable behaviour seems to be using protest methods which break the law. But the disclaimers offered, and the apparent protection of 'disruptive activism', are nothing more than empty platitudes given the wider context of anti-protest and anti-association laws subsequently introduced by state governments. These include anti-protesting laws that expand police powers against protesters, laws that give public officials broad power to 'direct a person' to stop 'taking part in any gathering, meeting or assembly' on Crown-owned land, proposed laws aimed at punishing unlawful entry and disruption on farms – laws worded so broadly that arguably any 'inclosed land' will be affected (schools, mine sites, banks?).

Policy wording must be evaluated against government rhetoric. When, in 2018, animal-rights activists conducted nationwide coordinated protests and action targeting farms and abattoirs, bringing one of Melbourne's busiest CBD intersections to a standstill, the backlash was fierce. Scott Morrison condemned the animal-rights protesters as 'shameful', 'un-Australian' and 'green-collar criminals'. Protesters who broke into abattoirs were described as 'domestic terrorists'. In Queensland, a government crackdown on protests by the climate-action group Extinction Rebellion in 2019 was justified because they were 'radical' not 'peaceful' protesters. As climate change protests increased in 2019, governments' rhetoric and responses to protests and 'disruption' escalated. In a speech addressing the Queensland Resources Council in November 2019, Prime Minister Scott Morrison referred to such protests as 'this new absolutist activism, anarchism', commenting in a radio interview that same day: 'It's not okay for environmental, well, they're anarchist groups ... to be able to disrupt people's jobs, their livelihoods, to harass people as we saw down in Melbourne'. Not only is disruption apparently *not* a 'legitimate expression of freedom of belief and free speech' as claimed in the RAK, Morrison went further, characterising environmental protesters as 'anarchists', and vowing to introduce new laws targeting environmental groups that campaign against businesses providing goods and services to mining companies (as well as seeking to prevent such boycotts from spreading to other sectors, such as gas projects, abattoirs, airlines and the sugar-cane industry).

Why does the RAK, a policy document drafted in 2015, matter? For two reasons. The first is that it's a government publication, addressed to and aimed at students. On paper, the 'right to protest' is seemingly protected and distinguished from 'illegal direct action'. But in the years since the RAK's publication, it's clear that the policy wording rings false. Indeed, what are young people to make of it when their forms of lawful protests are treated with contempt and ridicule?

When, in 2018, up to 150000 Australian students skipped school to participate in the School Strike 4 Climate movement, staging coordinated lawful protests around the country, they were criticised, and in some cases mocked, by politicians and sections of the media. The message from the Prime Minister Scott Morrison was categorical: 'We don't support our schools being turned into parliaments. What we want is more learning in schools and less activism in schools.' With the 2019 Global Strike 4 Climate, protests were again met with criticism from the government. Federal education minister Dan Tehan blamed 'green political activists' for encouraging the students, a patronising denial of young people's agency. The protests were 'just a disruption' and should instead be 'held on weekends' so as not to 'disrupt business, schools, universities'. Students would 'learn more at school than at a protest rally'.

It's clear that the kind of distinctions made in the RAK don't translate into how governments in reality differentiate between direct action (such as the above-mentioned animal rights activists) and youth mobilisations. This is more than just 'skipping school'. When it comes to climate change, young people are obviously rejecting the implied government line to trust in 'mainstream organisations', 'moderate' their vision, adopt 'philosophy' over 'action', work 'broadly' not in targeted ways, all codes for maintaining the status quo.

That youth climate-change activist Greta Thunberg has become a lightning rod for criticism is a case in point. She represents everything a neoliberal state fears: a young person who refuses the status quo, who rejects the rhetoric of trickle-down and gradual change. The language with which she is attacked is also revealing in its patronising dismissal of young people's agency and intellect. Young people are aware of how they are perceived as immature, incomplete. As Yassir (17, Syrian-Australian, Orthodox Christian, Blacktown) told me: 'I'm not powerless just because I'm young'. Another student, Adam (17, Irish/Jewish, Kings Langley), wrote this in response to a task asking students to reflect on growing up in today's social and political climate: 'The fear of individuality is what is coming, the fear of us millennials. Societies that continue to praise individuality, also continue to crush it before it blossoms.'

In her 2018 TEDx talk, Thunberg responded to those who criticised her protest, and told her to instead 'study to become a climate scientist', by questioning the claims made by neoliberal capitalism: 'what is the point of learning facts in the school system,' she asked, 'when the most important facts given by the finest science of that same school system clearly means nothing to our politicians and our society?'

In a neoliberal society that privileges the individual over the collective, there is deep and growing anxiety within governments and other powerful institutions about youth anger being harnessed to make concrete demands, challenge ideologies, refuse free-market rationalities, and reject political slogans and false promises.

Which brings me to the second reason why CVE policies like the RAK can't be ignored. Words like 'radical', 'extreme', 'disruptive' have been weaponised against Muslims in the war on terror to stifle their dissent and protests long before #freeKaren became a trending hashtag. 'National security' has been used to justify all manner of violations of Muslims' rights and liberties without pushback from the wider community (like I argued in my introduction, when a nation can turn a blind eye to the ongoing systematic abuses of Indigenous people's human rights, it's little wonder that what happens to Muslims is 'business as usual').

Take, for example, the widespread outrage at Scott Morrison's 2019 vow to crack down on boycott campaigns. Since 2005, Palestinians (myself included) and their supporters (including anti-Zionist Jewish groups) have been campaigning for the global Boycott, Divestment and Sanctions (BDS) movement against Israel. BDS advocacy has been condemned as anti-Semitic, met with lawsuits or flatly disregarded, as in the case of, say, SBS screening Israel's hosting of Eurovision in 2019. Notably, there has been widespread silence about the right to advocate for BDS, and state suppression of BDS protest rights have largely gone unnoticed. In 2011, Victoria Police arrested 19 protesters at a peaceful BDS action organised by the Coalition Against Israeli Apartheid. During a bail variation hearing at the Magistrates Court of Victoria, the police 'acknowledged that the demonstrations had been peaceful, that solidarity activists hadn't damaged property and there was no record of police or any member of the public being injured'. Alarmingly, they also confirmed that 'for some of the activists arrested on 1 July ... a decision had been made to arrest the protesters before the demonstration', with those in leadership specifically targeted. Police also testified and 'acknowledged that police infiltrators had been sent to pro-Palestine solidarity meetings in order to monitor the activity of BDS activists'. For Muslims and Arabs, particularly Palestinians, the state has long sought to regulate which causes and forms of protests are permissible, and which aren't.

The capacity for Muslims to choose how, where and when to express their political subjectivity has been constrained in some astonishingly egregious ways, such as a council in Victoria seeking to impose a 'ban on any political discussion' as a condition on a mosque planning permit. What Muslim communities have experienced as 'suspect communities' since 9/11 set the stage for the increasingly draconian crackdown on protests, dissenting speech, civil disobedience and rebellion we see unfolding today. But still, I can't make this argument without pointing out the obvious: that state efforts to punish and control Muslim political agency have been practised par excellence against Indigenous people and their supporters. Consider that local councils which have cancelled citizenship ceremonies on Australia Day – because the date 26 January marks the invasion, dispossession and genocide of Indigenous people – have had their right to hold citizenship ceremonies stripped by the federal government. Government is there, determining what counts as 'good' and 'bad' protest and dissent.

It is important to connect the dots between the war on terror, or the language of radicalism and extremism being used against environmental activists, or the patronising and paranoid containment of youth dissent. State power has expanded to control, as Nicholas De Genova puts it, 'the ever-mobile, and always receding, target' of the 'ever-amorphous, unbounded and limitless' global war on terror. In other words, the war on terror is about more than stopping the next 'bin Laden' or finding the next Muslim 'lone wolf'. It's about nation-making: protecting the neoliberal capitalist nation, the imperial democratic nation, especially when more and more people are pushing back against false promises and market agendas, challenging the very foundations of how nation states are imagined and structured. National security is leveraged in many ways, across multiple fronts.

Youth have always been the site of crisis and collective angst, burdened with both hopes and fears about the future as the next generation. Even as they are expected to change the future, their imagination of the future is managed and constrained. A neoliberal logic underpins this approach to youth, a logic Australian academic Cameron Smith identifies as 'reproducing neoliberal capitalism' by compelling young people to 'make the right "choices" within a strictly delimited market of acceptable ideological commitments'.

Policies such as the RAK, addressed to young people, are government articulating to young people who they should become. Directing them as to what kinds of political subjecthood, expression and participation are acceptable: contained, moderate, passive. In fact, one of the university students I interviewed, Rokaya (whom we met in chapter 1), made this exact point to me.

Rokaya told me that in 2018 her mother received a telephone call from ASIO requesting a meeting. Rokaya's mother had no idea why she was being contacted. Her first reaction was to ask Rokaya if she had said something at university. Rokaya started feeling paranoid: 'I was doing a politics subject on the Middle East and I'd been doing online research'. In fact, ASIO wanted to speak with Rokaya's mother about a comment somebody had left in response to a Facebook post Rokaya's mother had made. The post had been about prayer and war. Rokaya explained:

> Mum's Facebook friend had commented, something like the West being responsible and having their day eventually for the harm they've done. I think the lady fit the *criteria* for who they think is a typical ISIS sympathiser, young Arab niqabi woman who posts a lot of religious and Islamic posts. All harmless but would look *extreme* to those who demonise the faith.

Rokaya explained that her mother told the ASIO officers to 'go and deal with real problems'. Rokaya was struck by how ASIO could find this comment by this woman on my mum's Facebook page and contact her simply because she posts religious and political stuff, but I literally read comment after comment calling for Muslims to be killed, on social media and the gaming sites I play on, and nobody says or does a thing. So, yeah, the whole thing made me paranoid about my online research, and I'm careful about what I google now.

A year after our interview, Rokaya contacted me again. She was writing her thesis on online White supremacist communities. She told me:

I'm waiting for the day I get a knock at the door because I'm researching these communities, or for my Middle Eastern politics classes. There's always this engrained surveillance despite doing nothing wrong. We were talking about it in class last week, and the typical response by non-Muslim students was, 'If you have nothing to hide then why are you worried about the surveillance?'

I asked Rokaya how this made her feel. 'They have no clue what this is doing. How the bigger goal is about creating docile citizens.'

Indeed.

CHAPTER 6

PROFILING IN SCHOOLS

We are locked in a global struggle with cynical
manipulators who exploit vulnerable young people
and children to commit acts of terror.

—*then NSW Premier Mike Baird*

The introduction of a countering violent extremism (CVE) policy specific to NSW schools occurred in January 2016, as part of an expansive range of measures targeting schools under Premier Mike Baird's Liberal state government. The measures were rolled out with 'special urgency' in response to the tragic shooting of a civilian police employee, Curtis Cheng, by 15-year-old Farhad Jabar outside NSW Police Force headquarters in Parramatta, Sydney, on 2 October 2015. The NSW policy is a good case study for understanding the more general problems of turning the CVE gaze on schools.

Developed by the NSW Department of Education, Catholic Schools NSW and the Association of Independent Schools of NSW, the *School Communities Working Together* (SCWT) strategy comprised 'Management guidelines for Department of Education executive staff' and an 'e-learning awareness module'. The strategy seeks to 'offer practical guidance to NSW Public School executive team members on how to manage *anti-social and extremist behaviour*' (my emphasis), defined as a *combination* of these two behaviours. Anti-social behaviour is behaviour that threatens the safe and secure atmosphere of the school, including bullying, harassment, discrimination, racism, illegal or criminal acts, physical violence or damaging school or other property. Extremist behaviour is demonstrated when a person believes that fear, terror and violence are justified to achieve ideological, political or social change.

The SCWT guidelines outline three ways schools can 'prepare for and respond to' issues of anti-social and extremist behaviour. The first is fostering resilient and inclusive school communities to help reduce the opportunity for extremist organisations to encourage young people to engage in their cause. The second is identifying and supporting young people who need additional assistance to help protect them from becoming vulnerable to extremist influences. And the third is having effective incident management and support systems in place to assist schools to manage anti-social and extremist behaviour impacting the school community.

The SCWT guidelines characterise ideal school communities as places that 'champion the values of respect, responsibility, participation, care, fairness and democracy', as places that foster 'a positive school culture and enhance respectful and inclusive school environments'. Teachers' responsibilities include 'reaching out to students and noticing changes in behaviour'. Education professionals are acknowledged as best placed to maintain discipline at school and provide safe, supportive and responsive learning environments. Also acknowledged is that teachers are in a position to make judgments about their students and are encouraged to raise their concerns with a nominated member of a school's executive. Completion of the online awareness module is encouraged but not mandatory. It was against this backdrop that I interviewed and ran workshops with students.

WARNING SIGNS

Indicators that 'may suggest that something is wrong' in a student are listed. According to the SCWT guidelines, what distinguishes 'typical teenage behaviour' from a student 'becoming vulnerable to anti-social and extremist behaviour' is 'a pattern to the behaviour, a sudden significant change in behaviour or if the student displays a number of the signs'. Signs include increased interest in or devoutness regarding religious beliefs, significant change in appearance, significant change in behaviour or language in line with an extreme ideology, dialogue that may try to justify violence as a solution to an issue, statements of moral superiority, or searching for answers about faith, identity, ancestry and/or belonging in an inappropriate way. What is deemed 'inappropriate' is left open.

At this first stage, teachers are responsible for identifying and supporting young people they deem to be displaying signs of vulnerability, conducting risk assessments and implementing management plans if needed. They are also encouraged to seek risk-management advice from the Specialist Support Team.

The SCWT guidelines impose a *duty* on schools to report to the police, to an Incident Report and Support Hotline or one of the designated support units if they become aware of concerns about a potential or an actual incident of anti-social and extremist behaviour. The duty is activated if there is a report from an external source, such as a parent or carer, peer, police, or a member of the community, that a student is displaying anti-social and extremist behaviour. This could be while the student is at school or during an off-site school activity or a post on a social media site. The duty is also activated if there is a notable and sudden change in a student's behaviour and it's discovered that the student is associating with people involved in anti-social and extremist behaviour.

Examples given of reportable incidents are threats made to a school via the school's website or social media site such as 'ISIS is coming'; graffiti in the school relating to extremist or terrorist organisations; a student threatening other students, in regard to religious practices or beliefs; a noticeable change in a student's behaviour, including the student posting pro-terrorist related information on their own or other's social media site; a student writing and sharing violent or threatening racial comments; and a student who says they want to travel to a country where there is conflict and fighting occurring.

Once a report is made, a case manager is assigned to assess the incident and commence case management at the school.

A legal issues bulletin released by the Legal Services Directorate of the NSW education department in March 2018 clarifies schools' duties. Schools are *not* permitted to investigate allegations of anti-social and extremist behaviour. When an allegation is received, schools have an obligation to notify the appropriate authority (in cases of imminent risk, the police, and for all other cases, the Incident Report and Support Hotline). The examples of anti-social and extremist behaviour cited in the bulletin are the same as those set out in the SCWT guidelines, with one notable addition. 'Expressing support for an extremist group' is listed as 'anti-social and extremist behaviour' and must therefore be reported. Let that sink in: expressing support is a reportable incident.

'RACE-NEUTRAL' POLICY TARGETS

Race works quietly, confidently, behind the scenes, to signal who the protagonists and actors, audiences and subjects are in the SCWT guidelines. Like in the *Community Awareness Training*

Manual and the *Radicalisation Awareness Kit*, the language poses as race-neutral. But in a political climate in which extremism is, in the words of race academics David Tyrer and Salman Sayyid, a 'floating signifier' that has, through a sustained discursive regime, stabilised its meaning to 'Muslim', it's reasonable to see how the common-sense implied target of the SCWT guidelines is the Muslim student.

Consider the fact sheet for students. The opening paragraph addresses students and their family and friends who are 'affected by conflict which is taking place overseas or instances of violence here in Australia. Some students may have family or friends who live in parts of the world which are affected by the conflict reported through the media.' The primary audience is one with transnational ties to conflict zones in the context of the 'war on terror' (that is, Muslim countries, the Middle East). This is how this document immediately contains its message as Muslim-specific. And so, when the fact sheet proceeds to make the following statements to students, it stands to reason that these exhortations are being made with a Muslim audience in mind: it's never okay for people to force their views on others or use threats or violence to get their opinions across, or to solve problems; growing children are in a stage of exploring their values and beliefs and may search for and push the boundaries of acceptable, responsible behaviour during this process; parents concerned that a person in their community is 'showing possible signs of terrorism' are encouraged to call the National Security Hotline.

To suppose that this information applies to 'all students' is to be grossly naive of the work done by CVE national and state policy to entrench the idea that SCWT addresses a Muslim problematic. It's not white students who are on 8chan or gaming sites with 'Brendan Tarrant' as their profile name, as my friend told me, who are targeted. It's not the parents of White supremacist students who must call hotlines and monitor their circles. When then foreign affairs minister Julie Bishop appeared on the ABC's *7.30 Report* in 2017 following the June London terror attacks, I noted how emphatically she came down on 'the kinds of posts that incite hatred and violence and radicalisation and teach people how to carry out these savage, positively medieval attacks, then there should be an ability to take that kind of – that kind of post down immediately'. I noted this part of her interview, in particular, because of how striking a double standard it was, given the flood of online posts inciting hate, violence and murder against Muslims on social media sites and in the comments sections of the most popular news sites and blogs. I noted how my Muslim friends routinely have their accounts suspended after political posts, while accounts calling on 'setting up abortion clinics in Lakemba', for example, are allowed to remain.

In September 2016, nine months after the SCWT guidelines were introduced, the NSW Department of Education hosted a one-day workshop titled 'School Communities Working Together: exploring the current climate with a panel of experts'. Topics discussed at the workshop included: the 'Current NSW threat environment', 'CVE, radicalisation and Australian Muslim youth', 'Outlaw motorcycle gangs', 'Student resilience programs for anti-social extremism behaviour (ASEB)' and 'CVE in NSW and the education sector'.

Attending the workshop were the most senior members of the Department of Education, senior officers of NSW Police and the Australian Federal Police, and senior representatives of the NSW government's Policy and Programs. There was one academic presenter, who spoke about 'Student resilience programs for ASEB'. The remaining two expert presenters were Muslim: NSW's Muslim Chaplain for Corrective Services, who presented on the topic of 'CVE, radicalisation and Australian Muslim youth', and the CEO of the Muslim Women Association and United Muslim Women Association, who presented 'An overview of reality'.

'How did this terrorist stay in the shadows, hiding among us in plain sight?' asked Prime Minister Scott Morrison after the Christchurch attack. Well, where were the experts on the influence on young people of the increasingly prominent rise of far-right, White nationalist and Islamophobic movements at the conference? Where were white community members?

But it gets worse.

In the March 2018 legal bulletin issued to NSW schools, the NSW Department of Education emphasises that 'gender, culture, nationality, religion, descent, ethno-religious or national origin' are not 'in and of themselves an indicator of anti-social and extremist behaviour'. Instead, 'the context of the behaviour (for example the difference between a rational debate in the classroom or staffroom about passionately held views and a heated exchange in the playground) is important'. The bulletin reassures educators that it's not a breach of discrimination law to notify that a person *of a different race* has engaged in anti-social and extremist behaviour, provided the notification is prompted by the *person's behaviour and not their race.*

This is critical. For Muslim students, the stakes get higher depending on how race is defined. Sure enough, the bulletin follows the federal *Racial Discrimination Act* and NSW's anti-discrimination laws to narrowly and problematically define race as 'colour, nationality, descent and ethnic, ethno-religious or national origin'. Religious groups are excluded from the definition of race unless narrowed to 'ethno-religious groups' (that is, Jews and Sikhs). Discrimination on the basis of a person's religion is, by this definition, exempt.

Let that sink in.

In a policy strategy that so clearly envisages its audience as

Muslim students, this is alarming. Islam does not count as race. Therefore, simply *being Muslim* can be 'an indicator of anti-social and extremist behaviour'. Far from obscuring the reality of CVE's racialisation of Muslim subjects, the legal bulletin brilliantly illuminates it.

To look like 'an extremist', to engage in practices tied with 'extremism', ascribes being Muslim in a certain stereotyped way as dangerous, threatening. A Muslim academic peer attending a CVE symposium in Canberra recounted to me how a CVE 'expert' turned to her and explained that a Muslim girl who stops plucking her eyebrows (a prohibition normally associated with Wahhabi religious edicts) is a 'warning sign'. The CVE gaze reaches deep down into the most intimate, personal spaces of the Muslim's life. A beard on a Muslim guy, unplucked eyebrows on a Muslim girl: both are potentially infused with the capacity to affect as extremist. The SCWT guidelines enable teachers to flag increased religiosity and changes in appearance as potential 'signs'.

The direction to school staff as to what does *not* constitute anti-social and extremist behaviour is, on its face, pedagogically sound and consistent with aspirational statements about what schools should offer students. Namely, 'safe environments' where students can 'genuine[ly] attempt to process and understand a situation', where everyone can discuss, explore and debate 'world issues'. It is, however, as law and policy so often are, 'disembodied from its subjects' in the words of academic Victoria Sentas. The SCWT guidelines can't be reduced to their policy wording. Policy plays out in lived social relations, where debates around national identity, extremism, the 'limits' of multiculturalism and 'Australian values', and the 'war on terror' seep into embodied habits of thinking and speaking in the intimate spaces of everyday life. It's not simply that the CVE gaze risks racial and religious profiling: it's that the CVE gaze expects racial and religious profiling.

CHAPTER 7

TAMING 'JUNIOR JIHADIS'

Teachers 'must ID radical students'.

—The Australian, *9 June 2017*

The teachers look to me whenever they need to be reminded that it's the Boys of Punchbowl who are wrong, who are lesser beings. But then, when we're on the outside, Fatala and I are the same – we are sand niggers, rejected and hated and feared.

—The Lebs, *Michael Mohammed Ahmad*

Almost 3000 articles referring to Islam and Muslim, 152 incendiary front pages, all in one year. Those were the results of a year-long investigation conducted by Muslim Australian media group OnePath Network. Tracking coverage of Muslims and Islam over 2017 in five News Ltd newspapers – *The Australian*, *The Daily Telegraph*, the *Herald Sun*, *The Courier Mail* and *The Advertiser* – OnePath found 3000 articles referred to Islam or Muslims alongside words such as violence, extremism, terrorism or radical. 'With the number of incendiary front-pages in 2017 about government and police policy regarding terrorism', OnePath argued, 'a casual observer would not be faulted for thinking that Australia was actively engaged in daily combat on its streets'. One topic that received extensive coverage in 2017 concerned Punchbowl Boys' High School, a public school located in the South Western Sydney suburb of Punchbowl, with News Corporation leading a frenzied charge against the high school concerning the dismissal of the school's principal and deputy. In a policy environment that lacks transparency, this is a good case study for unpacking government expectations around the operation and role of the *School Communities Working Together* guidelines in NSW schools. It's also important to trace how such a media frenzy creates feedback loops for young people, particularly students attending schools outside of Western Sydney. We'll soon meet young people who live in the north-western, eastern and northern suburbs of Sydney who associate Punchbowl and its surrounding suburbs with crime, danger and radicalisation. It's therefore important to understand how these negative associations, cultural idioms and terms of reference circulate in public commentaries, debates and media headlines, and become embedded as 'common sense'.

THE PUNCHBOWL MORAL PANIC

That Punchbowl Boys' High was at the centre of a moral panic over 'radicalisation' was not surprising given the school's controversial history, notorious particularly in the 1990s for 'drive-bys, gangs and drugs', barbed-wire fences and surveillance cameras. Under the leadership of Jihad Dib, who was principal from 2007 to 2014, the school turned around this reputation, with improved student enrolments, performance and graduation rates, and stronger connections established between students, teachers and parents.

The News Corp story broke with a report in *The Australian* on 3 March 2017 alleging that Chris Griffiths, the principal of Punchbowl Boys' High, had been sacked 'for excluding female staff from official events'. *The Daily Telegraph* soon followed, quoting a spokesperson for the NSW education department that a departmental appraisal had raised multiple issues at the school, alleging 'a high level of staff disunity and disharmony, plus increased disengagement of the school from its local community'. The article also quoted anonymous 'police officers' claiming there were 'concerns about radicalisation' at Punchbowl High and that 'the students were being led down a dangerous path by the principal', who 'one officer said converted to Islam in 2014'.

When Department of Education Secretary Mark Scott was interviewed by 2GB radio shock jock Ray Hadley, he was unable (or unwilling) to challenge Hadley's claim that 'things had gone off the rails' at the school since Griffiths had converted to Islam and 'shoved' Islam 'down the throat of children'. The 2GB interview was reported in *The Daily Telegraph*, including additional claims that the 'newly converted Muslim' had been dismissed for 'refusing to run a deradicalisation program'. The article also claimed that the principal and his deputy, Joumana Dennaoui, had been sacked because of 'serious concerns [the principal] was planning to only allow Muslim students into the school after he recently converted to the faith'. Further, the article stated that Griffiths had 'alienated non-Muslim teachers – including senior female teaching staff – and excluded them from key school events'.

Buried towards the end of the article, and therefore rendered invisible, was a denial by Mark Scott that Griffiths had attempted to 'create his own Islamic school' and a quote by Scott that 'some of the allegations made against Mr Griffiths were unsubstantiated'.

It was the conclusion to the article that was most interesting, in terms of the final impression it sought to convey about the school. The article profiled the replacement principal, Robert Patruno, who came to Punchbowl High from his role as principal of Reiby Juvenile Justice Centre, a 'hardcore maximum security children's prison, where young boys were strip-searched if pens or pencils went missing from the classroom'. The article concluded with a quote from an interview with Patruno during his time at Reiby: 'Some of these kids come from such a dark place that we try to provide some light in their life … They have been exposed to things that no one should be. We develop positive thoughts and resilience here – we have set up an environment that is like any classroom.' In ending the article on this note, the line between Reiby and Punchbowl High was completely blurred. And why would it not be, given the appointment signified in no uncertain terms how the education department viewed the school and the boys in it? The distinction between a school and children's prison, between students and child prisoners, dissolved.

In further coverage, two '19–20-year-old unidentified men', 'both of whom were said to be of Middle Eastern appearance', were reported as allegedly threatening Robert Patruno outside the school gates. Passing reference was then made to 'students chanting "bring back Griffiths" in classes' and a community petition of 'more than 1600 signatures calling for the pair's reinstatement'. Such a community response was framed as a security issue, and not one which questioned the department's decision or claims. The article noted, in light of parental backlash and the case of the two men, that Patruno and the school 'had not requested additional security'.

Linking the 'threat' by two unidentified individuals with legitimate protests by a parent body enabled a larger field of meaning about Muslims and the school as sites of danger to be made. The language used to describe both the principal and the school confidently invoked familiar racial motifs regarding Muslims and

Western Sydney. References to Griffiths, the dismissed principal, always foregrounded the principal's conversion to Islam and his refusal to implement the CVE program: the principal, 'who had resisted intervention from the department'; the principal, 'who converted to Islam in 2014'; the principal, 'an Islamic convert'. Even once he was reappointed as principal to a different school in Western Sydney, in 2018, newspaper headlines described Griffiths as the 'Islamic convert principal'. In other words, he joined the wrong side – don't forget it.

The lexical choices in the various descriptions of the school conjured up a familiar train of essentialised, stereotypical tropes about Muslim bodies and spaces: 'besieged Punchbowl Boys High School', 'troubled school', 'hit by allegations of discrimination, threats and violence and a fractured relationship with police', 'a Western Sydney boys school at the centre of Islamic radicalism fears', 'the state's most troubled school', 'one of the country's most controversial public schools'.

In a cynical attempt to link the story to a similar 'radicalisation in schools' beat-up in the UK, *The Australian*'s coverage noted that NSW education minister Rob Stokes, studying in Oxford at the time the story broke, would be seeking advice from British education officials on 'Birmingham's infamous Operation Trojan Horse scandal', defined in the article as 'an attempt by Islamic school officials to introduce Islamist and Salafism principles into the public education system in Britain by marginalising or forcing key teachers out of several schools in Birmingham'. The next line noted that Stokes maintained there were no parallels between Punchbowl and Operation Trojan Horse – a buried and therefore worthless disclaimer.

An *Australian* editorial titled 'Who will stand up for fundamental Australian values?' argued that 'vital questions' arose 'about the basic values that underpin education in this country', because of the controversies at Hurstville Boys and Punchbowl Boys – 'two government schools in Sydney's southwest, where many Muslims live' and where 'there are worrying links between disaffected youth, crime and jihadi sentiment'. 'Schools', the editorial declared, 'are not exempt from the war for the soul of Islam'. The handshake controversy at Hurstville Boys High was being dragged back into the public light. The editorial quoted federal education minister Simon Birmingham, who said then Prime Minister Malcolm Turnbull's government 'expects schools to uphold and promote Australian values and is monitoring the response of states to these issues, including their application of appropriate deradicalisation programs'.

Each media report added a new 'twist' to the Punchbowl controversy, almost always based on anonymous sources. According to a *Daily Telegraph* report on 10 March, with the headline 'Punchbowl parents vent their fury', 'angry parents' were complaining 'their kids felt "pressured" into daily prayer meetings, Koranic lectures and even cutting their hair by other Muslim students, as it can be revealed almost 20 NSW schools have been identified as "at risk" of radicalising Islamic children'. Despite the headline and article referring to 'parents', only one parent was quoted, alleging that 'their son had been bullied for having long hair and badgered by his peers for not joining in prayers'.

Teachers were reportedly trying to 'defuse tensions' with students, and 'female and male teachers' were greeting students at the front gates and 'shaking hands' with them. Asked if 'the "hand shaking" was part of the deradicalisation program', a department spokesman noted it was 'part of the school's regular morning routine'. The article then contextualised this 'gesture' by referring to the 'furore' at Hurstville Boys. The fixation on handshakes would be the stuff of comedy, if the context wasn't so dangerous.

The story was picked up by Ten's evening news that same day

under the headline 'New evidence that terror training starts in high school', and repeated most of the claims made in the article.

A feature article in *The Weekend Australian*, with the headline 'Inside Punchbowl Boys High School: a battle for hearts and minds', attempted to provide more context and background, but ultimately it still resorted to a frame which inscribed Muslim students, their school and the suburbs in which they live, with violence, danger, 'otherness' and inferiority.

The article suggested that 'an intriguing internal political battle over how to run a school' appeared to be 'at the centre of the controversy'. The dismissed principal had reportedly changed direction, 'shutting out the local community', adopting an 'authoritative style', been 'less open and engaged' than his predecessor, Jihad Dib, which education department secretary Mark Scott admitted was a factor in his removal.

The article also offered more insight into how parents responded to allegations that Griffiths had been 'zealous': parents were 'dumbfounded' and strongly rejected 'claims he was implementing strict Islamic rules at the school'. Such revelations, which contradicted the basic premise of the department's dismissal and claims made in the media coverage, had minimal impact.

The underlying premise of the story hinged on stereotypical tropes and assumptions. One particularly disturbing 'taken-for-granted', 'common-sense' ideology was the role of the police in the school. The article had this to say about the principal's 'difficult relationship with the police':

Punchbowl might not have been the war zone it once was but it's still a tough neighbourhood. The school has a high concentration of Muslim students from disadvantaged backgrounds. And while there is no evidence it was, or is, a hotbed of radicalisation, there is the potential for that to change. With about 90 per cent of the school's students now Muslim, concern has grown among local police in that it could also be, or become, an incubator of potential terrorists.

The article went on to quote 'police sources', who said that 'while Griffiths was running the school, they had no clear idea what was going on inside it. They say he was openly hostile to counter-radicalisation programs rolled out in response to Islamic State propaganda.'

Police involvement in a school with a 'high concentration' of Muslim students is taken for granted as an unquestionable, common-sense expectation. A principal's deference to police involvement, to CVE interventions in his school triggered by the demographics of the school rather than any actual incident, is accepted as reasonable.

This normalises the dehumanising reduction of young Muslim students to a homogenous category of 'becoming terrorist', always cooking away in an incubator of potential terrorists. There is a clear line of argument here: disadvantage plus a large population of young Muslim means there is always, inherently, potential for *them* to become terrorists. It made no difference that the reporters wrote there is 'no evidence it was, or is, a hotbed of radicalisation'. Too little, too late.

What began as a scandal over Punchbowl High quickly expanded to include Punchbowl Primary in stories that hit the front pages of *The Daily Telegraph*, with the headlines 'Allah Allah Allah, Oi Oi Oi' and 'Behead of the Class'. What were these but typical examples of what the late brilliant scholar Edward Said called 'thought-stopping headlines' designed to intentionally create visceral fear in the media industry's 'covering Islam'?

The articles that accompanied these incendiary headlines were based on the claims of an anonymous teacher 'blowing the whistle on Islamic extremism' and consistently connected Muslim youth with extremism and radicalisation. The articles asserted Punchbowl Primary was 'a hotbed of radicalisation' with kids in year 5 'using religious language' and 'chanting the Koran', as well as claiming the 'infamous' primary school was disrespecting women and police, and had Islamic prayer group bullies who supposedly targeted children who didn't pray.

The article referred to 'three teachers' having taken stress leave, received counselling, or been paid compensation 'because of bullying from Islamic students'. The primary-aged students were described not just as students but as a racialised category of 'Islamic students', such that their actions laboured under the weight of every stereotype and trope that category imagines.

In one 2014 incident, a teacher complained that two students had been kicked out of class for being 'repeatedly uncooperative and disruptive' and that when placed in 'time out' they apparently 'began audibly chanting the Koran in Arabic'. The 'concerned teacher' 'could give no explanation of their behaviour'. In another incident, alleged by the 'whistleblower' former teacher, 'two Year 5 students pushed her into a corner and chanted the Koran in Arabic around her'. The education department confirmed 'an incident occurred matching that description' and that the students had been 'counselled and put on detention'. A range of allegations were made from 'threatening death notes' to the teacher's family, to walking out of class at prayer time, to making racist comments to a peer. The article referred to an 'incident report' describing 'how boys were teasing each other about eating sausages and seafood because they were doing work related to food in the classroom'. According to the teacher, 'this lack of discipline at the school encouraged extremist behaviour'.

A denial by the department of any religious-related violence at the school was lost in the litany of bizarre claims. That the replacement school principal, Robert Patruno, confirmed students were, in fact, respecting their female teachers, and that he had found no evidence of 'Islamic State sympathisers' at the school, was lost in the incendiary headlines and sensationalist, exaggerated claims. A 'prominent Sunni community member Jamal Daoud' was interviewed in an article, with the headline 'Radical swamp for years', and he claimed that 'radicalisation problems' had been rife for a while. The strategic reliance on quotations from sources affirming the line of argument was clear.

The indexing of students' alleged conduct within the context of radicalisation claims complemented official radicalisation narratives promoted by government and 'experts'; namely, approaching 'radicalisation' as an empirical task legitimised by the industry of 'experts' claiming to use scientific typologies to draw conclusions around who is 'becoming terrorist' and what behaviour counts as suspicious – in this case, using religious language, reciting the Qur'an, disrupting classes, even joking about eating 'sausages and seafood' in a class are presented in a taken-for-granted way as 'signs'. Religious rituals – praying five times a day or reciting the Qur'an – are pinned with suspicion and treated as risk indicators. The misbehaviour of primary school-aged children is coded as 'becoming terrorist' when performed by 'Islamic students'. It makes me wonder what *The Australian* would report if they came to my house and heard my son screaming 'Allahu Akbar' as he jumps on the trampoline, or how his phase of loudly chanting 'bismillah al Rahman al Raheem' as he plays with his *PJ Masks* figurines would be interpreted.

On 18 March, Channel 9's national program *60 Minutes* featured a 'special investigation' inside 'the Australian schools at risk of extremism', headlining its story 'Lessons of hate'. Presenter Karl Stefanovic introduced the story as follows:

> In the past two weeks, Punchbowl Boys High School
> has been at the centre of a bitter row over schoolyard
> radicalisation, with accusations not enough has been done
> to stop students being swayed by extremists. The dispute
> calls into question our very approach to tackling this
> insidious threat – and the radicals who recruit them.

As part of the investigation, Stefanovic interviewed Department of Education Secretary Mike Scott. Scott claimed that the principal had been removed because he had failed to report threats of violence made by students against staff and that under Griffiths's control, Punchbowl High had turned from a 'poster school' to being 'isolated' and 'locked away' from the community: 'I was concerned that he was given three occasions to welcome that program into the school and he decided not to, and it was on learning that I decided I wanted a full appraisal at that school'. The program Scott is referring to is the *School Communities Working Together* program. The case of Punchbowl High demonstrates the program is mandatory and the serious consequences for principals refusing to implement it.

After Mike Scott's interview on *60 Minutes*, even the popular parenting website Kidspot chimed in, promoting the program as an insight 'into this very real and dangerous threat facing our schools' and noting its alarm that schools, 'meant to be a safe haven for children', 'are being targeted by Islamic extremists as possible breeding ground for junior jihadis'. Parents around Australia worried about lunch-box ideas or how to plan the ultimate birthday party could add concerns over 'junior jihadis' to their list.

Every Islamophobe's dream native-informant 'expert' on Islam and Muslims, avowed 'apostate' Ayaan Hirsi Ali, who describes Islam as 'a destructive, nihilistic cult of death' and 'the new fascism' and has said the West is 'at war with Islam', then weighed in. Ahead of a speaking tour in Australia, she wrote an opinion piece in *The Daily Telegraph* pontificating that it was 'worrying but not a surprise' that students were 'acting out radical Islamic ideology'.

I remember Hirsi Ali's article clearly. I was sitting in the foyer of a Catholic high school in South Sydney, waiting to deliver a writing workshop to students, when I received a text from a friend, sending me the link to the article. I read it. Oh, the irony of reading her demand for Islamic schools to be shut down as I sat in a school foyer surrounded by statues of Jesus and Mary.

Hirsi Ali cautioned: 'Whether it is in Raqqa or Punchbowl the Islamist strategy with regard to children is the same: indoctrinate them, prevent critical thinking, then accept and implement sharia law'. 'Raqqa or Punchbowl': in other words, Punchbowl becomes a metonym for ISIS. Hirsi Ali warned against focusing only on 'terror' and 'violent extremism', as the real danger was 'nonviolent' Islamist groups espousing extreme viewpoints: 'In focusing only on acts of violence, we have ignored the ideology that justifies, promotes, celebrates and encourages those acts. We need a new anti-dawa strategy, designed to check the advance of political Islam as an ideology and a movement.' Thus, for Hirsi Ali: 'While the children in Sydney's western suburbs are not being handed guns, they are play-acting the violent instructions of political Islam. In this case, the weapon Islamists use is the mind ... We in the West' need to 'recognise that the weapon of the mind is what must be defended against by waging a war of ideas' and 'to map the individuals and organisations who promote dawa within Western borders'.

To that end, she called for Sydney Islamic schools to be shut down 'to stop the indoctrination of children'. While Christian and Jewish schools were acceptable ('they are different'), Muslim schools were 'political ideology masquerading as a religion infiltrating the institution of learning, preying on really small children and filling their heads up with these extreme ideas'.

Despite the crude language, the logic underpinning Hirsi Ali's calls for a focus on nonviolent extremism, a focus on 'the mind', on thoughts, beliefs and ideas, is no different to the logic governing the CVE agenda. It may also seem easy to dismiss Hirsi Ali's views as belonging to the conservative far-right, if it were not for the fact that she is a darling of the liberal establishment, given prominent speaking platforms such as on the ABC's *Q&A* program and the annual feminist program held at the Sydney Opera House, *All About Women*.

TAMED BOYS

The point about the media and political commentary on the war on terror and radicalisation is that nothing involving Muslims is ever an isolated incident. It's always made to mean something bigger. The local is 'contextualised', inflated to the national, to the global. Punchbowl/Birmingham; Punchbowl/Raqqa. These stories become an opportunity to talk about how the Muslim must be tamed.

One year after the Punchbowl controversy, *The Australian* published a follow-up article, working to the headline 'Scandal ridden school's radical change – Punchbowl Boys High'. Reading the article, I was reminded of the citizenship test introduced by the Howard government in 2007, which was soaked in jingoistic, cringe-worthy, masculine and conservative references and unabashedly glorified 'diggers, explorers and sportsmen'. The reporter introduces Punchbowl as 'the school famous for its extremism and anarchy'. Unlike the previous year's coverage, this article, however, sings the school's praises under the leadership of Robert Patruno, who is reportedly undertaking a 'radical transformation' of the school. *This* 'radical' change is positive, though, and the article recounts the various initiatives introduced into the school – an insight into the work involved in producing the 'good' Muslim student. These include 'talks by a former SAS officer and a cadet training day at the Holsworthy Barracks on Remembrance Day', taking an 'oath to be an advocate for women's rights' on White Ribbon Day, a 'wellbeing room', the rolling out of the *School Communities Working Together* program, a 'renewed relationship with police', cadet training and police career sessions. Although Muslim prayer sessions are still being held, we are quickly told there is 'an equal focus is on what it means to be Australian' with students taught 'traditional Australian values of respect and tolerance'.

The programs and messaging don't even try to hide what the school and Department of Education are trying to do, which is 'fix' Muslim male youth and compensate for what they are 'lacking': valorising Anzac Day, loyalty, defence and service to nation, respecting women and trusting police and authority. 'Respect and tolerance' have been learnt – despite the continuation of prayer. In other words, the values of respect and tolerance are *external* to Islam. One almost expects the article to end with a reference to handshakes! And so we come full circle, to the social engineering at the heart of CVE work in schools, which is ultimately about nurturing Muslims who are compatible with a White, patriarchal cultural imagining of what it means to be 'Australian'.

These policies and the common-sense regime surrounding them follow young people, even if those young people are unaware of them. I don't mean that every speech act by a young Muslim is policed with reference to a clause in the CATM, RAK or SCWT, or that Muslim and non-Muslim students are in direct dialogue with what is happening at the level of law and policy when navigating their own identities, judgments and interactions.

The common-sense of radicalisation, extremism, risky behaviour and speech is not assembled in any particular coherent order. The political culture and racial ideologies mobilised in these policies circulate and regenerate in community dynamics, media coverage and public debates. When we understand this inventory, we can appreciate how the fragments and traces of race and Islamophobia trickle down into young people's everyday lives.

So, let's hear more from these young people.

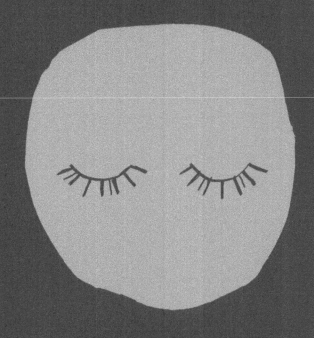

AN INVENTORY OF FEAR

CHAPTER 8

VELCRO BODIES

**One minute you're a 15-year old girl who
loves Netflix and music, and the next minute
you're looked at as maybe ISIS.**

—*Jamilah (15, Algerian-Australian, Inner West Sydney)*

Over the years, and especially since 9/11, I have observed, researched and personally experienced how Muslim bodies, behaviour, symbols and spaces have been increasingly and more intensely encountered as threats, different, out of place, jarring, uncomfortable, unwanted. For my generation, there is a clear difference in the intensity of this experience before and after 9/11. For the generation growing up in a world at war on terror, the Muslim experience has always been one of the hypervisible 'Other'. This is the common sense they have grown up with, reinforced by the policy frameworks and public discourses discussed so far. As Jeena, a spoken-word artist and first-year university Arts student (whom we first met in chapter 3), told me:

> I don't know how to describe this, but I'm just going to say it: I've always had this almost preconceived guilt attached

to who I was. Like, every time something happens on the news, even though I know I'm not guilty of anything, I feel like because of everything that happens, I feel like I've kind of accepted this guilt attached to me. It's like I've just sort of absorbed a million different ... the million messages in the media, politicians, popular culture, all these little things that add up and add up.

For many of the Anglo, non-Muslim students I interviewed, this inventory of ideologies that have been put to work in the war on terror has left few negative traces on their everyday lives, although it has left traces on how they perceive Muslims. The majority of non-Muslim youth I interviewed or who participated in writing workshops, from all over Sydney, acknowledged that they were for the most part either desensitised to the war on terror or unaffected by it other than, as many cited, long waits in airport security (and even then, they acknowledged that this was 'normal' and they'd 'never known any different'). Some of the most common responses from non-Muslim students were: 'It's unfortunately become a normal thing when I see something in the news ... I feel that the automatic internal reaction is, *Damn, that sucks*, and then you go on living your life without thinking about it again'; 'It seems like a thing far away from me'; 'I'm a little surprised by how unaffected I am by the war on terror'; 'I feel mostly safe most places I go. I guess I am a white male, so I guess it's more comforting.'

As part of my research, I held writing workshops in Sydney schools and local libraries. For one writing workshop exercise, I asked students to write a short story in response to a prompt: waking up to news of a terrorist attack in a Western country. Ben, 17, is an Anglo-Australian and attended Grammar College. He wrote:

It's cold in the winter. My feet are purple with the grip of
the morning chill. My cereal is mostly dry due to the lack of
milk that was left in the carton. My mum walks in and starts
speaking, so I put my spoon in the bowl and take out my
earbud.

'A man in Canada killed some worshipers in their mosque
yesterday,' she tells me.

I let out a long sigh and think about it for a moment:
'We need more milk.'

During the class discussion, Ben spoke about his story: 'The war
on terror doesn't mean much to me as it doesn't affect me at all.'
He described feeling desensitised:

It's kind of, like, with these terrorist attacks, whenever they
happen, I'm just like, oh, here's another one. And that's not
to be rude and say it doesn't matter. It's like seeing a car crash
on the TV, it's like, oh, it's another car crash. It's just kind of
expected, almost …

Another student, Tiyana, also 17 (Anglo-Australian, North Western Sydney), said 'terrorism' is 'background noise': 'it's pushed to
the front centre of the media, then it drops back, and then it's
pushed again. It falls back and forth in place.'

There were non-Muslim students, particularly those who
lived and went to school in Western Sydney suburbs with large
Muslim populations, who displayed empathy by imagining what
the war on terror means for their Muslim peers. For example, Josh
(17, Anglo-Australian, Merrylands) admitted that, 'The war on
terror doesn't affect me but obviously affects people of Islamic and
Muslim background, like, with discrimination in the media'. Blake
(17, Anglo-Australian, Granville) thought it was 'rude that all

Muslims are often assumed to be radicals and have to face racism as a result. The war on terror doesn't really affect me personally, but obviously it's still important. It makes me sad how fear makes people aggressive, racist towards Muslims.' Toby (16, Anglo-Australian, Granville) also wasn't affected in his 'day-to-day life' but added, 'Islamophobia is a result. I can see that for Muslims. People don't care as much as they should about that.' During the writing workshop, one student, Matt (17, Anglo-Australian, Blacktown) wrote this extraordinarily sensitive story from the point of view of a Muslim:

> There has been another act of terrorism.
> *Oh no, not again*, I think to myself.
> I'm sick to my stomach. I know today will be harder than normal. The friends I've managed to get to know will turn their backs on me. I sit on the bus and look out the window. I see all sorts of people walking the streets. White, Asian, African. I spot another Muslim, her head down.
> There will be no looking up today, for either of us. No chance to feel as others feel. Just guilt that doesn't belong to us.

Another non-Muslim student, Joy (16, Anglo-Australian, Kelly-ville), similarly wrote from a Muslim point of view:

> The stares intensify, piercing into the back of my head.
> I hear them whisper, 'Do you think she knew him?'
> Another girl whispers back: 'They're all the same.'

Dara (15, Korean-Australian, North Western Sydney) wrote:

She tilts her head back ever so slightly. A look of embarrassment crosses her pale face. People stare at her, silently whispering to each other. These remarks are never made about me. I can experience the luxury of no fear or judgment.

Some of the non-Muslim students I spoke to were also trying hard to push back against dominant narratives. They were aware of the contradictions, the damage done by assumptions, the complicated but important work of checking oneself against a tide of stereotyping.

For example, Caley (17, Anglo-Australian, Grammar College), whom we met in chapter 1, told me: 'There's a difference between having a fear and, I guess, actually acting on that fear. And I guess the prevalence of fears in our society and the fact that people are starting to act on them is, I guess, scary. But it'd be scarier for Muslims.' Steven (16, Anglo-Australian, Grammar College) understood that he was

definitely a product of the society I've grown up in. So terrorist equals Muslim, that's the first image that comes to my mind. But then when I see a Muslim, that's not the first thing that comes to my head is that they're a terrorist either. So it's kind of on one end, yes. But on one end, no.

Emma, the Chinese-Australian Grammar College student we heard from in chapter 1, told me that after the Parramatta shooting, her mother questioned her over breakfast, 'about the people around me, are there any people who are a bit violent or can do something wrong like that'. Emma had no suspicions about 'anybody at school', because 'it's a very close community, everyone knows each other'. On the other hand, 'if you walk on the street and you see … if you drive past some areas and you can see Middle Eastern people that are smoking and swearing and stuff, you do get that sense of urgency to leave'.

Michael (17, Anglo-Australian, Grammar College) spoke to me about the disconnect between what he saw on the news and what he saw and experienced in everyday life, living next door to a Muslim school. He told me that when he walks the dog, he sees Muslims in the area, 'so when we hear something like "war on terror", "terrorist bombing", it's almost very hard to connect what we're hearing with what we're seeing, because we have these nice people walking across the street, doing nothing, just being normal citizens'. Michael found it difficult to reconcile what he saw in the media with 'the same kind of people behaving completely normally'.

Nick (16, Anglo-Australian, Grammar College) pointed to the media:

> It's very hard to imagine someone who isn't of Muslim
> background, because I mean, off the top of my head, it's
> really, really difficult to think of an instance of terror that I
> know that's been somewhat large scale that hasn't had some
> Muslim influence. I don't know. I feel like that's definitely, it
> must be wrong. There's no way that it could be like that.

Caley also blamed 'the media and politicians, there's definitely a strong correlation, I think, between the emphasis of a potential attacker being Muslim'. Caley was thoughtful and reflexive about the impact this had on her own thoughts and feelings:

> I think there probably is somewhat of, I guess, tension,
> which is … frustrating to admit in the respect that you, I
> guess, don't want to be affected by the media and politics and

what you see online, and I don't want to … Like, I obviously believe in equality and the treatment of everyone equally. But I think … I would say there is a slight kind of tension, slight. Depends on who's next to me, where I am. I'd say my hesitations would probably be more towards adults than children.

Brayden (16, Anglo-Italian, Grammar College) also highlighted the role of the media:

I see it in the newspapers and everything, where it's just framing them. I try not to think of it, but I guess it's always there, and I guess from what I know there's kind of a culture behind it. But at the same time not. There's so many people who aren't, that it's not fair to frame a whole culture around it. It's confusing but it shouldn't be too.

As for Tom (16, Greek-Australian, public school in Parramatta), he said he

wouldn't avoid a Muslim man that you see in the street, I wouldn't walk away from him like that. I wouldn't judge them immediately and terrorism isn't the first thing I'd think about. But I guess a part of me still feels there is a relation between terrorism and Muslims.

These young people are growing up in a world that is bombarding them with a litany of labels, images, myths, public commentaries and folk summaries about terrorism and Muslims. But not every non-Muslim young person swallows these narratives without question. It's important to acknowledge the times young people hesitated when they expressed being unsettled, to whatever degree, by 'Muslims'. Sure, many did so from a position of White and class privilege. Some did so after making problematic statements of generalisation. But there were some who allowed for the possibility that their prejudices were exacerbated by the media and political discourse. Others acknowledged how Muslims their age were vulnerable to suspicion, isolation, in the aftermath of a terrorist attack. The students here are taking the first but crucial step of acknowledging that emotions, reactions, feelings are not psychological but structural, bigger than just an individual's response. They are understanding that their emotional orientation towards Muslims as potential threat has emerged because they have been conditioned to think and feel this way.

In her groundbreaking book *The Cultural Politics of Emotion*, feminist, queer and race studies scholar Sara Ahmed challenges the common understanding of emotion as something that begins inside our bodies and moves outside. Sara Ahmed argues we should avoid thinking about emotions as internal states. Instead, we should think about how emotions circulate by moving 'outside in', meanings impressing *onto* bodies and objects. In other words, emotional impressions, like fear, disgust, danger and so on, come to be shared because of how emotions move around, accumulate, endure and 'stick'. Like the way 'threat' gets 'stuck' onto black men's bodies in America, for example, or 'fear' gets 'stuck' onto Muslim male bodies. These emotions (threat, fear, etc.) 'stick' to bodies and objects through constant circulation. Ahmed shows how these emotions depend on 'past histories of association' that often work through concealment. These students are 'sticking' potential terrorist onto Muslim bodies because of the history of media headlines, policies and political debates that have reinforced this association.

But these young people are doing something else too. They are arguing back and forth with themselves, thinking through how they make meaning out of their feelings, how they code their emotions. This is something Ahmed also takes up in her book, when she argues that emotions involve 'reading the bodies of others, such that "they" become the source of affect'. This is important, because so often in debates around the war on terror, people will say, 'I'm scared of Muslims', and their 'fear' is presented as the end of the argument. Their fear becomes a Muslim problem: I am scared, therefore *you* are scary; *you* are the cause of my fear. These young people are taking the first steps to understanding that fear and suspicion are lived and made, and that there are power relations inherent in those who are fearful and suspicious, and those who are seen to be the cause of that fear and suspicion.

BEING TARGETED, FEARED, SUSPECTED

So what is it like to be a Muslim girl and have fear, disgust, hate, 'jihadi' stuck to you? Or, put another way, what is it like for Muslim girls and young women to live in the everyday of racial stickiness? To simultaneously feel one's body as *sticky* – depending on how one dresses or talks, for example – and to feel *stuck* by the judgments that adhere to you?

Every Muslim I interviewed could not avoid, at least at one point in their life, being drawn into the category of Muslims as a racialised collective. But this collective identity intersected with other variables – their ethnicity, gender, social class, the urban locales they lived in. For example, Muslim students from Hills Islamic School sometimes had a lot more in common with their non-Muslim peers than they did with Muslim students from Western Sydney suburbs. In reality, 'Muslim' and 'non-Muslim' are fluid, messy categories, which is why it's important to unpack the multiple and cross-cutting axes of identities and social categories when we try to understand how power and difference work in young people's everyday lives.

The girls I met had a lot to say about their hypervisibility, but one thing instantly became clear to me: I couldn't approach 'Muslim' as a master category that explained one single dimension of an oppressive experience. There were 'privileged' positions affording (relative) safety, anonymity, immunity within and between intersecting social categories of religion, race, gender, class. In making sense of this, I find the notion of identity as a question of performance and practice – of acts of *doing*, not an essentialised *being* – compelling. I'm of course gesturing towards Judith Butler's work on performativity, but specifically how her work is extended and applied to Muslim/Arab identities by academics such as anthropologist Ramy Aly in his book *Becoming Arab in London* and Sherene Idriss in her book *Young Migrant Identities*. Both books provoked me to think more deeply about how to make sense of identity as temporary, contingent. Being a parent who is actively raising her children 'as Muslims' confronts me head-on with the question of identity as doing rather than being. When my third child started school this year, he started reciting the Qu'ran, learning to pray. What does it mean for a five-year-old to 'be a Muslim'? It means nothing except that he is learning to do and enact the rituals and lessons of Islam, until he is old enough to start to understand what these rituals and lessons mean. But those meanings will vary, fragment, be variously within his control and out of his control. Like in his swimming lessons, he's learning each stroke and skill, being taught the ethical and moral foundations underlying his skill set, in anticipation of him comprehending what will make sense in different ways as he grows and matures.

'Categorical labels,' Ramy Aly writes, are 'best understood not as a form of authentic "being" but as repertoires of "doing", achieved through the imperfect repetition of culture over time and space. One is not born an Arab in London, instead Arabness is a process of becoming through acts, enunciations, objects, spaces, bodies and settings.' Likewise, Muslimness is a process of becoming through 'acts, enunciations, objects, spaces, bodies and settings'. I started this book by analysing what 'Muslim youth' is made to mean in public discourse and policy. In an environment where young Muslims are expected to perform ways of doing Muslim girl or boy (do moderate, do apolitical, do *not* angry, do 'Australian values' and so on), Muslim youth engage in different performances of Muslimness, gender, class and ethnicity depending on their setting and context. As we will see, in some settings, Muslim is clearly a resource; in other settings and contexts, a burden. In some settings, Muslim is erased, hidden, distanced; in other settings, it's asserted, embraced. In fact, it's part of the universal vernacular among English-speaking Muslims to talk of 'practising Islam', 'a practising Muslim'. The language itself gestures to this idea of religious identity being a matter of active investment, repeated actions, rites and rituals. To be a practising Muslim is commonly understood as somebody who does Islam, is *doing* Muslim. Young Muslims growing up in the age of terror are on a journey of learning how to practise, how to do, their Muslimness. 'Doing' here connotes a degree of computing and measuring how much Muslimness one performs: a little or a lot and so on. But in the war on terror, external discourses and politics about how much Muslimness is acceptable undoubtedly seep into embodied ways of acting, enunciating, performing.

Most of the Muslim girls I met, especially those who were not fair-skinned, or who wore hijab, were acutely aware of the 'hypervisibility' of their bodies. There was a shared feeling among the Muslim girls I interviewed that this sense of hypervisibility intensified after reports of a terrorist attack in a Western country.

Indeed, there is quantitative evidence bearing out the girls' stories. In 2017, the Islamophobia Register Australia released its inaugural report examining almost 250 verified Islamophobic incidents reported to the register between September 2014 and December 2015. Like the Australian Human Rights Commission's *Ismaع* report 14 years earlier, it found that veiled Muslim women, particularly those accompanied by children, were more likely to be targets. Perpetrators were reported to be predominantly Anglo-Celtic males. The report also found that after every heavily reported incident of terrorism overseas perpetrated by Muslims, there was a correlating marked spike in Islamophobic incidents in Australia. A further report released in November 2019, analysing data collected in 2016–2017, again found that the predominant targets of Islamophobic incidents were Muslim women and girls in the form of verbal abuse, profanities, physical intimidation and death threats in public places, most often while shopping, and most often by Anglo-Celtic male perpetrators.

Sara, 17, a Muslim of Syrian/Palestinian background, had been one of a handful of Muslim students at a public school in the eastern suburbs for two years. Fair-skinned with light blue eyes, Sara was candid about how 'my looks mean I get away with a lot, people never look at me and see Muslim or Arab. I get mistaken as an Aussie.' At school, Sara likes to keep it that way. 'It's easier', she said. Note how Sara, born in Australia, still positions herself outside the category of Aussie, which she uses to denote the white Anglo majority. This rhetorical slippage was something my friends and I routinely did, too, growing up. Indeed, it's something I still hear among many first, second and third generation friends and family, for whom the word 'Aussie' denotes Anglo-Australian. Sara has learnt that doing Muslim and Arab and fair-skinned in school means passing as White, hiding her Muslimness and Arabness.

Farhaana, 17, attending a public school in the North Shore, is of Muslim Indian background. She understood

> people see me and say, okay, yeah, that's an Indian girl. And I guess there's a certain stigma attached to Indians, like various things that I guess you could draw upon. But because I don't wear hijab, I could be Indian Catholic or Hindu, so no one's ever called me a terrorist.

Farhaana let out a laugh. 'I've got one less racist thing to deal with.' Without outwardly performing her Muslimness, Farhaana is raced as Indian only, and her comments suggest there is some relief contained in that.

This is how intersectionality and identity as performance draw attention to multiple positions of power inequalities within groups, and also how individuals can strategise with multiple identity performances, making use of privileged aspects of identity as a form of resistance or protection. In Sara's case, her skin and eye colour, and concealing her religious and ethnic heritage, gives her proximity to 'Aussie'. In Farhaana's case, her darker skin exposes her to one layer of exclusion, while her lack of hijab protects her from another.

Not surprisingly the hijab figures as the major axis of difference. Abear, in her first year of university, is an Australian-born hijabi of Syrian/Lebanese background whom we first met in chapter 1. She recounted to me the 'struggle' she experienced on public transport to and from her girls' high school in Liverpool after she started wearing hijab, and especially after 'certain incidents that are amplified in the media': 'I just felt sick about having to get back on that train and hav[ing] to commute to school'. Abear was used to 'people already looking me up and down every single day on the train', because she had altered her school uniform to be a long-sleeved shirt and a long skirt, so 'I already stood out'. After 'any attack and media', Abear said she would be nervous before school, thinking, *What's going to happen now? It's going to be even more alienating, it's going to be even more of an exclusion kind of going on.* Abear spoke to me about waking up after the Lindt Café siege:

> I felt properly ill, and I said to my mum, 'I don't know how I'm going to face this. How I'm going to go out in my hijab and deal with this now?' I didn't feel safe going out. I never thought about taking off my hijab. That's been my source of strength throughout everything, but I just felt sick.

Abear talked about how she 'mentally prepped' herself. She had to 'first get through the train ride … I was more alert and more vigilant and just looking around to feel I was safe if I was going to be harassed'. And then, after the train ride to school, was 'getting through school … facing people who've got all these questions, wondering what I'll say if the topic comes up in class'. There's a particular imagery to this feeling of 'getting through', as though the train and her school are blocked, barricaded. To get through these blockades, Abear had to be active – alert, vigilant, anticipating harassment, primed to respond to any questions or classroom discussion. This is an exhausting mental load for a high-school girl, in year 10 at the time. But Abear's fears were not exaggerated. When she first started wearing hijab, in year 9, she was walking to the train station when

> some guys from a boys' school bus threw things at me from the bus. So the bus would drive past and they would throw things. More than once. I had to get my school involved, because they would spit and swear at me, and I was just

alone walking to the train. At first they'd call me a terrorist, and then one day they started yelling out 'ISIS'.

To switch from 'terrorist' to the specificity of 'ISIS' shows how the geopolitical and the everyday can become deeply entangled. That a busload of schoolboys can make this discursive shift tells us something about the kind of 'low-hanging fruit' of vernacular Islamophobia that media and political debates have made easily available for the picking – including for a group of schoolkids.

We can see that to live in the everyday of racial stickiness has flow-on effects that extend well beyond the threat of being physically attacked: the mental load a schoolgirl carries to and during her school day whenever an incident is playing out in the media.

Jamilah, 15, is of Algerian background and attended a public school in South Western Sydney. She wrote about her experiences at the airport:

> My sister and I travel with my mother a lot to Dubai, where my father is working on an expat contract. Every time we travel, somehow it's always us that they stop. We've had one-way tickets, and those times there's lots of questions, searching our phones, our bags. My mother's English isn't too good, so I have to speak to the security staff. I become the advocate for my mother and sister, but the irony is I'm just as confused and intimidated. My mum eventually explained to me it's because they think we're going to join ISIS. One minute you're a 15-year-old girl who loves Netflix and music, and the next minute you're looked at as maybe ISIS.

Interviewing young Muslims in the UK, sociologists Gabe Mythen, Sandra Walklate and Fatima Khan write about how young Muslim people experience a risk reversal. The routine surveillance, suspicion and questioning of young Muslims in public life means that 'the relatively safe are being contrarily represented as risky'. At airport security, Jamilah the innocent schoolgirl is interchangeable with possible danger. Hiba (15, Afghan background) was another student I interviewed at Inner West Islamic School. She recounted to me that on a road trip to Melbourne with her family during the 2015 summer holidays, her mother made her change her hijab: 'We were leaving the house and my mum's like, "Don't wear a black scarf", and I was confused as to why not. She was like, "Just don't wear it". I didn't understand why, and she said, "because some people just get all weird around black hijabs".' Amira, 16, is of Malaysian background and attends Inner West Islamic School. She told me about the time she was at a pet shop, giving her pet German shepherd a shower. Amira was with her 20-year-old brother, and a woman approached him to ask if Amira was his wife. The woman then remarked that German shepherds 'sniff for bombs'. Amira was shocked and upset. She said she didn't know how to respond and started to feel embarrassed walking around with her brother. For a while after the incident, Amira avoided being alone in public with him.

Abear, Jamilah, Hiba and Amira are coming of age while embodying the double bind of what Australian Muslim gender-studies scholar Shakira Hussein calls 'victim to suspect', simultaneously stuck with the labels of 'oppression' and 'danger'. Amira's experience also speaks to how the slippery categories of child, youth or adult become even slipperier for Muslim girls. To wear a hijab beside a man and be taken as his wife is to be propelled out of childhood and youth into child bride, into forced womanhood, with the mere utterance of an assumption.

The self-policing of the mundane – the colour of a veil or hanging out in public with your brother – shows how even the most banal and intimate aspects of girls' lives become politicised in the war on terror. Muslim girls are turned into what I call *velcro bodies*, easy to stick 'weird', disgust, terrorist, 'child bride', etc. onto.

None of these girls projected victimhood or defined themselves by a sense of injury. Nor did I get a sense that Islamophobia, the war on terror, was constantly at the forefront of their minds. Their self-presentation and lines of narration to me were responding to the theme of my research, so they were sharing stories with me in the context of me hailing their Muslimness front and centre. What was clear, and sobering, was how matter-of-factly they related their stories to me. They didn't seem surprised by their experiences. It was just part of the common sense of growing up in the age of terror.

When I separately interviewed the girls, I asked each of them if their friends at school were aware of these kinds of experiences. Jamilah, Hiba and Amira all said they 'didn't really talk about that kind of stuff' with their friends, whether Muslim or non-Muslim. Jamilah said: 'We don't think about it much. We talk about TV shows, funny stuff online, that kind of thing mainly.' The other girls said similar things to me. I didn't get the impression that for these girls this lack of talk was strategically calculated, a kind of self-imposed protective bubble. It wasn't so much an attempt at normalcy as it was that the everyday of racial stickiness coexisting with everyday life as a schoolgirl *is normalcy*. On some days, these girls' Muslimness was summoned in ways that made various demands on them. On other days, their Muslimness was in the background.

Abear, on the other hand, did attempt to share her experiences with a friend at school. At the time of the Lindt Café siege, she sent a text to a schoolfriend, Jennifer, telling her that she didn't feel safe, didn't want to go to school and have to deal with everything. Jennifer never responded, despite the message showing it had been delivered and read. The next day at school, Jennifer made no mention of the message. 'It was really like the elephant in the room', Abear told me. 'We just never spoke of it, but it was there. It was really awkward for me, but she acted normally at school, as though nothing happened.'

Although Abear and Jennifer were 'quite close', the 'driving force' behind their friendships was their 'similar interests and priorities – we were both high-achievers, we watched the same shows, had the same sense of humour'. The girls were in a lot of the same classes and also 'kind of competitive'. Abear said that 'despite my wearing the hijab, it was more just two girls getting along, and we almost forgot about our religious differences'. It was only when Jennifer didn't respond to Abear's text message that Abear's religion surfaced. Ironically, it surfaced through Jennifer's deliberate silence. In texting Jennifer, Abear had brought attention to her religious identity, complicating Jennifer's defining of their friendship as predicated on not acknowledging religion. Abear told me, 'I think talking or messaging about it would have made it real in her mind, and she didn't want to do that'. The friendship continued, albeit Abear understood it was conditional on her not bringing up her Muslimness.

Abear also shared with me her experiences with another friend, Chloe, who had become an ex-friend after a series of overtly toxic episodes. After a major terrorist attack (Abear couldn't recall which one), Chloe was walking with Abear from the train station to school, when Chloe turned to Abear and said: 'I'm scared now, and I don't know what to do. Why are they doing this?' Abear told me she 'was gutted', telling Chloe, 'I know as much as you. I was born here. What do you want me to tell you? I don't know what's going through the minds of these people.' Chloe's reaction was to joke, 'It's all right. If someone comes to my door, I'm just going to get a towel and put it on my head and say salam alaikum.' Chloe continued to ask Abear to explain what was going on, insisting she should know as a Muslim: 'She kept saying, "I don't feel safe, I don't feel safe"'. Abear couldn't get her to understand that 'it's not my responsibility to tell you about this or answer these questions, because I know as much as you'. Their friendship ended at a farewell party a year later. Abear presented Chloe with a hamper of gifts and a card, and Chloe joked, 'I'm getting a cat, and I'm going to name that cat after you. I'm calling it ISIS.' Abear realised that there was nothing more she could do:

> You can try to talk to a person every day and try to get
> them to change their mind, but if they're going to be
> ignorant, there's nothing you can do about it. It's not your
> responsibility to deal with it. You've got a million and one
> things to do. It's not my job to try and convince her that I'm
> a good person and that Muslims are good people. I tried for
> five years, and I got nowhere.

Sonia, 17, is of Sikh Indian background and attends Grammar College. She complicated my understanding of vulnerability and fear, and which bodies are made to become velcro bodies in the war on terror, when she spoke to me about how scared she felt after the Lindt Café siege. 'Scared because we're Sikhs,' she said, without a hint of irony. Sonia lives in the North West Sydney suburb of Glenwood, near one of Sydney's largest gurdwara. She said,

> we get a lot of hate from people who think we're Muslim.
> The first time the temple opened up, because they didn't
> have, like, Sikh Temple written there, just because there's
> a dome on top of a building, people used to come out and
> throw rocks at the windows. And then when they got Sikh
> Temple written, it reduced.

After the Lindt Café siege, Sonia 'didn't go out for a week'. She told me she usually walked all the way to the gurdwara and back with her family, but they 'didn't do that for a week'. When I asked Sonia what she was afraid of, she said, 'Terrorists. And racism.' Sonia's story reveals how in the war on terror, sticking processes serve to both stick guilt and hate onto innocent Muslims who are mistaken for 'terrorists', and stick guilt and hate onto non-Muslims who are mistaken for Muslims.

'BUT I'M SPEAKING AS A MALE'

To be exposed as a Muslim girl, especially after a terrorist attack, was something the Muslim boys and men in these girls' lives were also acutely conscious of. There is obviously a gendered dimension to this exposure. Many of the students I interviewed told me that after a terrorist attack, their families were on high alert about how it might affect the veiled females in the family. Abdul-Rahman, a 16-year-old student at Hills Islamic School, told me that after

> any big terror attack, me and my brothers advise my sister and my mum not to go out alone. And to always, if you're going out, make sure, you only go to, like um, you only go to your friends' houses. And if you go out ... to the shops or something, you make sure there's someone with you, to make sure you're protected.

One boy at Hills Islamic School told me during a classroom discussion at a writing workshop, 'generally, in day-to-day life, the war on terror doesn't affect you, but I'm speaking as a male. I can't be identified as a Muslim. For women wearing a scarf it's different.' Another boy chimed in,

'Like, you're at a normal shopping centre and everyone's
… usually after an attack, everyone's looking at you, well
not necessarily you, but you can still feel that sense of them
judging you on what they saw on the TV … when I'm walking
with my mum or sister or my cousins and they're scarfed'.

Girls told me about taking time off school, off work, 'for a few
days after an attack'. A few told me about their parents changing
their work arrangements for a few days so that they could drop
them to school rather than have them take public transport. So-
called fear *of* Muslims (by wider society) becomes fear *for* Muslim
girls and women within Muslim communities. Fear for Muslim
girls becomes a constraint, a self-management of mobility and
exposure, another way the war on terror weighs down Muslim
women's lives especially.

Fatina (whom we first met in chapter 4) was in year 11 at
Inner West Islamic school. She described herself as 'a bubbly, outspoken girl that always gets her way. I'm very proud to be Lebanese. Extremely proud. And I take religion very seriously. And I'm
always up for a good time, basically.' There was a lot of bravado
in how Fatina presented herself, as though she was performing a
resilient and proud Muslim hijabi. But Fatina soon revealed how
affected by living in the everyday of Islamophobia's stickiness she
actually was. She went from 'always get my way' to:

I feel like I see myself always staying in my comfort zone,
always with Muslims. I don't tend to go anywhere else.
Or seek anything else. And you're always, like, a victim
wherever you go. 'Cause there's always going to be someone
that's going to say something to you. Or someone's going to
play you some way because of what everyone else is doing.
Especially being in Australia and Muslims being a minority,

you are, basically, in danger. At all times. But I do have hope for future that things will get better and racism to the word Muslim will slowly die down. But currently, it's hard because of everything going on around the world.

For Fatina, 'girls who wear the scarf, the abaya, guys with beards, that's the image that gets splashed around. So people see you and you know they have the thought in the back of their head.' Fatina spoke to me about how this 'sense' has built up:

At the beginning, as a child, you don't really notice, you don't really think much. You always had an idea that the people hate Muslims for a certain reason, but you were never told or you never knew. So you were always a bit iffy about it, but at the same time you didn't really notice, you didn't really care. But as you go out all day – I have this Westie accent and I'm a dark Leb – you tend to get, oh if you decide to wear the headscarf, you tend to get even more looks. You draw more attention to yourself. And you tend to see the racism that exists within society as you go out all day.

During the writing workshop, Fatina wrote this story:

My mum turns up the radio as we crawl through traffic. A girl with a heavy backpack and a plaid shirt walks past us as the newsman informs us that a Muslim man has run through a crowd in London. My mum tsks gently and shakes her head. I watch the dirt particles floating in the sunlight.

'Always stay close to walls when you walk in the city,' she says to me. 'Always be careful.'

I nod and shift in my chair. Mum changes the station, adjusts her hijab. She glances at me, pauses.

'Maybe you shouldn't wear the hijab today.'

I shake my head. I adjust my hijab, grab my heavy bag and smooth out my uniform as I hop out of the car.

'Be safe,' she tells me. 'Stay close to walls.'

I nod.

It feels like the walls are closing in.

Fatina relayed her experience to me about a trip to the Gold Coast. Driving up, the family stopped for a meal at McDonald's. Fatina went to the bathroom and was washing her hands when a young girl, maybe ten, walked in with her mother. They stood at the sinks, and then the girl looked at Fatina and said, 'Stay away from me. I don't want to be next to you.' The girl's mother then said, 'Yeah, God knows what she can do'. Fatina recalls the 'filthy looks' they gave her as they left. Fatina felt shocked by how young the girl was: 'that girl's too young to come up with that on her own. She's learnt that from home.' Fatina's story echoes so many stories of racism in Australia. Indigenous AFL player and Australian of the Year Adam Goodes being called an 'ape' by a 13-year-old girl during the AFL's Indigenous Round in 2013 left him feeling 'gutted' and 'shattered': 'it's what she hears, in the environment she's grown up in that has made her think that it's okay to call people names.'

As Fatina spoke to me, I was reminded of a story my father had recounted to me, about his first experience of being racially abused in Australia. It was 1973, and he was walking along Cleveland Street, towards the aeronautical engineering department at Sydney University, where he was studying. A woman walked past him, carrying a toddler. The toddler looked at my father and said, 'wog'. The only reason my father remembers the incident so clearly, he tells me, is because the word stung so much more coming from a child. 'A toddler imitates', he said. 'He was playing out what had been role-modelled to him by the adults in his life.' Forty-six years later and my father says he still vividly remembers the toddler's face, the shock he felt hearing that word.

Fatina told me that the next day, the family woke up to get ready for a trip to Movie World. That morning, a lone gunman, Man Haron Monis, held 11 people hostage in the city of Sydney's Lindt Café. Fatina told me that 'the parents were all not sure, but they decided we'd still go'. There were probably 20 of them in total, 'big Leb family, many of us in hijab'. Fatina recalled:

> Some people were screaming from their cars at us, saying that we're terrorists and things like that. It made me feel sort of disgusted that people assumed that because of one person, a group of people had to take blame and the consequences. It ruined my day. You constantly have to think about it during your day …You're expected to be a victim when things like that happen. It was in my mind as we were queuing up for rides. I was paranoid, on edge, you keep looking. Who's staring? Why they staring? Who's going to say something? Do you have people around you? Do you have your family around you? Even if you want to walk by yourself, your parents wouldn't let you. To that extent, if you want to go to the bathroom, you had to have someone with you, in case someone wants to say something or hurt you.

The Lindt Café siege was happening in Sydney, but it followed Fatina into the Gold Coast. The freedom to just be a teenager on holiday at a theme park was denied to her. Was this what she meant when she wrote about 'walls closing in'? Fatina was left paranoid, vigilant, second-guessing every look, every encounter. This is how other people's suspicions and prejudices stick onto bodies, and how those bodies then get stuck encountering the world from a position of vulnerability, victimhood, target.

Fatina is intelligent, confident and charmingly sassy but was acutely conscious of the labels and judgments that stuck to her hijab, her 'Westie accent', her dark skin. When I started the writing workshop, she put up her hand and in a bold voice declared (it wasn't really posed as a question): 'You're not gonna censor what we write?' At one point in the workshop, she yelled at some of the guys, who were laughing and chatting among themselves, 'Shut up, will youse? Walk outside with the hijab, and we'll see if you're still mucking around.'

Whether it was recounting her trip to Movie World, or telling me so matter-of-factly 'people hate Muslims', or being conscious of her accent and skin colour, or qualifying her dreams ('I want to be a lawyer, but I doubt I'll get a job with hijab', or 'I can't wait for uni, but I'm scared to be outside my comfort zone'), Fatina was clearly struggling to make sense of how to do Muslim, Western Sydney, hijabi girl in the context of rising Islamophobia – proud, confident, ambitious, resigned, paranoid or scared? At one point in the writing workshop, she raised her hand. I noticed how some of the other boys and girls stopped writing or talking to listen to what she had to say. Fatina had an undeniable charisma and presence in her classroom. She ordered me to turn on the voice recorder: 'I want you to record this', she said. 'You can add it to the interview we did.' I agreed and raised the voice recorder towards her as she shooshed the class.

'You know, miss,' she started,

I'm writing and I'm thinking – I tend to always have the thought, well, they're scared of *me*. I shouldn't fear *them*. Like, it's a little kid or, like, an adult, *they* feel scared. I feel like I cope with it, saying to myself, '*They're* scared of me.

I shouldn't be scared of *them*.' But the thing is like, miss, fear like … doesn't hold people back all the time, does it? So their fear, in their heads, becomes like my fear, like in my actual life, you know what I mean?'

Some of the boys and girls erupted into wild cheers and applause, playful calls of 'ooooof, Fatina!' It was as much that her words had resonated, as it was that the class were playfully teasing her for being the 'good student', as it was that the students were enjoying the chance to make some noise around – but also for – Fatina, who sat beaming, gesturing with her hands to keep up the cheers even as she half-heartedly scolded the boys to 'shut up'.

In that moment, I felt like ripping every policy document into a thousand tiny pieces and throwing them to the wind. The violence of words like *at-risk, vulnerable, radicalised* has no business in these classrooms and communities.

As I drove out of Fatina's school, I could not stop thinking about her words. How profoundly insightful they were; how eloquently 17-year-old Fatina had articulated what the politics of fear and resilience in the war on terror means for so many Muslims.

CHAPTER 9

THE MUSLIM PERFORMANCE

During airport security, I was the only person pulled
aside. Everyone else was allowed through the gates
except me, being a young Muslim guy. It was so obvious.
My bags were checked and messed around. I went
through security as a kind of accused not a passenger.

—*Mesut (17, Turkish-Australian, Muslim,*
North Western Sydney)

Hasan was on a roll: 'Imagine you yell Allahu Akbar going
through security?' The class laughed. Mehmet raised his hand
and, with indignation, said, 'You get bomb-tested and they act like
it's random!' 'Nah, man, they need to bomb-test you', the guy sitting behind him joked, and Mehmet and the others laughed. 'We
can't just walk through', said another boy, Ali.

I was running a writing workshop with a year 11 class of boys
at Inner West Islamic School. Airport security stories seemed to
be the running theme. The young Muslim males I interviewed
were acutely conscious of their bodies' capacity to negatively affect
others, to have certain stigmas and suspicions 'stick' to them. They

were enjoying the chance to be subversive, to play around with stereotypes.

During the session, Jalal, 17, said, with a grin: 'I was at another school before I came here. I was called "Taliban" at school!' The rest of the boys laughed. I asked what was funny. One of the students explained: 'He's Iraqi' – which made me chuckle – prompting another boy to call out, 'They should have called him ISIS'. The boys, including Jalal, all roared with laughter.

One thing that struck me about the Muslim boys I was interviewing and working with was that joking and banter were a very obvious and organic part of the boys' classroom dynamics, even when it came to the topic of the war on terror. This is, after all, what characterises most schools. Bullying, exclusion and conflict occur in what are fundamentally places defined by noise, laughter, teasing, joy, banter and kids clowning around. In his article exploring the strategic use of humour in stories of racism, Kevin Hylton writes, 'the use of techniques of humour enables feelings of subordination and humiliation to be transposed into forms of resistance, while its physiological and psychological benefits can lead to inter-racial relief and catharsis'. This was evident among the boys, who were clearly aware that 'ISIS' and 'Taliban' stirred up connected histories and stereotypes and had become sticking devices on Muslim bodies. And they enjoyed 'taking the piss' out of this reality. Abdul-Rahman (whom we heard from in the last chapter) explained: 'We try to at least make jokes about it, at least among ourselves, yeah. Because we understand how, how serious it is … We know it's not who we are. Especially our religion.' The boys switched between poignant accounts of Islamophobia – told without a trace of self-pity, in dispassionate, matter-of-fact tones – and moments of irreverence and ironic self-awareness.

I read Abdul-Rahman's account to me as young Muslim guys using humour, irony and bravado to reclaim some power in the face of widespread dehumanisation. But also, as teenagers, there was a natural youthful exuberance in these boys' personalities, an instinctive rebellion against performing solemnity and sacredness by performing insensitivity as an act of defiance and independence.

During class discussion, Jacob, 15, shared his experience about being the only Muslim on his local soccer team: 'Like, the terrorist attack that happened in Bourke Street Melbourne recently, they're like, do you know this guy? Have you seen him at the mosque recently?' Jacob was animated: 'How dumb do you have to be?' Another kid called out, jokingly, 'You should have said you know him'. Jacob and some of the others instantly grinned, and Jacob said with a laugh, 'The thing is, I didn't even know about any Bourke Street situation! I told them we're not all related just because we're part of the same religion, but I had no clue what they were talking about.'

Some Muslim students engaged in joking and ironic takedowns of terrorism only among other Muslims. Abdul-Rahman, attending an Islamic school, explained to me that when he made jokes with his friends, 'we're careful about doing that in front of a non-Muslim teacher. If we do that, we make sure it's acknowledged that it's a joke. I think they get we're joking, but it's also for them a concern of, *maybe they're not joking.*' I doubted all the boys in Abdul-Rahman's class were as sensitive to how their jokes would be interpreted. It struck me that those who didn't care were engaging in a powerful act of defiance, a refusal to be measured against 'warning signs'. As I wrote earlier, these boys would probably have no idea about the existence of the CVE policies that apply to schools, and yet they have internalised the common-sense idea that to joke about terrorism as a Muslim is inherently dangerous and risky, because of how it can be misinterpreted as something more sinister than just insensitive or callous.

For some students, though, misinterpretation is the point.

Deena, a 14-year-old Australian-born Palestinian Muslim, attended a public high school in South Western Sydney. She told me about a boy in her year level, Ayman, of Afghan Muslim background: 'He's really smart but he acts like an idiot, tries to act hard. He randomly brings a red and white tea towel from home and puts it on his head'. Deena rolled her eyes.

> He once started saying 'Allahu Akbar' in class. He was trying to scare this girl, because she's non-binary, well we think she is. And I had to reassure her. He was pissing himself laughing. She was kinda freaking out. The guys and me, we were telling her, 'It's okay, it doesn't mean anything'. He kept saying it.

In a culture and society shadowed by the war on terror, young people – Muslim and non-Muslim – are clearly attuned to the stereotypes and folk fears attached to the symbolic 'paraphernalia' of 'Muslimness' and 'Arabness'. Ayman is subversively manipulating climates of fear and suspicion, ironically performing 'Muslim terrorist' not as a defence mechanism, but to contrive a 'hard' reputation in the playground, on the one hand, and to cruelly taunt another bullied minority, a student 'suspected' of being non-binary, on the other. *Passing as terrorist* is fun for Ayman; watching his peer misunderstand the words he chants is his objective. He uses the stereotype of terrorist to effectively 'terrorise' another student, an easy target because of their gender identity. This story might tell us no more than that Ayman is a nasty person. That much is clear. It might also show us the futility of trying to fix people's identities into discrete categories of 'Muslim', 'victim'. What does it mean to be a young Muslim? Is your story one of victimhood, subjection? Or is it one of agency, grit and resilience? Or can we think about all the points in between the process of learning to *do*, learning to *be* – or not *do*, not *be* – Muslim? Can Muslimness be experienced as subjection (to a war-on-terror climate and all the stereotypes that come with that) *and* simultaneously an opportunity to 'punch down' in certain circumstances, to reclaim discourses of fear and suspicion in service of one's biases (here, homophobia), a way of accumulating a measure of power and authority? Joking, 'taking the piss', can offer a space for young people to do just that.

'A turn toward laughter', Liz Sills writes in her article 'Hashtag comedy: from Muslim rage to #MuslimRage', 'is a natural and common trend for people responding to an unfriendly stereotype'. But more than this, Sills sees humour (in her case, a hashtag inspired as a response to an incendiary article by Ayaan Hirsi Ali) as an expression of critical consciousness. Sills quotes Frank Furedi, who says, in the war on terror, 'instead of acting as the audience for yet another performance of the politics of fear, we can try to alter the conditions that give rise to it'. Individuals can 'directly question and alter these conditions and become performers of their own philosophies as a collective, potentially weaponised mass of individuals'.

One student I interviewed, who attended a boys' public school in South Western Sydney, brilliantly weaponised humour to 'alter conditions' of fear. Sami, 16, seemed determined to defy every convention and expectation about how to behave in the context of fears around terrorism. He recounted to me the day his school 'went into lockdown'. Sami was in year 8 at the time, and someone had graffitied 'ISIS are coming' on one of the brick walls (this is no doubt the source of this example being included in the *School Communities Working Together* guidelines as a 'sign' of anti-social and extremist behaviour). Sami recalled:

It was period three, I remember, English. The school got a phone call that someone said they were gonna bomb up the school … We went into lockdown, we turned off the lights, went under the tables. I started to scream 'cause I knew it was a joke. And I was laughing and then I started pretend praying. And the teacher was like, 'Just sit down, go under the table'. And I didn't like this teacher. And she didn't like me. We had our history. And I gave her hell for about two hours in lockdown. After I made it a joke, they all thought it was a joke. I'm an influencer.

I asked Sami why he thought it was a joke. Was it just about teasing the teacher? He snorted: 'It's Revesby. Who's gonna bomb us? If I was in the city and I was at, say, Parliament House or 52 Martin Place, and then there was a bomb scare, I would be shit scared. But, like, who the hell is going to bomb our school?'

Sami found the entire situation hilarious and deserving of ridicule. He explained: 'some kids did call their parents. I just said, "I'm not going to call my mum, she's not going to care". She's going to laugh.' Sami's mother was equally dismissive of the paranoia around terrorism: 'She thinks it's politics'. Sami continued:

After a while the teachers were pissed off, mainly because it was BS and they missed out on teaching, so they were irritated. It was on the news. I remember them saying in an assembly, 'Don't speak to the media'. Because, the media was outside the school wanting to interview us, and I so badly wanted to talk to them and tell them, 'Oh, we were all scared and frightened and praying to Allah to save us from ISIS here in freaking Revesby! It was such a bad experience.' Yeah, they would love it. They'd lap it up. It would be on replay for the entire month. But I didn't 'cause they threatened to give me a detention.

Sami paused. 'It's a serious issue, yes. But it's also laughable in some cases. That's weird. But 9/11's been meme-ified.' I asked Sami if he worried about how others perceived his irreverent attitude. He told me other students mostly felt the same way. As for the teachers who misunderstood him, he enjoyed it that way.

When I asked Brayden, 16, from Grammar College, what he understood about the war on terror, his first and immediate response was, 'I'll have friends, they'll be in a game and they'll throw the ball, but they'll just pretend to throw a bomb, saying, "Allahu Akbar!" Stuff like that. Just out of context, just randomly. It's a joke now.' For Brayden, the war on terror was what happened in the school playground. I asked Brayden if these friends who were making these jokes were Muslim, to which he replied, 'Oh no, non-Muslims, obviously'. I asked him if this happened in front of Muslim students, and he said, 'There's not too many Muslims in our school, like in our year, so not a lot. I don't think that they would have really noticed.' Jokes and racist banter are practices embedded in the dynamic flow of interaction among students in schools. Brayden seems to implicitly understand that such jokes might be offensive to Muslims when he emphasises they're jokes made by 'non-Muslims, obviously'. Because the cohort of Muslim students is small, he assumes they wouldn't notice. Brayden said such jokes were random, 'it's a joke now'. The 'now' is telling, as though 'Allahu Akbar jokes' are part of today's Zeitgeist, perhaps 'once' unacceptable but normalised 'now'.

During a writing workshop at a library in Blacktown, students from a few public and Catholic boys' schools in Greater Western Sydney attended. During the discussions, one boy, of Indian Hindu background, said, with a grin: 'Sometimes we call the Arab kids "9/11" and they call us back "7/11"'. The boy's friends, Arab, sitting next to him, laughed in agreement.

Here was humour as 'convivial sociality', what Sarah Winkler Reid found in her study of race and humour in a school in London as interactions which have 'cross-cutting, counter-balancing or liquefying effects'. I like this description. It points to how humour can dissolve tensions, cut through differences or re-adjust the power differential in relationships. The boys are playfully appropriating stereotypes, but it's reciprocal and lateral, rather than hierarchal, hence the grinning and laughter. I asked the students if non-Arabs and non-Indians made the same jokes, and a few were swift in their response: 'From us, it's okay. From others, it's different. It's not okay.' Two of the boys disagreed: 'It depends', said one. 'If it's a friend, I know he doesn't mean it. It's just a joke.'

'Could you make a terrorism joke about a non-Muslim?' I asked.

Most of the boys shook their heads. Karim explained: 'Like, jokes about bombs is what you expect if you make a joke about a Muslim. But it depends on who says it.'

Among peers, the jokes, sarcasm and quick-fire banter happen so fast that it feels contrived to sit and analyse the intent and dynamics of these interactions as if the boys are consciously making statements about race and identity. What fascinates me is these evolving social conventions in the war on terror, how shared laughter is a product of a certain social, cultural and political context. In her classic essay 'Jokes', anthropologist Mary Douglas writes, 'We must ask what are the social conditions for a joke to be both perceived and permitted'. One student tells us, '9/11's become meme-ified'; simulating a bomb sound seems to be the way you make fun of Muslims *now*; 'Allahu Akbar' is part of the common vernacular, deployed as a joking threat, standing in for menace. For students to use these kinds of scripts in their everyday interactions points to how humdrum 'the war on terror' seems to be in their lives.

HIDING AS A SURVIVAL STRATEGY

The everyday of racial stickiness for young Muslim males in Sydney has a specific and longer history than 9/11 that can be traced back to a cycle of moral panics around the Muslim male Other, the male 'of Middle Eastern appearance', in the late 1990s and early to mid 2000s. A substantial body of Australian scholarship has charted the emergence of this racial profiling descriptor and analysed how it contributed to the formation of the Arab/ Muslim Other. 'Of Middle Eastern appearance' has invariably targeted young people, as criminals, potential terrorists, gang members, threats to public safety and 'bodies out of space' when they dare to move outside of 'the western suburbs'. These associations have been firmly implanted in public consciousness. The figure of the male 'of Middle Eastern appearance' endures and is an example of what Sara Ahmed calls 'past histories of association', racialised scripts and stereotypes that are easily recalled because of how they've become historically embedded.

In 2013 and 2014, I conducted fieldwork, interviewing mainly Anglo-Australians who were affiliated to different degrees with various anti-Islam movements (the Q Society, the Australian Protectionist Party, Party for Freedom and Rise Up Australia) as well as 'everyday' Anglo-Australians who were on a spectrum from strongly anti-Muslim to those who negotiated more complex and ambivalent feelings about Islam and Muslims. That research, along with this project, demonstrated to me that hegemonic Orientalised narratives and images about Islam, Muslims and

Arabs mediate, shape and animate interpersonal encounters. The archive of Islamophobia and race bears down heavily on encounters, sorting difference (in this case, Muslim difference) according to racial codes, making sense of 'the Other' via racialised scripts.

These codes, scripts and histories of association are traced by the late, brilliant Edward Said in his seminal works such as *Orientalism*, *Culture and Imperialism* and *Covering Islam*, and imagine the Muslim and Arab as interchangeable, constructing the Arab/Muslim male as deviant, criminal, hypersexualised. 'Arabs only understand force', Said wrote of these Orientalised representations, 'brutality and violence are part of Arab civilization; Islam is an intolerant, segregationist, "medieval", fanatic, cruel, anti-woman religion'. These Orientalist representations, which flesh out the Muslim Arab male in racist, exotic and inferior essentialist form, proliferate in popular culture. Not only par excellence in Hollywood films, as meticulously documented by the late US scholar Jack Shaheen, but also in Australian film and television depictions, as explored by sociologist Mehal Krayem in her book *Heroes, Villains and the Muslim Exception*.

With moral panics over asylum seekers in Australia in 2000, and then the 9/11 attacks, the concept of the Other morphed and collapsed Muslim, Arab and 'third-world looking', as anthropologist Ghassan Hage wrote in *White Nation*, into invading hordes of 'boat people' and 'queue-jumpers', either potential terrorists or carriers of illiberal practices that 'threatened' the 'Australian way of life'. Following the emergence of ISIS in 2014, the civil war in Syria, and fears of 'homegrown radicalisation' and Australian citizens joining the war, the figure of 'could-be terrorist' became detached from particular (Arab Muslim) bodies and became stuck to any brown body, as Sara Ahmed has written.

How this archive bears down on encounters is exemplified by Nick, 16, who attends Grammar College, and who spoke to me about his mother being 'more intimidated by men rather than women'. He told me that his mother doesn't react to veiled Muslim women, 'but definitely men, Muslim looking or ... just not Australian looking'. He shook his head with disapproval as he spoke. I asked Nick what he made of his mother's reaction, and he shifted in his seat. He paused. I waited for him to gather his thoughts. And then he said, 'I don't really know that many Muslim people at all ... But, I guess in my mind, I don't see all Muslim people as bad or evil.' Nick paused again, placed his hand on the table and slightly drummed his fingers. 'I guess when I think of terrorism, I just think of, I kind of think of the events, I think of ...' Another pause.

> If I was really to put a face to a figure, I guess my first thing
> would probably be maybe a Muslim guy. Like with the
> long beard, like that, whatever it's called, the dress ... But I
> wouldn't say, Muslim terrorist. I wouldn't say, oh yeah, every
> Muslim is bad. Stay away from them. But yeah ... that's the
> image that comes to me.

The pauses in between Nick's sentences, the hesitancy and qualifications by which he offered his thoughts to me, meant just as much as his actual words. What archive, what filing system was Nick reaching for that gave him the 'image that comes' to him during those fleeting moments?

The 'image that comes' to Nick is an image the Muslim males I interviewed were familiar with. It's the reason why Abdul-Rahman, Lebanese Muslim, is 'scared of being accused'. He referred to 'a meme image of Muslims being, like, bearded and, you know like, wearing Arab kinda clothing'. He told me about video games 'like *Counter-Strike*, with the Arabic writing on the walls, and you shoot up guys who look Arab'. *Counter-Strike*, a

2002 video game which has attracted more than 7.5 million users, requires players to kill or convert non-Christians, all of whom have 'Muslim-sounding names', and has been used as a tool to recruit young men into the US army. The images and meanings around terrorist and Arab and Muslim men are intertextual, moving between government websites, policy documents, public discourses, social media and gaming.

Some of the Muslim males I interviewed were affected enough by the stubborn sticking of terrorist to Muslim that they felt the need to tame their Muslimness, to strategically erase and conceal their identities. I met Ali, 17 and of Iranian background, at Grammar College. He wrote this short, devastating piece about assimilating:

> The war on terror has impacted many aspects of my life and my family, but you can't get more impacted than having your parents change your name from Ali to Christian. I come from half-Iranian heritage and I'm very connected to it. Throughout my life, me and my family have been the main target of racism. I've had many racial slurs thrown at me, been discriminated against, and attacked because of this. Me and my father are always pulled aside at airports and are searched extensively. Me and my family are not allowed to travel to countries such as the US, due to our heritage and connections with it. This issue has impacted my family so much, that we have had to change our last name to a more Anglo name in an attempt to stop being subject to this hatred and stereotypes. When I started at this school, my parents decided I'd start as Christian. To avoid any assumptions. I'm a Muslim and even though I don't practise, when I'm at school as Christian, I feel I've lost a part of myself and my identity.

This need to hide resonates with what UK anthropologist Ramy Aly found in his research, vividly captured in his book *Becoming Arab in London*. Part of the 'project of cultural survival' can involve appropriating whiteness, passing for white. In Ali's case, he is attempting to pass as *not* Muslim and so adopts the name Christian — not just any 'white' name, but one that unequivocally avoids being assumed to be Muslim. But as Ramy Aly notes, appropriating whiteness is not necessarily 'motivated by "desire" to be white *per se* but by the need to be socially intelligible and to survive'. It's a strategy, as Ali/'Christian' writes, of avoiding 'hatred and stereotypes'.

In the workshop Ali wrote, 'I'm a Muslim and ... I don't practise when I'm at school'. Again, we see here an understanding of Muslimness as something that is done, and something that can therefore be undone by practising another identity: 'when I'm at school as Christian'. Identity is performed as a matter of self-preservation in certain contexts.

Farhan, 16, is also a student at Grammar College. He's of Muslim and Indian background but told me quite quickly in our interview, 'there's a lot more to identity to me than just the nationality or religion'. His statement confirmed to me the frustration of Muslim youth being defined solely in terms of their religion. Farhan spoke to me about what it's like to be the only Muslim in class when you don't even '100 per cent identify as a Muslim'. Farhan said he wasn't sure if he was 'speaking on behalf of other Muslims', whether he was 'a good spokesperson in this environment at least', but he had to fall back on the fact he was 'more Muslim than anyone else in the room, so I have the most right to have an opinion on if it is a Muslim issue'. Farhan doesn't have the space to work through his own ambivalence around his identity and the religion he has inherited from his parents, because he still feels a responsibility to 'be a spokesperson'. He's in a state of flux, between hiding his identity and feeling a duty to 'speak up'. He's conscious that because of the political environment, he is faced with a choice between doing his Muslimness in hiding or openly. Farhan told me,

> At school I don't hail myself as a Muslim to anyone … I guess the stigma that's been attached to it recently, it has kind of deterred me from saying that I'm a Muslim or at least I'm a second-hand Muslim and I've been to mosques and my mother definitely promotes me to go to those places. I don't know how people would perceive me if I was to tell them that.

Like Ali, although not so drastically, Farhan resists expectations on doing Muslim openly and proudly. But unlike Ali, he does feel compelled to occasionally speak up, to perform the role of ambassador, defender of the faith.

Many of the students I interviewed felt frustrated by the burden of representation. Not simply the sense of being loaded with a responsibility outside of their control (forced to act as 'global Muslim spokesperson' to challenge accusations of terrorism, as the Human Rights and Equal Opportunity Commission found in its study way back in 2003), but the fact that they were being expected to perform Muslimness when they were still trying to make sense of their Muslimness.

Tahminah, 17, for example, an Afghan-Australian attending a public school in the eastern suburbs, vented her frustrations over having to perform her religion, gender and ethnicity. She was annoyed at how 'Middle Eastern is synonymised with radical Islam and terrorism' and how 'Afghans sit at the top of the pyramid. We're the most associated with the war on terror.' For a long time, Tahminah felt ashamed of saying she was Afghan because of how it conjured up 'the image of a country that's in a state of conflict all the time'. Ironically for Tahminah, born in Australia, she conceded that she ('and all my cousins') had an Australian-socialised imaginary of Afghanistan: 'My vision of Afghanistan is dirt and terrorists walking around and harming people. Our vision of Afghanistan is the war on terror. That is what we see Afghanistan as. Dirt, guns, Taliban, ISIS. That's all we see. Everyone is in danger.' She spoke about the dissonance at the age of 12 between her impression of Afghanistan and her mother's descriptions of 'the greenery', of having family in Afghanistan: 'People have phones. There is internet. There are schools. There are shopping centres. There are houses.' Tahminah was conscious that her 'idea of Afghanistan is so shaped by what the media is. If that's me, I'm pretty sure everyone else in Australia probably thinks Afghanistan is like the Sahara Desert.' For Tahminah, this presented her with a constant battle: compelled to over-invest herself in an ethnic identity and heritage that was foreign to her:

> I would be in Legal Studies, and the teacher would bring up something related to a terrorist event and people would automatically turn to me like, *What's her opinion on it?* It was almost like people waiting for me to put my hand up and say something on the issue. The teachers, they would feel a bit uneasy. For most of [my] senior years, I was the Middle Eastern person in the room, even though I'm Afghan, I was the only one, because there weren't many of us at my high school.

Tahminah refers to herself here as 'the Middle Eastern person'. She understands she has been assigned an identity that has nothing to do with the actual fact of her Afghan background (let alone how fraught that is for her). The need for students and teachers to ask questions erased her particularity, as Afghan, making her a Muslim universal, in other words, 'Middle Eastern':

> It was almost like they wanted our opinion on these topics all the time, like, *What does she think? Does she think it's okay?* We always would discuss it. It wasn't a lot, because I feel like my generation isn't as bad as others, but some people would say it's because 'They're Muslim', and 'It's part of the faith, and the faith is Jihadist', and all that kind of stuff. It was a pressure on me. What if I don't identify with Islam and stuff, but I'm here standing up for it all the time and expected to say something?

Tahminah found it difficult to always be 'a spokesperson', especially

> in terms of my personal identity and all that kind of stuff ... I was speaking up for the community. I need to change people's minds and people's perceptions and tell them what the real situation is. These people are radicalised. It was draining sometimes. When those events would happen, I'd dread going to school the next day.

Farhan and Tahminah say they are Muslim, Afghan, but these words don't seem to belong to them. Like an item of clothing that they are struggling to fit into, to feel comfortable in, they feel forced to wear 'Muslim', 'Afghan', even 'Middle Eastern', whenever 'a Muslim issue' comes up in class. Muslim is summoned as a performance into Farhan and Tahminah's lives at school, in the classroom, under the weight of wider debates. They both reveal they're struggling enough to come into their identities without the added burden of being entirely or primarily defined by their faith, by the homogenising lens of Islam.

EATING BACON TO FIT IN

'I instantly felt guilty. I was embarrassed. I was humiliated.'

Salim, a year 12 student at a public boys' high school on the lower North Shore, was telling me about the time he ate bacon to 'fit in'. When Salim 'hit year 7' at his 'majority Asian and Anglo' school, he started to feel uncomfortable about his Afghan Muslim background. He felt self-conscious and started to change himself 'because the problem is no one knows about it that much. But you get the kids, the teens get, like, exposed to social media ... their parents tell their kids stay away from certain ethnicities. That is what I was told from people in my school as well.' For Salim, it was about avoiding the mental network of associations he 'knew' other kids were making:

> Because Islam is tied in with the Afghans and most Arab
> backgrounds. I started to realise that because I'm Muslim and
> Afghan as well, my identity started to weaken and become
> more Australian. I tried to conform, be more like Anglo, and
> I did successfully, and it was an easier way out.

Reflecting on his 'year 7 self' as a year 12 student, Salim was able to look back and see how his conformity was 'the normal teen-age thing of wanting to not stand out, but in my case standing out wasn't about my hairstyle or any of the normal things kids get picked on for, but about being Afghan and Muslim'. Salim remembered the hardest times were in years 7, 8 and 9,

> when kids call you 'terrorist', or, 'Are you going to bomb
> me in school?' It's just those jokes that would be, like, daily,
> but you just get used to it. Okay, who cares? If you keep on
> focusing on that kind of banter, it gets in your way. Just block

out all the hate. The kids didn't know any better as well. I
feel like you couldn't really blame them, because they weren't
brought up with the proper knowledge of Islam and stuff
like that. They just know about the negativity and not the
positivity.

Salim was being generous here. Kids do know better and understand the meanings behind certain words and jokes. Salim's 'who
cares?' and 'blocking out all the hate' translated into a desperate
attempt to perform being a Muslim in hiding. Because assimilation is not passive. It's a series of acts and practices. Salim angli-
cised his name to Sam and recounted 'the worst thing he did',
which he regretted 'the most':

> I was at one of my friend's house with just all my Aussie
> friends, and they offered me bacon and eggs and stuff. I was,
> like, to myself, okay, if I don't eat this thing they're going
> to start deep questioning me like, 'Why don't you eat this?
> Why do you want to be this background?' ... I was very
> uncomfortable about it, and I was like, *I'll just take a bite*, and
> I did. It wasn't – that was when I was very vulnerable, but
> now I'm not afraid to show who I am. I instantly felt guilty. I
> was embarrassed. I was humiliated, but with that bacon I had
> somehow become more Aussie.

Now any non-Muslim reading this might think *bacon*? *That's* your
worst thing? But for Muslims, even those who don't observe most
of the Islamic rituals, bacon is a massive taboo. Every observant
Muslim knows a Muslim who unabashedly drinks alcohol or gam-
bles (also two major taboos) but who would freak out if they were
served a pepperoni pizza. Even Aziz Ansari's TV series *Master
of None* devoted an entire episode to its protagonist Dev eating

bacon and the wider political narratives associated with his hesitant admission of this to his parents. What is important to note here is how Salim's eating bacon took on the magnitude of a rite of 'Aussie' passage. To fit in required him to move closer to the White mainstream: to become Australian meant eating bacon, performing what he perceived as quintessential Australian and quintessential *not*-Muslim.

This is how political and media debates and policy trickle down into small, mundane, everyday spaces and bear down on identity practices and performances in the project of cultural survival. Growing up, you become attuned to what counts as Australian, Western, White; you pick up hints, clues, implicit and explicit messages about what markers of identity need to be tamed and suppressed to keep you safe from exposure, and what markers need to be strategically embraced to prove yourself. Salim was just about to finish year 12 when I interviewed him. He had reached a point where he was no longer practising being the Muslim in hiding. He told me it had taken him a few years to realise the goalposts for 'being Aussie' would always change, so there was no point in trying.

'I WAS EVEN WEARING A POPPY'

Ahmad was one student who, in year 12, was still trying.

Precocious, high-achieving, ambitious and cocky, Ahmad attended a boys' public school in South Western Sydney with a large Arab and Muslim student body. Ahmad clearly delighted in being the provocateur, telling me he was a political conservative in a family of artists and lefties. He seemed to enjoy the shock value of performing Whiteness, of being an Arab-Muslim minority member of the Young Liberals, of stirring his Arab and Muslim peers in classroom debates by playing the contrarian.

As we spoke, Ahmad recounted two experiences to me. The first occurred when he was in Melbourne, on work experience at the Magistrates Court. During his lunch break, Ahmad's aunt, an artist, took him to the National Gallery of Victoria. Ahmad mentioned that he was 'in quite a nice suit, and she was dressed up quite well too'. Ahmad seemed to think this detail was important, and of course it was, because class, race and gender are always performances. Ahmad recounted to me that security followed them the entire time they were walking in the gallery. 'We were the only people in some sections,' he said, 'and they would just follow us. And we would speak about it, "Oh, why are they following us, what have we done?" "Have we touched something?" We didn't know.' Ahmad then jumped to a similar incident, a few months later, this time on a visit to the Museum of Modern Art exhibition with his aunt: 'It was packed this time. But again we were the people who the security were looking at, and I could see, I was making eye contact with them, and I could see that they were focused at us. I was wearing a three-piece suit that time.' I asked him, 'Do you think that makes a difference?' He didn't hesitate: 'Yes, absolutely. But I felt exposed, kind of. Like, "What have I done wrong?" My aunt, well, she was in trackies, God love her.' At this point he chuckled. 'Maybe that's why they were looking at us.' Here again we see how Ahmad is cultivating a certain class and race persona. I raised my eyebrows and smiled. 'Do you genuinely think it was because she was in trackies?' I asked. Ahmad smiled back and then said: 'I see myself as Australian, but they must have seen me as …' He stopped, just shrugged. I coaxed him to continue: 'What do you think was actually going on?' He replied:

There's obviously a reason that they're following us. And, the reason is they see us as a security threat. Maybe it's because someone stole a painting a month before, I'm not sure. But

again, I think it's just a consequence of the society that we
live in. I guess Indians get stopped, Greeks get stopped.
Anyone who looks a smidge Arab gets stopped.

Ahmad seemed to be arguing against himself. On the one hand,
he was clever enough to believe in his instinct that these incidents
were racial profiling. On the other hand, he so clearly wanted
to believe that his 'nice suit' would make a difference; that there
might have been another reason why they were being watched
so carefully. Ahmad was reckoning with the painful experience
of being attributed as part of a suspect community. The act of
attribution comes from outside, from 'non-suspects who create
and define what it is to be a member of the suspect group', in the
words of Marie Breen-Smyth.

For Ahmad, *doing* Muslim and Arab changed, depending on
the setting. When I asked him about 'identity', he said:

When people ask, 'What's your nationality?' I tell them
Australian. And then they say, 'Oh, no, no, where are you
from?' I say, 'I'm from Melbourne'. And, then they say, 'No,
no, no, where are you from?' And I say, 'Oh, do you mean
where are my parents from?' They say, 'Yeah', and I say, 'Yeah,
Australia'. 'All right then, where are your grandparents from?'
'Oh, yeah they're from Lebanon.' And, then they say, 'Why
didn't you just say that?'

This dance is in and of itself a performance, a way of Ahmad using
his Muslim and Arab background as a resource to provoke and
unsettle the power dynamics in such an exchange.

Ahmad then told me about an argument he was having with
kids at school:

'What are you, Lebo or Aussie?' I told them, 'I'm Aussie with
Lebanese background'. So they go, 'So, you're not Lebo?'
And I said, 'No, neither are you. Neither is half the people in
the class.' It's now a recurring joke. *That Ahmad is not Lebo.*
I understand for some people, they feel marginalised in that
they can't identify with a country that … want[s] them to
leave.'

Here Ahmad is proudly at odds with many of his peers, who
embrace 'Lebo' as a response to racism and a strategy of defiance.
Ahmad's performance of 'Aussie with Lebanese background' (note
his ownership over 'Aussie', a term that many people of colour col-
loquially reserve for white Australians) is an act of refusal.

'I am Australian.' 'I'm Aussie with Lebanese background.' We
can see how these pronouncements are context-specific and seem
to speak to UK anthropologist Ramy Aly's assertion that 'Arab
identity is not an essence or a cause of behaviours and dispositions but an instrumental reaction to being hailed and subjected
by social institutions, hegemonic gendered norms, national and
international politics and media representations'. Ahmad dips
in and out of variations of Arabness, Lebaneseness, Muslimness
according to the context.

Ahmad told me about walking to the bus stop with his sister
after school, when 'a drunk Anglo-Australian came, he was walking down, and he screamed out, "Fuck yeah, Australia"'. Here
the perpetrator is 'Anglo-Australian', not 'Aussie'. Ahmad is consciously appropriating the language of belonging for his own pur-
poses. Ahmad continued,

My sister goes, 'What?' and then he said back to her,
'Oh, shut the fuck up, you bloody Muslim'. And I said
to him, 'Mate, I'm born in Australian, my sister's born in

Australia, my mum's born in Australia. I think I'm a bit
more Australian than you because I at least tolerate other
people.' He was smashed, told us to piss off, go back to where
we came from, and I said, 'I would be happy to go back to
Melbourne. You're paying for my ticket.'

This is sensational stuff. In such a short space of time, Ahmad
engages in gender, class and race performances. His response to
the drunk ravings of the 'Anglo-Australian' is calm and poised, as
though he is trying to subvert the stereotype of the angry Arab
male. Ahmad, a 'bloody Muslim', calls the man 'mate', a cheeky
and no doubt provocative appropriation of 'Aussie' masculinity
codes. He schools him and responds to his 'piss off' with deadpan
confidence and humour.

Ahmad then shared another incident with me, which revealed
the painful edge of keeping up such performances. I so keenly
felt Ahmad's longing to not be misidentified, to be included on
his own terms, to prove himself as 'Australian' that I publish his
responses to my questions here as a narrative:

So, it was Anzac Day this year, and I was the guest of the
veterans affairs minister for NSW, and I went to the dawn
service at Martin Place, again in a nice three-piece suit. So
after the service I wanted to get Macca's. On my way to the
Macca's at Circular Quay, I stopped at Government House,
and I buzzed in and I said, 'Your flags aren't at half-mast'.
And they said, 'Yep, all right, we'll get it down'.

I went to Macca's and on my way back, I noticed the
flags were still up. So I buzzed in again and told them. The
gardens were open then, which meant the house was now
open. I walked through the gardens, drinking my Macca's
coffee. Then I walked up to this kiosk thing, thinking that it

211

was the tourism box or the tour box, because I wanted to go do the tour of the Government House. I've done it before. It's really nice. But then the police kind of like jumped out of it, and I was shocked because I didn't know it was a police box. And she says, 'Hey, what are you doing?' I said, 'I'm looking'.

She wasn't angry, just a serious tone. She asked for my licence and I said 'Yeah, of course'. I gave her my licence. She walked in and I was angry now, because I did nothing wrong but walk. She took it inside and said, 'I'll be five minutes'.

She was about 10, 15 minutes. I think she was doing a background check on me or something. There was a bench right in front of the box, and I sat down and went on my phone. After about 20 minutes she comes back out, gives me the licence, and says, 'Yep, it's all fine'.

So I asked her, 'What was that for?'

She's just like, 'Oh, you know, just you have to have increased security with the times that we're in'.

And, I told her that, 'You know, I'm here to celebrate Anzac Day. I'm not here to do anything stupid. Why would I?'

I was even wearing a poppy.

She goes, 'Well, I can't help it'.

And then I said, 'Do I look like someone who would want to do something?'

And she said, 'No, but you have a Middle Eastern look'.

And I was like, 'Do I look like a terrorist?'

And she goes, 'No, but you know, some people fit certain descriptions'.

Then I walked back to the Anzac Day march, and I went to the government headquarters, because it's in Martin Place. Because I was the guest for the minister. And I sat down there with the police, because I know the police officers there, and I charged my phone until the march started. We marched all the way to Hyde Park and I was in the VIP section for the memorial service at lunch. I met the foreign minister, the Governor again. I walked back with the veterans affairs minister, and I spoke to the Turkish Consul General, because I've met him a few times before. And then I told the minister, 'This and this happened to me'. And he said, 'Yeah, I've been stopped too. So have some of my staff.' He doesn't look Arab at all, but I don't know. He knew it was profiling. But he was just trying to make it better, the situation.

What we can see here is a pretty devastating example of postcolonial scholar Homi Bhabha's seminal concept of *colonial mimicry*. In colonial relationships, mimicry, 'one of the most elusive and effective strategies of colonial power and knowledge', emerges when members of a colonised society are encouraged to imitate and take on the culture, norms, traditions of the coloniser. Here is Ahmad – Australian? Aussie with Lebanese background? Not Lebo? – in an Anzac Day ceremony. A ceremony that has become the hallmark of a White male patriarchal national identity, one that has been extensively analysed as linking 'national identity to the supremacy of the Caucasian race'. Here is Ahmad, with his three-piece suit and Macca's coffee. He's doing everything right in the mimicry game. He looks the part; he's so attuned to cultural rites that he reminds authorities the flags aren't at half-mast, not once, but *twice*! But as Bhabha writes, 'mimicry is constructed around an ambivalence; in order to be effective, mimicry must continually produce its slippage, its excess, its difference'. Miming whiteness produces people who are 'almost the same, but not quite'.

Ahmad's narrative poignantly captures this ambivalence. I see Ahmad, with his dark hair, dark eyes, olive complexion, sitting on the bench in the lush grounds of Government House. The irony is excruciating. He's sitting on the bench because he innocently approached what he thought was a tourism kiosk, only to find it was a police box. Ahmad isn't even aware of 'his slippage, his excess, his difference'. He's sitting on a crisp Sydney morning in the grounds of Government House, a teenage kid from a Western Sydney public school, sipping his Macca's coffee, waiting … for clearance, for his 'slippage, excess, difference' to be accounted for.

As Ramy Aly notes, applying Bhabha's concept of 'miming whiteness' in relation to similar narratives he encountered in his research with young Arabs in London, 'superficial identification' with whiteness 'is more to do with the promise of a common humanity and recognition, a recognition that the colonial relationship places out of reach. Where one mimes whiteness, one may appear White, but will never be White enough'. Ahmad's experiences demonstrate so palpably how there are no winners in the game of 'good Muslim/bad Muslim'. In the war on terror, risk is not either/or, it's always a matter of degree. For all of Ahmad's efforts to be counted as the moderate Muslim, the Australian first, Lebanese second, he was still condemned to the racialising logic of the war on terror. His three-piece suit; his proximity to power (he *knows* the police officers, the delegates); his performance as the Arab Muslim guy who wears a poppy, notices the flags aren't half-mast, embraces the rituals of Anzac Day, didn't spare him.

There is something so pitiful and therefore profoundly sad about how clearly Ahmad believed he was the exception. What is even sadder, perhaps, is not that he had been seduced into believing the fantasy, but that he pursued it when a part of him knew that no matter how much he strove to deny it, he would always be an *Arab Muslim* wearing a poppy, in a three-piece suit.

CHAPTER 10

'GEN Y JIHADISTS'

'Radical Islam in the playground'

—*ABC News, 28 July 2015*

'How to spot terrorists'

—*news.com.au, 24 May 2015*

'Islamic State: does Australia need
to monitor young Muslims?'

—The Courier Mail, *3 May 2015*

'Online extremists harnessing anger
of youth for lone wolf attacks'

—Sydney Morning Herald, *3 October 2015*

On 24 July 2015, *The Australian* broke a story of a counter-terrorism investigation of a year 12 student at Epping Boys High School over allegations he had been preaching 'radical Islam in the schoolyard'. A *Sydney Morning Herald* story with the headline 'Radicalisation of pupils: Epping Boys High not the only school investigated by police' reported that the police had not named the other schools being investigated. A story on news.com.au high-lighted quotes from the police and NSW's Premier about increasing radicalisation among young people and the need for adults to signal their concerns about any 'signs' they pick up. They described the boy as 'reportedly sport[ing] a scruffy beard', but that he did 'not wear a skull cap'.

I-once-ate-bacon Salim attended Epping Boys at the time of the incident. He recounted to me what school life was like during the media and political outcry:

> It affected me a lot, school wise. I cut all ties with the Muslim community in my school because I just didn't want to be associated … I used to go to the Friday prayers. I mean, a couple of the boys, we just stopped going because there was talking that we were being watched … It kind of made me mad, that just, like, one or two people in, like, a community can just ruin the total name of your culture. I didn't see the point of what [the boy under investigation] was trying to do as well. It angered a lot of us as well, and you'd walk to school and would see the TV cameras you'd be like, *Oh, do I even want to come to school knowing there's gonna be cameras outside?* Especially, like, looking for the ethnic people, trying to record them, trying to interview them for a hot take. What we and the other Muslim boys did was – Afghan boys, you could say, Arabs – we walked through the back bus routes we had, which took us slightly

longer, you'd wait for the bus an extra 30 minutes, but it was all just to avoid the media. It was, like, a month later, they left us alone.

Salim went from denying his Afghan Muslimness in year 7, to learning to embrace it, to again retreating to the safety of anonymity – to the Muslim in hiding – in response to the racialising impact of a sustained media and political beat-up. From withdrawing from his Muslim peers, to abandoning his prayers at school, to taking different routes to school to avoid being hassled by the media, this is how wider debates, and paranoid political and media campaigns, play out in the everyday lives of students. More disturbing was the chilling effect the controversy had on Salim:

> I got dragged into an argument, they were saying
> something about me following the same religion as these
> terrorists, and I was saying, 'Well, what do you know about
> my religion? You know nothing about it. You haven't read
> any books on it. There's nothing wrong with it.' But the
> way I said it, my tone … I came off very aggressive. You
> can't be monotone or, like, happy with that because you're
> not going to get anything through it. Sometimes anger
> gets you to where you want. Sends the message through,
> I guess. But then I was scared, because that's what people
> think of as radical extremists … In their mind. I felt like
> I'd be taken straight to the principal and you would have to
> deal with that. So I shut up. The only person I could talk to
> was my SOC [Society and Culture] teacher. One on one.
> No one else.

Salim learnt to tone down his anger. He learnt that anger is read as aggression, and aggression as potentially being 'radical extremist' *in their mind.* The Orientalist trope of the angry, humourless, irrational Muslim/Arab (because in the public imagination they are synonymous) is longstanding and pervasive. Salim knows he is working against a figment of other people's imaginations, judgments and prejudices. And still he decides to 'shut up', 'control himself', 'shut down'. That Salim understands that presenting as angry works against him reveals how effectively this deep-rooted collective image of the 'angry Muslim man' manages Muslim speech.

The incident at Epping Boys escalated into a wider story about the radicalisation of schoolkids and the safety of prayer groups in NSW public schools. An alleged incident involving one boy was extrapolated by media, politicians and police to a general crisis. Indeed, to emphasise the point, the NSW Police Assistant Commissioner stressed that Epping Boys High School's situation was 'not unique' and that 'the radicalisation of young people, including school students, was a worsening problem', concluding: 'it stands to reason that any of these young people would be in the education system or may have recently been at school'. Media reports quoted the state Opposition's education spokeswoman, who said that 'the threat of schoolkids being exposed to radical ideologies at school was deeply troubling'.

A few months before the incident, in May 2015, the Australian Government had announced its plan to introduce a national 'deradicalisation in schools' strategy. Widely reported as the 'jihadi watch' strategy, the media referred to a 'confidential council briefing paper' highlighting 'the broad reach [Islamic State] had in Australian schools' and the strategy being introduced 'as terror experts, Islamic leaders and the government talk about the best way forward to manage the growing issue of the Islamic State terror threat through schools'. The 'jihadi watch' scheme was reported as showing 'teachers and students how to spot the signs of a potential terrorist including behavioural shifts such as getting into trouble, having fights with people of differing ideology and drifting away from friends'.

The targeted strategy in schools was not surprising. A federal government review of counter-terrorism laws earlier in the year had identified an increased threat of 'homegrown' terrorism and 'a rise in small-scale terrorist attacks' by 'lone actors'. Attention was also focused on young Muslims joining ISIS as 'foreign fighters', a group dubbed 'gen Y jihadists' by an Australian Strategic Policy Institute report. Rising concerns about how to predict who would be radicalised were intensified by a number of high-profile cases involving young Australian Muslims in 2014 running away and allegedly joining ISIS. Entrenched, loose and mobile racial summaries attached to, and arranged, young Muslim bodies (for example, wearing beards), spaces (suburbs, schools) and words ('Allahu Akbar') as 'risk factors', as 'radicalisation'. Muslim youth's 'vulnerability' was framed as part of a wider problem of the war on terror being a 'battle for young minds', in which terrorists manipulate 'disillusioned teenagers', 'exploiting with ruthless efficiency the uncertainties and angers of youth'.

Against this backdrop, it's no surprise that both media and political commentary around the Epping Boys incident reinforced the problem of Muslim youth radicalisation as rife, and portrayed Western Sydney schools – with large Muslim populations – as sites of crises.

The week after the story broke, the NSW government announced a government audit of 'prayer groups in public schools', because of 'concerns about a small number of students being potentially exposed to violent extremist ideologies'. The qualification of 'small number' was meaningless in the context of the work already done, and which would continue to be done. In announcing the audit, then Premier Mike Baird said: 'I don't think any one of us could have imagined four or five years ago the concept of 13- and 14-year-olds being involved in extremism and signing up for terrorist activities. That's something almost beyond comprehension.' Police training for the education department 'on radicalisation and extremism' was also announced, with Premier Baird explaining: 'This is an appropriate step to ensure extra rigour, extra care, extra sensitivity to movement, words [and] actions that we may see that might be appropriate to report and take action against'. The Department of Education and NSW Police Force issued a memo to NSW public school principals providing a new 'Safety and Security Directorate Hotline' for reporting suspicious behaviour.

The eruption of media coverage, political rhetoric, and disproportionate policy and legal action triggered by one student at Epping Boys clearly fits the classic model of a moral panic. Indeed, the story went beyond Australia, typifying the global circulation of local panics that has become key to the globalised war on terror. BBC News reported the story with the headline, 'NSW school prayer groups audited for extremist ideology'. *The Straits Times*, Singapore's highest selling paper, also ran the story, under the headline: 'Probe into ISIS subversion at Aussie schools', reporting that an audit would be conducted following 'revelations that students have been preaching extremist propaganda in classrooms and playgrounds'.

Unsurprisingly, the state audit, which concluded in September 2015, didn't uncover radicalisation in prayer groups. Rather, it found only that 'some schools' were not following 'departmental guidelines' by obtaining parental permission before students could participate in 'voluntary religious activities'. There were no retractions of the initial media coverage.

In response to the audit, the Department of Education issued a memo to schools reminding them of the requirement that they monitor voluntary religious activities and obtain parental consent, provoking a backlash by some Muslims and an online petition that argued that 'it is not the role of teachers to police their students, nor is it to act as intelligence officers spying on children on behalf of the government'. Concerns were raised about how such a register 'might be exploited in the future', exacerbated by one school incorrectly advising parents that students who attended prayer groups would be placed on a federal government register.

Jeena, the spoken-word artist and university student we first met in chapter 3, told me about attending a girls' public school in Western Sydney, where her wider friendship network included a family member of a teenage boy who is in a supermax (that is, one of Australia's supermaximum security prisons, Goulburn Correctional Centre). Jeena had very clear memories of the furore over Epping Boys and prayer rooms. Suddenly the teachers at her school 'went into paranoid mode'. The rule now was that the girls couldn't pray 'with the door closed'. Jeena explained:

> The thing is, I felt like they were scared of … us, but also …
> I also didn't know if they were scared of the policies that were
> coming out, and that they'd have to follow them, or police
> would come in, and it would just be messy. Like, I felt like it
> was just a bit of both.

There was no discussion or explanation by the teachers, just a direct reaction to the controversy that was happening outside, and departmental pressure being exerted on public schools. Jeena then went on to talk about the September 2014 counter-terrorism raids across Western and North Western Sydney: 'You know, my mum used to threaten us with the police when we were little. 'Cause we used to get scared of the police a lot when we were little. I don't know why. I think it's just growing up being Arab. Or maybe crazy mums.' Jeena laughed and continued: 'But then, when I was older, my mum used to tell us, "Don't be scared of the police if you haven't done anything wrong". But some of the terror raids really proved that statement otherwise to me.'

Jeena told me that even though she

> felt safe, some people that were raided were completely innocent or whatever ... but I still felt like I was more innocent. So, I was scared, but scared for other people, but not that scared for me, even though I don't know what I thought made me special compared to them. You know?

Jeena's words are telling. For suspect communities, guilt and innocence are distributed unevenly. If one can be 'completely innocent', another can be 'incompletely innocent'. One can be 'more' innocent, another can be 'less' innocent. That innocence is *relative* can become a way some Muslims end up viewing each other, internalising a sorting mechanism shaped by the collective racialisation of communities, spaces and suburbs. Jeena's self-awareness here is admirable. At her age, she is interrogating her own even fleeting feelings around innocence and guilt.

When two new deputies joined Jeena's school, around the time of the counter-terrorism raids, there was a crackdown on school uniforms. Some of the senior school girls at the school were 'very religious' and had been permitted to wear black jilbabs over their uniforms. The new deputies came in 'very, very strict about uniform'. Jeena recalled the girls praying at lunchtime and being intercepted by the deputies on their way back. One of the deputies told the girls they could not wear their jilbabs. When pressed why, the teacher replied, 'Safety issues. What if it gets caught on fire?'

Jeena said the girls conceded the point. They 'got it', but then, to their surprise, the deputy continued:

She kept going, saying, 'We don't know who you are if you are covering your face with that, we don't know your identity. You could be hiding something under that. You could be hiding a weapon under there. You could be hiding a bomb under there. We don't know!'

And everyone was like, 'What? Where did that come from? We're not even hiding our face.'

Jeena said they pressed the deputy to explain:

'We're in hijab, do you mean hiding our face with our hijab?' The deputy's response was, 'If you were hiding your face, we wouldn't know who you were'. And we were like, 'Where is this coming from? And then she called the girls 'ninjas' because their jilbabs were black, even though under their jilbab, the whole school uniform was correct.'

Jeena then paused. 'I'm trying not to completely demonise her. Like, even if you're upset that it's the wrong uniform – regardless of what you think, as a teacher, an educator, you know the political context of the world right now, Australia right now – you shouldn't be making those comments about the uniform'.

And Jeena was spot-on in referencing the wider political context, given that only a few months earlier Australia had been in the grip of yet another 'ban the burqa' debate. In fact, new rules had been introduced by the Australian Parliament's Department of Parliamentary Services requiring 'persons with facial coverings' (a clear reference to Muslim women visitors wearing the niqab) to sit in glass enclosures segregated from the public gallery. The public gallery, it should be noted, is where schoolchildren are seated, a rather neat signal of the way Muslim women are both infantilised *and* posed as threat. The rule was subsequently abandoned, not before the usual public commentators weighed in using Muslim women's bodies as a site for debates about 'national security', and the limits of religious freedom and multiculturalism.

The girls reprimanded by the school deputy asked Jeena to take the matter further, given she was a member of the School Representative Council. She reluctantly asked for a meeting with the deputy, while the principal acted as a 'mediator'. The deputy refused to apologise and defended her comments on the grounds that she had 'lived in Western Sydney [her] whole life' and was genuinely upset that her comments had caused offence.

This is a good example of what sociologist Robin DiAngelo has coined as 'white fragility', in which 'a minimum amount of racial stress' can 'become intolerable, triggering a range of defensive moves' for white people. Rather than acknowledge the hurt caused, the deputy principal exposes her fragility at being confronted. 'Living in Western Sydney' takes the defensive trope of 'I can't be racist because I have a black/person of colour friend' to the next level. Western Sydney is often used as a stand-in for 'diverse', 'multicultural', used interchangeably with person of colour or 'culturally and linguistically diverse' as a way of White people from Western Sydney giving themselves licence and authenticity to speak on, and control, issues concerning race. Being a White person from Western Sydney can often be used as 'diversity street cred,' a way of positioning oneself *as diverse*, not simply proximate to diversity. The deputy's response isn't like saying, 'I have friends who are persons of colour'. It's like saying, 'I *am* a person of colour'.

The deputy's response is also a good example of what writer Ruby Hamad chronicles in her book *White Tears, Brown Scars*, in that the deputy uses her emotional state ('genuinely upset') as a 'weaponised defensive' against Jeena and her Muslim peers who have raised concerns over her Islamophobic comments. The deputy's feelings end up derailing the students' attempt to open up a conversation about Islamophobia, placing the energy on the hurt feelings of the deputy rather than her racist comment. Jeena said that the incident 'badly damaged' any trust the students had in the new executive. I'm not surprised.

CHAPTER 11

NARRATING CLASS

Here we can forget what's happening
outside and just be.

—*Aamenah (17, Egyptian-Australian,*
Muslim, South Western Sydney)

One of the clearest examples of how wider discourses train and socialise people to be affected by Muslims is the language around *suburbs*. Emotions circulate, accumulate, endure and 'stick' not only to bodies or symbols, but to *geographies* too.

Many of the young Muslims I interviewed who lived and went to school in suburbs in Western Sydney, with large Muslim populations, experienced certain pockets of Western Sydney as geographies of comfort and protection. Australian academic Rhonda Itaoui's research on the 'geography of Islamophobia' in Sydney attests to the way public space shrinks for young Muslims as they create 'mental maps of Islamophobia across Sydney'. Itaoui found that 'the absence of Muslim populations across space appears to be a stronger indicator of racism, and vice versa – greater Muslim presence in an area is associated with a stronger sense of acceptance across space'. Itaoui draws on the concept of a 'pedagogy of unbelonging' developed by sociologists Greg Noble and Scott

Poynting. This refers to the way in which racism can transform the spatial imaginaries of Australians from migrant backgrounds by 'teaching' them to feel less comfortable in certain neighbourhoods and the wider national space simultaneously. An anticipation of racism therefore creates 'inventories of the spaces of fear' among racialised minorities. This is exactly what many of the young Muslims I interviewed revealed to me. They felt unsafe 'in the city', at certain beaches, in areas where there was a small population of Muslims. They anticipated Islamophobia and racism and therefore remained wary in those areas.

One student, Haroon, 20, whom we first met in chapter 1, attended the private Catholic university of Notre Dame, located in the city. He told me 'most of the students were from the eastern and northern suburbs'. According to Haroon, Strathfield, a suburb about 12 kilometres from the city, 'was as far west as most had travelled'. Haroon lives in Mount Druitt, 50 kilometres west of the city, and he was 'always up against stereotypes. They thought I had to keep my car windows up, doors locked.' Mount Druitt was the focus of SBS documentary *Struggle Street*, a three-part television series that followed the lives of residents in Mount Druitt and attracted a huge backlash, including from residents who participated in the series and felt the series used them as 'poverty porn', exploiting and dehumanising them. Haroon told me, 'I was always up against a two-factor defence: always the Muslim element and always the Western Sydney element'. For Haroon: 'The Western suburbs is home. Always home. Always right. In Sydney I'm a tourist. I recoup in the West. I don't feel safe, comfortable, until I'm in the Western suburbs.'

Aamenah is a 17-year-old devout hijabi of Egyptian Muslim background. Homeschooled until year 11, she was now attending an Islamic school in Strathfield and living in Greenacre. She told me that she feels 'good most of the time. It's only once there is an attack and the news is broadcasting and defaming Muslims that I don't feel great anymore. I feel scared.' Aamenah told me that attending an Islamic school

> is a bubble for me. My parents could have sent me to a fancy private school out in the Hills where we used to live, where my mum grew up. But they decided to move us to Greenacre, like, *Let her be with her own in these times*. In a way, I can see their point. Here we can forget what's happening outside and just be. I don't know if that's a good thing or a bad thing, to be honest.

When Aamenah says she can 'just be', she is hinting at how living in Greenacre and attending an Islamic school offers a space where certain performances are not needed (except perhaps in front of non-Muslim teachers, as other students have already mentioned). That's not to say Aamenah and her peers aren't performing aspects of their gendered, raced, classed identities, but that the demands of those performances are different. It's telling that Aamenah's parents understand these dynamics and have chosen an Islamic school precisely so their daughter can 'be with her own in these times'. The Islamic school and the move from the Hills to Greenacre offer a double geographical bubble of safety.

That the suburbs of Western Sydney that have high Muslim/Arab populations evoke fear or suspicion among some of the young people I interviewed who live in the Hills Shire or outside of Western Sydney didn't surprise me. As has been extensively documented, since the 1990s, Western Sydney, specifically the areas associated with Muslim and Arab residents, has been the site of racialised moral panics. A lot of work has been invested over many years by the media, politicians and writers to stick certain signs to these urban locales: 'Middle Eastern' gangs, radicalised young men, ethnic gangs, welfare cheats, law-breaking youth.

In their groundbreaking book *Kebabs, Kids, Cops and Crime*, Australian sociologists Greg Noble, Jock Collins, Scott Poynting and Paul Tabar explored the relationship between ethnicity, racialisation, youth and crime in Sydney in the late 1990s, interrogating the stereotypical link between Australian men of Middle Eastern background from Western Sydney, 'ethnic youth gangs' and 'ethnic crime'. The authors showed that anxieties surrounding the Muslim Other were spatialised, contributing to the creation of what they called 'landscapes of fear' in South Western Sydney. 'The imagining of a place called Gangland', they argued, 'provided a tangible entity onto which we could project our anxieties, giving them a concrete, spatial character as a place to avoid'.

This is why places like 'Western Sydney', 'Lakemba', 'Punchbowl' and 'Bankstown' are not neutral. They come to stand in for fear, suspicion and derision for those living outside those suburbs. And they can stand in for safety, familiarity, comfort zone for many Muslims living within those suburbs.

When I first moved to Sydney from Melbourne in 2003, I worked as a lawyer at a firm in the city. One day, as I was preparing to appear in a matter at Parramatta District Court, a colleague joked, 'Remember to take a bulletproof vest', to which I replied, 'Spoken by somebody who's never crossed the bridge'. I remember this well, because it was a repeated exchange with him anytime I had a matter in Parramatta. As fantastically absurd and ignorant as his comment was, it was a common gag among so many of the lawyers I encountered, who lived in their White North Sydney ghetto and only saw Western Sydney as low class, crime-ridden or having the best charcoal chicken.

I recall, back in 2006, seeing an episode of *Today Tonight*, a tabloid, race-baiting national current-affairs program. Reporting on a 'hoon crackdown', the story followed a police operation in the city of Sydney, in which 'modified cars' were being targeted by traffic police working with the Middle East Organised Crime Squad. Several young Australian Lebanese men in modified cars were apprehended, one complaining to the reporter that he's 'being picked on. Look, I'm in my [pyjamas] and I'm out for a drive. It's because I'm a wog, because I'm from Auburn, it's a ... reason to take my car.' I remember this story vividly as my cousin, in his late teens at the time, drove a modified car and was forever fighting with my aunt and uncle, ignoring their warnings that he was making himself more vulnerable to being picked on by the police 'as an Arab kid'.

This idea of Arab/Muslim and Western Sydney as 'threat', 'trouble', has a long history and its resonances linger. Many of the young people I interviewed living outside suburbs with sizable Muslim communities invoked certain images about those suburbs: 'more gangster crime', 'a bit, like, ghetto', 'they stick to themselves', 'where a lot of the extremism and terrorism comes from'. As Ryan Al-Natour writes, Western Sydney is generally perceived as 'gritty' and a 'Muslim ghetto'. There was a clear looping and circulation of tropes and stereotypes among many of the young people I interviewed. The teenagers spoke to me in almost common-sense terms about the threat and problem of 'radicalisation', 'trouble' being located in suburbs with large Muslim populations.

Michael, a year 10 student at Grammar College, speaking to me about the shooting by Farhad Jabar of police accountant Curtis Cheng in Parramatta in 2015, acknowledged that his school was 'kind of removed from that sort of environment'. He then made a sweeping statement: 'I can see how in those problem areas you have issues with the parents and the children. Something's not quite right at home, that affects a child and then they become more easily into extremism.' I asked Michael to be more specific about what he meant by 'problem areas' and he said: 'I guess, I could be wrong, but I mean like Lakemba, Greenacre, Auburn, those areas where there's bigger Muslim populations compared to where we are here'. Michael then told me about his mother, who he said avoids going to 'suburbs where there's, like, bigger populations of Muslims because she feels anxious'. He explained to me that one time they had to go to Greenacre, and his mother

> was, like, clutching my younger brother's hand as we walked down the street, giving funny looks if a guy with a beard, who looked Muslim, walked past. Not so much the women with the headscarf, more the men. I think it's unreasonable, but then I also can't say that I don't understand where she's coming from … It's not a good thing, but it's really, really hard not to have that kind of, I don't know, human instinct when you've been told that that is potentially dangerous by the media.

Michael is describing the reverse position I observed among some of the Muslim students I interviewed who, as I wrote earlier, prefer to stay in places where there are lots of Muslims because they feel safe. In other words, Muslims stay close to Muslims because it makes them feel safe, and non-Muslims stay away from Muslims because it makes them feel safe.

Michael's mother offers a striking example of how a suspect community is created in the imagination of a suspicious public. Greenacre as suspect is an imagined creation, but real and present to Michael's mother as she walks its streets with her children, as she encounters Muslimness. Michael continued,

> whenever we went out of a shop, they'd make sure that we were with them. Because quite often if we go into the shops now, they'll just say like, 'Oh, go get something from the

frozen food aisle', and we'll go and get it, but something like that didn't happen. I think it's come out of generalisation. Just grouping people together under that one Muslim term. And then by doing that, lots of people who have nothing to do with it, simply because of religion, have been roped into becoming the enemies almost.

Xavier (16, Anglo-Australian, Grammar College), said he avoided

suburbs with questionable, like, that has a dangerous stigma. So, it's not just because of the race, it's just because of what I've been told about crime and stuff in those areas. When I think about a suburb that has a big Muslim population, I'd think of crime before terrorism. Just more the general stigma on those areas.

Emma (17, Chinese-Australian, Grammar College) expressed almost the exact same sentiment and told me she

tended to avoid those suburbs that are generally more like, I guess, a bit more with people with lower socioeconomic status living. Some of my friends now moved over to Western Sydney because of family, but I don't go much, my family avoids it. I guess you just don't feel as safe because you do have stories about people smashing car windows at night and things like that, and it's not particularly to do with race but more just the general vibe that a place gives off.

You'll recall from chapter 1 Emma recounting to me the racism she had herself experienced. It was therefore difficult to listen to her utter these words. Emma had an accent and it seemed, to my ears, even more pronounced as she repeated these myths. Her casual reciting of these kinds of stereotypes, inflected with her Chinese accent, revealed to me the heavy weight and burden of race. It told me another story: that even the raced can be seduced into racing others, seduced into repeating vernacular practices that pin people and suburbs with racist aversions. These accounts, and the automaticity by which the students connect certain Western Sydney suburbs with 'danger', shows us the intensity of race, how it's so 'ready to spring into action', as British academic Ash Amin puts it. A 'vibe' is no more than a socialised, trained response to suburbs that have been imbued with certain stereotypes and racialised, classed codes of meaning.

Not everybody felt the same way. Sonia (17, Indian Sikh background, Grammar College) found it 'crazy' that some of her peers referred to Western Sydney in the language of 'ghettos'. But Sonia had a connection to 'those suburbs'. She told me about her grandmother who is in an aged care facility in Revesby: 'literally she walks out, catches the bus, goes anywhere she wants, comes back home, nothing'. Sonia found it hysterical that 'people have this idea of Western Sydney as like, Arab ghetto and Muslim ghetto. As a history student, I love history, and ghettos are *not* Bankstown (laughs).' She mentioned that when she tells people at her school about going to Bankstown on the weekend, 'they're like, "Oh, there's a lot of Lebs there. A lot of Muslims." They don't say it in a bad way. It's like they just say it.'

They just say it. What slips out, what is noticed enough to comment on, to 'just say', is politically loaded. Like the image of a Muslim terrorist that 'pops in', there is a built-up comfort and confidence in 'just saying it' when we consider how readily media and politicians 'just say it'.

Mark, the year 11 Grammar College student we met in chapter 1, told me he lived a 'very middle-class life in Sydney hills suburbia'. When Mark walked into the interview room, my first impression was how stereotypically 'white, middle-class male' he appeared. Tall, with a blond crew cut and blue eyes, Mark had a polished, almost 'posh' elocution, but he was completely unpretentious, even a little shy.

During our interview, Mark said there's 'always been this stigma of Western Sydney where all the bad stuff happens or whatever'. Again, it was interesting to me to note how almost every student I interviewed in the Hills Shire spoke about Western Sydney as though it were a separate geographical region.

Mark's class watched a documentary about Claymore, a low socio-economic suburb in greater Western Sydney with majority public housing. Mark reflected that

the whole capitalist, I guess, idea of 'as long as you work hard, you'll get to succeed' doesn't always really seem true, because it seems like just through nepotism and just the fact you have to sort of have a degree of luck when you're born. And if you're unlucky, then you're going to have to either face prejudice, or you're going to have to face economic struggles.

Mark shows rare insight for someone his age about the myth of meritocracy upon which neoliberal democracies rely, even more so given we were sitting in a classroom in one of the Hills Shire's most elite schools, surrounded by hectares of bushland and state-of-the-art facilities and buildings. Mark said,

All those people over there, they were born there [referring to Claymore]. That's where their families are. And they're born into poverty. And that's where they're stuck, I guess. I don't really go over there that much. I assume they don't come over here that much for the same reason that they're stuck there.

It was refreshing to hear Mark reflect on what being stuck in poverty, and stuck by people's stereotypes, can do to people's mobility and life chances in *structural* terms. It was especially refreshing to hear this kind of analysis considering the systemic humiliation of people living in poverty through dehumanising policies and income support systems that blame people for their own poverty.

Mark added: 'Of course there's more crime over there [in Claymore] than over here. But I've never really seen crime as this sort of thing that's a product of bad people, which I think is what hip hop music taught me.' I confess I was completely taken by surprise when this Liberal Party poster boy brought up hip hop, a form of music that African Americans and marginalised people of colour created to speak back to power, as a platform for calling out racism, police brutality, poverty and for empowering the oppressed. And here was Mark, calling out how hip hop is 'accused of being bad because it glorifies crime and everything, but I think it … helps people be a lot more considerate to people who were born into poverty, where a lot of the time, crime can be the only way out'. Mark had a point – Tupac Shakur's posthumous single 'Changes' comes to mind with his lyrics on poverty and race; how it's hunger that drives him to steal.

Mark told me that because of hip hop he's 'never looked down on people for living in an area where there's lots of crime, because I think it's a product of the fact that, like I was saying before, they're stuck there. There is a system which keeps them there.' I found this to be an astute analysis, particularly given Mark's background and social location, and asked him whether this had any resonance in the way he thought about the war on terror. Mark said that he thought it was

> all linked together. Terrorism is obviously evil but, like crime
> and poverty, I don't see it as a product of evil people. And I

don't think anybody really understands why people can come from the exact same religion, but maybe different social and, like, economic backgrounds, and one person does a terrorist act and the other doesn't. I don't think anybody's really figured out that missing link, like the actual reason.

I couldn't help but smile when Mark said this. He had basically articulated what some of the most prominent critics of CVE have argued about the lack of any predictive evidence as to what *causes* somebody to commit a terrorist attack. It struck me that somebody like Mark was able to arrive at these kinds of conclusions because he was critical of grand claims, approaching class and race as structural problems. He partly credits his compassion and nuance to hip hop, while acknowledging its stigmatisation. As a white, middle-class male drawing knowledge and interpretive tools from hip hop, Mark is participating in a subversion of class and racial barriers, tuning into hip hop, as part of his political 'education'. This was an interview that lingered with me long after I pressed stop on the voice recorder.

OVER *THERE*

In my interviews, I showed students a series of media headlines and image prompts relating to specific incidents, such as the Lindt Café siege and the Parramatta shooting. I didn't want to make any assumptions about young people's knowledge of these events. It was quickly apparent that both non-Muslim and Muslim students from private and public schools in suburbs outside of South West-ern Sydney had less awareness (and in some cases none) of these incidents than their Muslim and non-Muslim counterparts from suburbs such as Greenacre, Lakemba, Punchbowl, Merrylands and so on. Farhan (17, Pakistani-Australian, Grammar College), for example, told me that while he heard about the shooting in Parramatta, he had 'no idea' about 'the debates about radicalisation and young people ... I didn't hear about it'. Farhan was a thoughtful young man and reflected on why this might have been the case as follows:

> We don't hear as much about these things in the private
> school system. Guess we're kind of isolated in our area too,
> since we're so far out from them. We do obviously hear some
> things. Maybe really far downstream where Punchbowl and
> Lakemba and stuff like where there definitely are greater
> Arab communities, you can say. We do hear about them, but
> the stuff you're saying about radicalisation and stuff it doesn't
> affect us nearly as much, so it's not a topic brought up.

Farhan slips into conflating radicalisation with 'Arab communities'. It's telling that Farhan, and so many of the students who live in the Hills Shire and areas outside of South Western Sydney, kept repeating the mantra 'it doesn't affect us', or 'it's not a topic brought up'. The notion that the war on terror, that 'radicalisation and stuff', is imagined as happening over there, not here to *us*, is a narration of privilege. It's symptomatic of a certain imagining of Sydney as divided into zones of danger, chaos, crime, and zones of safety, civility, order. Farhan was reflexive enough to understand this. He told me that he had been thinking about 'private schooling, as a concept, for a while'. He considered that it offered the privilege of disconnection and protection:

> To be at a private school, it brands you in a way, right?
> Because, like, if a public school person sees a private school
> person, they'd say, 'Oh, well they must be rich. They must

237

be of the highest standard.' … You see a Muslim kid, an
ethnic kid, in private school and people brand them better
than if you see a public school boy, for example, in the
western suburbs. That same sort of idea isn't attached.
They're more fast and loose with what they can say about
them. Like, 'Oh, it's just a public school guy. He could be
doing a variety of things.' You can't immediately say that,
'Oh, he's trying to further his education', or anything
like that.

Farhan is offering a candid assessment of how class, ethnicity,
religion mark students, exposing them to judgments and biases.
Students are 'branded' by their school status, where private school
privileges them with innocence, good sense, whereas public school
must work against a presumption of guilt. Branding students even
further is their ethnicity and religion, and even then Farhan is
honest in admitting that a Muslim and/or an 'ethnic kid' from
a private school will be 'branded' more positively than a Muslim
and/or an 'ethnic kid' from a public school.

Rania, a first-year Psychology student at Macquarie University, is of Pakistani background and attended a girls' high school
in the North Shore. She spoke to me about her circle of friends,
including family friends, 'mainly Pakistani background', when
growing up and at university. Most of them chose not to be 'very
political'. She felt that being Pakistani background, being 'non-
Arab', meant you could 'lie lower'. She felt that Lebanese Muslims
'get a lot of attention'. Rania perceives her Pakistani background
as a resource, in so far as it offers relative safety compared to
Lebanese Muslims.

I encountered Muslim students in the middle-class suburbs
of North Western Sydney who had their own perceptions about
'Muslims', specifically 'Lebos' of Bankstown, Lakemba, Granville

and so on in Western Sydney. Several students I interviewed at Hills Islamic School joked about 'Lebos' from 'those areas' as 'try-hards', 'gangsta', 'Adidas or Nike everything'. When I probed them about what counted as 'gangsta', it was telling that they were describing what academics such as Jock Collins, Greg Noble, Scott Poynting and Paul Tabar, Sherene Idriss, and writer-academic Michael Mohammed Ahmad, respectively draw attention to in their histories, research and writing on Lebanese-Australian youth identities. Performances of protest masculinity, Raewyn Connell's seminal concept, and youth cultures are sometimes defined by 'the performance of gang-like behaviour' and the mimicking of African-American hip-hop gangsta culture. This 'unique cultural identity', 'the Leb', Michael Mohammed Ahmad has argued, emerged in the late 1990s as a response to racism and marginalisation (poignantly and often hilariously recounted in Ahmad's critically acclaimed and award-winning novel *The Lebs*) and originated 'right here in Australia'. Significantly, it wasn't just people of Lebanese backgrounds calling themselves Lebs/Lebo or being *called* Lebs/Lebo. It was applied to all people, especially from the western suburbs of Sydney, who were from Middle Eastern and Muslim backgrounds and/or appearance, with Lebanese a marker of the Arab/Muslim Other in Australia.

I recall being on book tour in London in 2008 for the UK edition of my novel *Ten Things I Hate About Me*. The book is set in the mid 2000s and narrates the story of a Lebanese Muslim teenage girl from Guildford in Western Sydney. As I was being interviewed by a British-Lebanese radio host at the BBC, I was describing the context of my character's world in Sydney – the demonisation of her community as 'ethnic gangs, pack rapists, working class' and so on – when the interviewer interrupted me, horrified. In fact, I would go one step further and say he seemed viscerally offended by my description. I was 29 and, truth be told, naive about the nuances of class in the global Lebanese diaspora population. The host, his voice simmering with pride, said that the Lebanese I was describing were completely different to the Lebanese of Europe and America, who were affluent, successful and educated. The interviewer was fascinated by this new species I seemed to have introduced him to. I realised then that my character was thoroughly Australian, although I did not have the political language to articulate why at the time. (This probably explains why most of the fan mail I receive from readers in Europe and America in response to a story about a Lebanese-Muslim girl is rarely from Lebanese-Muslim girls!)

During the workshop one boy, Iraqi background, stood up and started acting out the 'try-hard Lebo' for my benefit – 'here, like this!' (as if I wasn't already well aware of the stereotype, and don't have nephews-in-law and friends with sons whom I recognised in the description!). The boy pinched his shoulder blades together, puffed his chest out, swung his arms slowly as he walked across the room, offering a quick upward nod as he said, 'Whattup, cuz? Wallah, bro.' He collapsed into giggles, joined by the others. The 'ghetto gangsta fantasy' was clearly on display. Notably, the students had no problem with the style being imitated, as most of them placed high symbolic value on hip hop and rap music and African-American popular culture. Earlier on in the workshop, one student, Hamza, Egyptian with Sudanese heritage, described himself as 'African, I'm black', insisting 'I'm not Arab, I'm black'. Ghetto gangsta was not the issue, whether self-consciously, as in Hamza's case, or more generally as a result of these students' consumption of global mass media.

Nor was being Lebanese the issue. I didn't sense any contempt for 'Lebanese-ness' (some of the students making these comments were Lebanese themselves). It was the subculture of 'Leb', defined specifically in terms of the performativity, the being a 'try-hard', that the students were mocking. In her book *Young Migrant Identities*, Sherene Idriss extends Greg Noble and Paul Tabar's work to highlight the importance of paying attention to intra-ethnic conflict and hierarchies of power among young Lebanese-Australian men themselves. In Idriss's case, some of the creative 'types' she interviewed disapproved of the image of 'the Leb' and rejected these kinds of performances of 'protest masculinity'. In the case of the students I interviewed, I read their disdain in the context of their class privilege, compounded by an instinctive youthful disapproval of the cardinal sin among young people: trying too hard. It was that 'Lebos' were showing off, *forcing* the 'ghetto gangsta' style. This was class in practice. For the marginalised and demonised, respect and recognition are sought through proximity to valorised popular cultural styles. For these middle-class Muslim students, including middle-class Lebanese-Muslim students, there were other forms of capital – private school education, good jobs, parents of higher socio-backgrounds – they could draw on in their pursuit of success, public space and social mobility.

DOUBLE LENS

Rania, the university student we met earlier, believes 'class is a difference'. Reflecting on her experiences at her North Shore high school, she told me that the academic standard 'was very high' and that she was lucky because of her parent's 'high educational background and my education setting'. She said she felt 'in a bubble of a good suburb and school'. I mentioned the 2014 counter-terrorism raids, and Rania said she had 'never heard about them. Here, that feels like another world to us. It's not even mentioned.' Rania said that as she 'grew older' and started university, she was 'exposed to more different people from other parts of Sydney, especially Western Sydney, compared to how many I interacted with in the North Shore'. She said that her

> exposure now has shown me there's a difference. I feel like they've seen more struggle and as a result they tend to be more defensive and ... I don't have a double lens when I'm talking to somebody, but they do. Not everybody, of course, but that's a thing I've noticed – they've had more experience, Muslim, even non-Muslim, there's like a double lens coming from Western Sydney.

Many Muslim students I interviewed from schools in Western and North Western Sydney were labouring under this double lens. Jannah is of Kurdish background and I interviewed her when she was in year 12, attending Hills Islamic School. Jannah expressed her disillusionment with 'the Muslim community'. She felt that what was 'really missing at the moment is like Muslims actually standing there and showing the rest of the community that we're against this kind of terrorism. Why aren't there any rallies of Muslims against ISIS or publicly showing people that we're not for this? This isn't Islam.' What Jannah said next points to why she felt this kind of public condemnation was necessary: 'Because I feel, as a Muslim, when I meet someone I just have to be extra nice', she told me,

> like smile extra ... I feel like I shouldn't really have to do that. I have to put out this kind of persona. And no one else from any other background really has to do that. When I'm going to a debate or public speaking at another school and I'm wearing the hijab, I'm wearing a long skirt, I feel like everyone's like, 'Whoa! Who are these people?' Because in this area we're the minority, so we stand out. And then they start talking and

they all sound so smart and, like, polished, I don't know how to explain it. So then when you go up on stage and you're like debating or you're talking to them, you just feel like you have to put in some extra effort, represent Islam, which is fine to an extent because I love my religion. But it's like you want to sound as fancy as them, plus not come off as the stereotypical Muslim, plus fight the stuff they see in the media, plus you're a girl, so you have to prove yourself even more.

Jannah is juggling so much at once. Her words to me reveal her 'doubleness' as she describes herself in terms of how she thinks she is seen by others, differentiated along the lines of class, religion, gender, ethnicity. The categories of marginalisation Jannah perceives herself up against compel Jannah to counter other students' misrecognition of who she is by adjusting her behaviour, engaging in multiple class, gender and racial performances. Jannah does not wear hijab outside of her school uniform, so this is a specific pressure felt when she's at school. I could sympathise first-hand with her instinct to 'represent Islam, which is fine to an extent'. Having attended an Islamic high school myself, I well remember the teachers' speeches to us whenever we boarded the school bus on our way to an excursion or inter-school activity. We were representing our school *and* Islam. Our hijab was a flag of Islam, a symbol of our faith. I sincerely believed this too. It was both burden and honour. To attend an Islamic school, back when I was at school and still now, is to labour under a constellation of complex, interlocking markers of difference and exclusion: the assumptions, sometimes disdainful, about Islamic schools as opaque, 'Other'; the assumptions about hijab as oppressive, about Muslim girls as 'foreign' and therefore less articulate, capable, worthy adversaries in debating competitions, for example; the scaling up of individual students to a global Muslim community.

It is unfair and frustrating that Muslims in Australia and around the world regularly endure the injustice of having to constantly explain themselves and attempt to prove that they are 'good enough', a 'model minority'. Nonetheless, when Jannah says 'this is fine to an extent', we should be wary of dismissing her response, in the context of this injustice, as coming from a place of disempowerment. There is some agency in her putting in 'extra effort'. Not simply agency in the sense of a defiant 'I'll show you', but something more than that. Something that is often glossed over: religious-motivated agency; a deep attachment to her faith, the hurt that comes with being misunderstood, and the way this can trigger a sense of religious obligation to rehabilitate and counter false assumptions.

Mapping out Jannah's allegiances, influences and orientations reveals yet another dimension to her story. It's one that shows that we can't assume that belonging to the category 'Muslim' means sharing in a bounded, stable, homogenous group. Jannah is Kurdish, and her passionate call for more protests against ISIS must be put into the interlocking context of her ethnicity and religion.

Jannah ended this part of our conversation by telling me that when she does speak in the debate or on the stage she can tell 'they're thinking, "Oh, okay! Well she's just like one of us."' Perhaps as a young person, this yearning to be accepted is particularly felt given that it comes with the vulnerabilities and emerging self-confidence of adolescence. To be accepted on one's own terms, yes. But there is often a relief, and therefore seduction, in being accepted by the majority as 'one of us'.

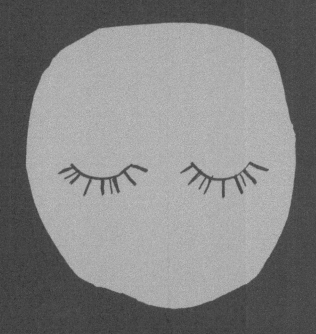

AN INVENTORY
OF TRUST

CHAPTER 12

RISKY SPEECH

I fear another Yassmin Abdel-Magied ...
the war on terror is a cone of silence.

—*Rania (19, Pakistani-Australian, North Shore, Sydney)*

In 2017, a Sudanese-Australian Muslim woman, Yassmin Abdel-Magied, went from being a 2015 Young Australian of the Year to what she dubs Australia's 'most publicly hated Muslim'. It first started with Abdel-Magied's appearance in February 2017 on the ABC's *Q&A*. Appearing alongside Tasmanian Senator Jacqui Lambie, Abdel-Magied expressed her opinion that 'Islam to me is the most feminist religion'. Lambie waged an unprovoked verbal assault on Abdel-Magied, and their confrontation was the catalyst for a media furore. Ten consecutive days of media coverage followed, with around 184 pieces across every major news site. Australia's broadsheet paper *The Australian* published an article with the headline 'Activist Yassmin Abdel-Magied "blind" to Islam's treatment of women'. Its tabloid News Corp stablemate *The Daily Telegraph* wrote 'What really happens when the "wrong" kind of guest appears on *Q&A*'.

On Anzac Day, 25 April 2017, Australia's national day of remembrance, Abdel-Magied posted a six-word Facebook post:

'Lest we forget. Nauru. Manus. Palestine'. The post generated national media outrage and launched an avalanche of hate and condemnation: 200 000 words worth of national media coverage, condemnations by the Prime Minister and foreign affairs minister at the time, debate during parliamentary question time, petitions in support and condemnation both garnering thousands of signatures, calls by politicians for Abdel-Magied to be sacked from her roles as board member of the federal government's Council for Australian–Arab Relations and as a presenter of an ABC program (her contract was not renewed). Abdel-Magied was maligned as a 'flea' who was both 'irrelevant and dangerous'. A politician tweeted that she should consider 'self-deportation', another that she should 'move to an Arab dictatorship'. A conservative radio commentator joked that Abdel-Magied was right to not feel safe and that she would be 'tempted to have run her over'.

Until then, Abdel-Magied had pretty much embodied the role of 'good moderate Muslim'. She was a youth activist, a mechanical engineer named one of the top 100 most influential engineers in Australia by Engineers Australia, founder of a non-government organisation (Youth Without Borders) at age 16, a member of the Australian Government's G20 Youth Steering Committee and the Federal ANZAC Centenary Commemoration Youth Working Group, an ABC presenter and a member of the Council for Australian–Arab Relations. She was 'moderate enough' to attend a Ramadan iftar held at the lodge of then Prime Minister Malcolm Turnbull, and to tour the Middle East promoting so-called Australian values. Abdel-Magied was in the game of 'performing safeness'. So when she expressed an opinion that deviated from the script Muslims must use when speaking publicly, she was quickly punished. After weathering months of intense Islamophobic backlash, including death threats, Abdel-Mageid left Australia and has made a new home for herself in London.

Abdel-Magied's experience has been described as a 'cautionary tale' to people, especially women, of colour. While this is certainly true, it's also true – and as a non-hijabi Muslim woman of colour, I can say this with confidence – that not all women of colour are mistreated in the same way. I've had my share of death threats, employment discrimination, trolling and experiences of censorship. But the ferocity with which Abdel-Magied was treated at a national level was undoubtedly intensified by the fact she is a black Muslim woman, as other black Muslim women, such as Indigenous Muslim woman Eugenia Flynn, have noted.

In her essay 'Once upon a time in the diaspora', Paula Abood refers to African-American feminist thinker bell hooks writing on 'back talk' or 'talking back'. Back talk, talking back, 'meant daring to disagree and sometimes it just meant having an opinion ... To speak ... when one was not spoken to was a courageous act – an act of risk and daring'. Paula goes on to write

> speaking back is an act of great courage. It is not always possible. But when it is, it can inaugurate a process of breaking down the heft of power. And I know that is never easy; I know that for many women it is downright dangerous ... For those in any kind of politically or socially precarious position, speaking back can get you abused, harmed or blacklisted.

Several of the Muslim and non-Muslim students I interviewed told me they were deeply affected by what happened to Abdel-Magied following the 'Lest we forget' post. They have witnessed what happens when a young, black Muslim woman 'talks back'. The abuse, harm and blacklisting. And it affects their own 'coming to voice', as Paula Abood describes it.

When I asked Rania, the first-year Psychology student I introduced earlier, whether she knew of Abdel-Magied, she was instantly animated. She sat up tall and her eyes flashed with anger. 'Randa, I was OUTRAGED!' she cried. 'OUTRAGED! How can that be taken offensively?! We talk about free speech in Australia and suddenly someone makes a comment and they're thrown out of the country! What does that make us as a Western democracy?' I asked Rania if other people in her circle felt the same way. She said that she had spoken about it with her Muslim friends at university 'and they all agreed with me, they all said they don't understand why it was taken offensively'. For Rania, the case of Abdel-Magied was 'a turning point'. She said, 'It has really stuck with me. I feel that is my grudge against Australia! I'm very hurt and disappointed about the whole thing.' Rania turned to her father for advice and support. This was their 'thing', ever since high school when Rania had first been confronted with a question about women in Islam and didn't have the knowledge to answer. 'My dad and I talk, and he teaches me how to debate, how to argue with facts.' Rania turned to her father to make sense of what had happened with Abdel-Magied:

> I said to him, you know, Dad, I was born and brought up
> in this country, and so was Yassmin, and I could have said
> something like that, and Australia could have treated me like
> that. And Yassmin, she's had to leave the country! Leave her
> own country! You know this could be me, this could be you!

For Rania and her father, Abdel-Magied was indeed a cautionary tale. It was proof that they 'don't enjoy the same privilege of free speech'. In the current political climate, Rania's 'main fear is not a terrorist attack'. It is, as she said in a low voice:

> Another Yassmin Abdel-Magied thing happening. That's the
> honest truth. I fear another Yassmin Abdel-Magied, where

an Australian Muslim is born and brought up here, and her opinions and beliefs are not accepted in an open, public conflict against Islam. That's my primary fear. Like, basically we become like Trump America.

After witnessing what happened to Abdel-Magied, Rania stopped engaging in discussions on her social media accounts. She continues to avoid any public voicing of her opinion: 'I consume now, I don't contribute. I feel like the war on terror is a cone of silence.'

DISCLAIMERS ON 'RADICAL' SPEECH

One year after Abdel-Magied appeared on the ABC's *Q&A*, the program hosted a special literary edition. During a discussion about a prime ministerial leadership challenge, one of the panellists, writer Sofie Laguna, said: 'I want radical change. I want radical change.' The conversation moved right along but her words – uttered so casually, received so casually – lingered in my mind. How different would the response have been if they had been spoken by a Muslim or Arab? Later on in the program, Michael Mohammed Ahmad, reflecting on the 'script' Muslims are expected to recite to soothe White anxieties in responding to racism, referred to what had happened to Abdel-Magied: 'How does that work out for the Muslim community when we follow that script?' Ahmad asked. 'How did it work out for our sister Yassmin Abdel-Magied? If anybody who knows her told you about her, they'd tell you she's the nicest person you've ever met, and she was still treated like a member of ISIS.' Ahmad then went on to make a point that would have resonated with every Muslim watching, and which certainly had me and my family cheering as he spoke: 'It makes no difference what kind of a Muslim you are', Ahmad said,

good Muslim, bad Muslim, ignorant Muslim, educated
Muslim, moderate Muslim, radical Muslim ... still Muslim.
I'm not interested anymore in reassuring bigots not to be
afraid of me. My position is actually quite the opposite.
My position now is this − if you're a racist, if you're a white
supremacist, an imperialist, a colonialist, an Orientalist, and
Islamophobe and a xenophobe, you *should* be afraid of me,
because I stand in solidarity with the majority of the people
on this planet, who will say no to you, and we are going to
stop this bigotry and hatred that you're spreading.

The response by *Q&A*'s host, Tony Jones, was extraordinary: 'Let's
be clear ... Mohammed,' Tony said, 'in your case, you're talking
about with your pen or your typewriter, correct?' This seemed
familiar territory for Ahmad, who replied, 'Um ... Because you're
worried that I'm implicating some kind of violent actions?' Jones
swiftly replied, 'No, I'm giving you the opportunity to say that you
aren't'.

My WhatsApp/Facebook Messenger/Twitter DMs were
buzzing! *'Did Tony Jones ACTUALLY SAY THAT?!'* My friends
and I were outraged. Because Tony Jones's response literally proved
Ahmad's point. The exchange vindicated precisely every trope,
every racist fantasy, every anxiety Ahmad was arguing Australian
Muslims have to contend with. In almost two decades of the war
on terror, every Muslim, even a prominent writer introduced on
the program as Dr Michael Mohammed Ahmad, invited to speak
about his lived experiences of racism on a national platform, must
be vetted, must prove they are *not* violent, *not* terrorist. A white
writer can casually yearn for 'radical change' without a demand for
qualification. 'Radical' speech by a Muslim writer must be offered
with a disclaimer. Jones no doubt understood Ahmad's meaning and was pre-emptively in damage control, 'giving' Ahmad

such an 'opportunity' in anticipation of how his words would be interpreted.

The Muslim who speaks in the context of the war on terror is damned from all sides: speak on your own terms and you will be presumed to be inciting violence. Clarify your speech, and you only prove yourself as a risk. The categories of 'good/moderate' and 'bad/extreme' Muslim are always there in the background, ready to pounce on a young Muslim woman's social media posts or a Muslim writer's television appearance. It seems Muslims are infected with a dormant virus and must offer an immunisation record; a reassurance that the strain of Muslimness they contain is safe.

FEAR OF AND FEAR FOR THE MUSLIM STUDENT

This censorship, tone policing and voice management is a canvas that hangs in the backdrop of the world in which the young people I interviewed are coming of age. The canvas offers cues, signifiers, hints and lessons as to what is sayable and what is not in the war on terror. Disparate and seemingly unconnected social, policy, media and political practices start to cohere, shaping a common-sense understanding of the risks of certain speech acts. In the war on terror, what are the boundaries of speech, of political agency and expression for Muslim youth? If the voices of prominent Muslims are encountered through the prism of security, potential threat, incitement and 'unAustralian', how do the young people I interviewed manage their own self-presentation, their own forms of political and religious expression?

I interviewed high school students who had found their political vocabulary and who faced pushback when they articulated their critique of certain narratives around the war on terror and Australian politics.

Shireen, a 17-year-old Muslim student of Bangladeshi heritage, attends a public school in South Western Sydney. She told me that when the Lindt Café siege was mentioned in class one day, she made a comment rejecting the description of Man Haron Moris as a terrorist: 'I said something like, he had mental issues, and if he was some jihadi radical, he was a pretty bad one getting the wrong flag'. During the siege Monis ordered hostages to fly a flag in a window that bears the Islamic testimony to faith. He then demanded the police bring him an ISIS flag. Shireen's teacher reacted angrily to Shireen's comment, accusing Shireen of being insensitive to the victims. Shireen was shocked. 'She wouldn't let me talk about it,' she said. 'It was like it was off limits. It was terrorism and that was that. She was always like that with me. It's like she was trying to always catch me out.' Shireen wrote an essay for the subject Society and Culture, arguing that Australia is racist because 'it locks refugees up but bombs their countries'. Shireen's teacher criticised Shireen for being 'too emotional, too angry, those were her words I remember, and in my head I was thinking, *Of course I'm angry!*'

Shireen was told to rewrite the essay.

Aamenah is the 17-year-old student of Muslim Egyptian background we met in chapter 11. Homeschooled up until year 11, she was now attending Inner West Islamic School. She recounted many incidents to me of being 'shut down' by some teachers 'because I love to argue and I question everything and I'm passionate about human rights'. Aamenah experienced being 'tone-policed' by members of her extended family ('they see me as the little girl who won't shut up') as well as being managed by some teachers in her school. She told me, 'We're having a debate about, you know, this terrorist act that happened recently and I couldn't say what I wanted, especially in front of the non-Muslim teachers. Supposedly you have to be a little bit more careful, but I haven't mastered that yet.' She laughed. 'I sort of blurt it out', she continued. 'I'm not justifying what I'm living on, I'm living on stolen land.' She paused and looked at me, sizing me up. 'I have some weird beliefs', she said.

> I think that, you know, the Aboriginals are kept in the situation they're kept in for a reason. Everything is being oppressed to an extent, because if you feel sympathy for these people you'll challenge the definition of democracy, which is supposedly to be civilised. The connotations of it, at least. And you aren't being civilised to Indigenous people. So then what's your democracy worth?

Aamenah shook her head, working herself up.

> So once I launch into that, it's sort of like, *What is this?! Don't talk about that! Don't challenge people's ideologies.* I'm not saying that we should all follow shariah. Islam says if you live in this country and this country's a democracy then you follow the democracy … I'm saying we need to be true to democracy if that's what you're going to follow. And be accepting. And not oppress people. But Ms Omar came and told me, 'You've got to tone it down. Don't say that.'

But it's not just teachers who were telling Aamenah to 'tone it down'. She found that students were too. 'They'd say, "woah, calm down, it's not good to say that". They get scared. Or maybe they don't care enough. They don't know who they are.'

Aamenah shared another experience with me. For a community and service project in year 11, she chose to run the 'Shoebox for Syria' campaign at her school. It was, in Aamenah's words, 'a disaster'. One of the non-Muslim teachers often clashed with Aamenah. She saw Aamenah as 'too political'. The teacher didn't approve, 'she said it's too Islamic. It's too typical of you. You should think of something more broadly. Westmead Children's Hospital, for example.' When Aamenah handed out fliers to students at lunchtime the teacher stopped her, so Aamenah took the matter to the school principal and her parents got involved.

In these teacher–student dynamics, there is *fear of* the Muslim student and *fear for* the Muslim student. Shireen's and Aamenah's teachers may not necessarily have feared that Shireen's criticisms, or Aamenah's 'too Islamic' project, placed them on the so-called conveyer belt towards 'radicalisation'. The thing about the cultural imaginary of the war on terror is that to remain in the territory of pre-suspect, viewed as inherently at-risk as a member of a racialised collective, is to be constantly scrutinised, judged as 'too political', as needing to be tamed.

By contrast, it's a fear of what Aamenah risks in expressing her dissenting views on Australia's political system that arguably drives her Muslim teacher's response. Tone it down: reduce your politicality, make it smaller, less visible, less threatening. The advice is clearly coming from a place of a Muslim teacher attempting to protect her student. The teacher knows what Muslim students who don't 'tone it down' risk. And it is a risk. Consider that in 2018 a year 12 student in Canberra was investigated by the Australian Federal Police after a tip-off by his teacher. According to media reports, the teenager was suspected of radicalisation because of an essay he wrote about Muslim terrorists and Western intervention, coupled with his travel to the Horn of Africa to donate sporting equipment to needy children as part of a compulsory volunteering subject. While the student was never charged, the experience reportedly left him shaken and affected his grades.

CHECKING AND HUSHING

The pressure to self-censor in classroom contexts was a common theme among many of the Muslim students I spoke to. This seems resonant with research in the UK context of Muslim youth reporting self-censoring and avoiding talk about politics following critical events, what UK academics describe in their research of young Muslims being educated under the UK's *Prevent* regime as 'checking' and 'hushing' practices used to demonstrate one's 'safeness'. In the US context, Sunaina Marr Maira has researched how young Muslims 'live in the everyday of surveillance'.

In their paper 'Being a "suspect community" in a post 9/11 world', Adrian Cherney and Kristina Murphy report that what Muslims observe going on around them, in terms of police or security agencies focusing on Muslims, can be experienced directly and vicariously, forming a perception of a 'community under siege,' shaping responses accordingly. When Abdul-Rahman, the 16-year-old Hills Islamic School student we met in chapters 3 and 8, tells me that he's 'very restrained' and 'I have to, like, control what I say', feeling able to 'talk freely with some teachers and restrict' himself 'with others', he is 'checking' and 'hushing' himself. The war on terror has created a kind of pedagogy of speaking politics as a Muslim. When Muslims speak on the phone and, after saying something controversial, jest, 'hey, ASIO, that was a joke', we see what Sunaina Marr Maira means by the 'everyday of surveillance'. If you're an outspoken Muslim, you expect your phone to be tapped, and the predictability of that expectation makes it all the more ripe for ironic humour.

What of the non-Muslim students I interviewed? Almost all of the non-Muslim high school students didn't feel censored, didn't experience a management or policing of their opinions in relation to the war on terror. 'I feel I can talk openly about things,'

Brayden told me. 'I pretty much talk about as much as I want to'. The common denominator among the most confident students was that they were white males. Several of the young men I interviewed looked genuinely puzzled when I asked them if they ever worried that the opinions they expressed about, say, foreign policy, or the war on terror, might be misunderstood as 'radical' or 'extreme'. They had never thought about these issues, let alone worried if they would get into trouble for speaking out. These were questions they had never needed to contend with. They took their 'free speech' for granted, because they had never been confronted with any costs.

ON NOT STANDING OUT

Race, religion, class and gender were the most salient social categories I traced in the students' narratives. But the one very clear and persistent narration line shared between all the students was the fact that they were adolescents, teenagers, young adults, youth – whichever category description one chooses to use. I soon realised it was too simplistic to expect to understand the 'everyday of surveillance' by reducing the picture to non-Muslim Anglo students freely speaking versus Muslim students self-censoring. As I was conducting my interviews and workshops, something kept gnawing at me. When a Muslim student told me they were holding back when they spoke up in class, was this because they felt judged through a security prism, or was something else going on? Was I reproducing totalising assumptions by treating 'Muslim' as a catch-all interpretive device? One Muslim year 11 male student told me he 'just wanted to cruise along in class' and 'wasn't interested in politics' or 'rocking boats'. Was this disinterest because he felt school didn't offer him a safe space to 'rock the boat'?

Therefore, why bother taking an interest? Alternatively, if he had felt free to 'rock the boat', would he still be interested and willing to do so? Another year 11 Muslim male student told me he had 'zero interest in the war on terror'. He knew 'what was happening in the world' but said, 'I prefer to let the world sort itself out'.

I confess, I silently cringed hearing this. I want young people, especially young people of colour, to be invested in leading political change, leading revolution. But I also felt guilty, because the expectation that young Muslims in this climate should step out of their bubble means prematurely exposing them to the pain that comes with confronting and fighting injustice. Perhaps for a limited amount of time, some of these young Muslims were enjoying the privilege of not caring. This is a privilege most young white people get to have their whole lives. Few young white people, and even few adult white people, are taught to care about these issues. That's why so many white people respond with shock or offence when issues of race and inequality are named as a problem – because they've been privileged enough their whole lives not to even realise there *is* a problem. For young Muslims, growing up in intensifying surveillance regimes is not simply and always a question of being scared to speak out. It can also be a matter of staying silent as strategic withdrawal. Yes, it's selfish; as a form of self-care it has to be.

And yet, one of the sobering consequences of this political climate is the implications it has on the kinds of young people produced by our education system. The political are largely managed, contained. But what of those who are disengaged, disinterested, generally apathetic and proudly so? When being docile, conformist and uncritical is rewarded, it's harder to arouse curiosity, make a case for political passion, especially when the costs of doing so are also starkly high.

Aamenah had things to say about this. She clearly stood out from the rest of her cohort and was in some way isolated because of how outspoken and passionate she was. She described an argument with a non-Muslim teacher at her school about the topic of Muslim women, and the surprising response of her peers. The teacher 'launched into this whole thing about women in Islam, that in the Qur'an women are told they're as good as camels'. Aamenah challenged the teacher.

> I was telling her, you know, in Islam, women are given
> a voice. Women were given a voice. Like, for example,
> al Ghazali, who taught al Ghazali? It was his mother.
> … Every case, there was a woman. It blows my mind
> how people just don't know, so I told her that. And she
> complained to the principal and the principal told me,
> 'You've got to tone it down', and I'm like 'Why?' and she
> said, 'You can't force your belief'. And I said, 'I wasn't,
> she was challenging my belief'.

I asked Aamenah how the other students had responded when she took on the teacher. She said,

> I looked around at them for support. But they played the
> mediator, like they wanted it all to stop, they're looking at
> me like, *What on earth is wrong with you? Just conform, shut up*
> … I can sense they're uncomfortable. Like, they just, they sit
> there. And I'm looking at them thinking, *You traitors, you're*
> *supposed to be on my side, come on.*

This has been a struggle for Aamenah.

> I was looking at them wondering why they weren't defending
> Islam. Then again, I shouldn't expect that of them. … We're
> so used to it. We read it, we watch it, we hear it. It's almost

cruel. And then they get scared because I have, like, an expectation, and they're like, 'What? You know, we just want to have lunch with you.' I'm talking to them about news I've read and I'll show them and they freak out, they don't want to know.

Aamenah couldn't work it out: 'I don't know if they're scared. Or if they want to stick in a comfort zone. Or maybe they don't want to speak about things that might provoke your thoughts further than what's already comfortable.' Aamenah believed it came down to identity:

the problem for my generation is you get the parents saying one thing, and you get the media and politicians saying another thing, and then you get your, you know, a whole bunch of other peers that are just as confused as you are. Are we terrorists or are we freedom fighters? All of that word choice.

Aamenah was emphatic: 'They don't have an identity. And you must have an identity to be able to be bold and loud and not fear the consequences.'

It takes self-knowledge and confidence to speak out. To 'rock the boat'. To not care about looking interested and engaged, especially, as I found, in the middle high-school years.

Even those who sit at the apex of privilege – middle-class white heterosexual males – like Tom, spoke about the vulnerability that comes with being opinionated, of being a non-conformist. Tom told me he didn't 'speak up a lot on political stuff', because he didn't want to look 'stupid and not knowing what I'm talking about, so I shut up'. To express an opinion means exposing your vulnerabilities; what you don't know becomes just as important as what you do. While Steven, a 16-year-old Anglo-Christian male, felt he could talk about anything, he worried about 'how I'll be judged as too smart, too nerdy'.

Steven told me about an incident on a school bus, where he pulled up a friend for a sweeping generalisation about Muslims and terrorists. His friend 'quickly backed down', because he realised 'I don't actually agree with him ... I think a lot of kids get frightened by that 'cause they just want everyone to agree with them. Teenagers also want to be liked. And so they're like, "Okay, I don't actually hold that opinion that strongly".' For Steven, voicing opinions 'wasn't just about courage'. It was also about the hesitation that comes with 'being not exactly sure how to disagree'. He believed this was as much true of comments around race as it was about, 'say, economics or something else in class. It's hard to know what your standpoint is. And so then those times you're quiet. But then if you come up with something good and you know you can convince them or you know that you can win, then you say something.' For Steven, speaking up in school, among your peers, came down to one thing: 'I think the big issue of fighting racism is teaching people how to win'.

This was a sentiment expressed by many students I interviewed. Even those who felt morally bound to speak up sometimes backed down or remained quiet on controversial topics, because they felt unsure of their facts, their ability to sustain a solid argument. Mark (the hip-hop loving student we met in chapters 1 and 9), felt this was a symptom of a wider problem.

> these days you can get exactly what you want and find your own little safe space which agrees with everything you agree with and then everything you believe. Like, they live in a different creative reality, which makes political discussion so difficult these days because the idea of, what was it,

'alternative facts' means how do you argue when science,
facts, evidence become meaningless?'

Daniella (17-year-old Greek-Australian, Castle Hill), whom we
met in chapter 1, felt 'everyone has their own opinion and it is
their truth ... but some people shouldn't be given the platform to
publish it, because they're publishing lies, publishing hate'.

Most of Daniella's schooling was at a Catholic school in the
eastern suburbs, until her parents divorced and she moved to
Grammar College. Daniella told me: 'People lack confidence and
are too scared to stand up for what they believe in, which I used to
be. Now that I found my voice, I feel like I can do anything really.
But there's still a cost. You get labelled.' Daniella felt students at
her school were 'more bystanders. They're scared to stand out in
a crowd. If something's wrong they won't say anything about it,
which breaks me.' Manuel (17, Filipino, Roman Catholic, Parramatta) was upfront about this: 'I'm embarrassed if my views and
opinions aren't the same as others around me'.

Both Muslim and non-Muslim students – including the
politically outspoken ones – often betrayed, if even fleetingly, a
desire to belong, to not stand out. So speaking out as a member of
a 'suspect community' wasn't just about how teachers would judge
you as a 'suspect' Muslim, but also how your peers would judge
you. Even Aamenah, as outspoken as she was, said that sometimes
she 'held back' because 'people see you as the social justice warrior, a know-it all'. She said that some of her Muslim classmates
had drifted from her, withdrawn because they perceived her as too
political. She wondered if they wanted to stay in a 'bubble' to protect themselves, or because they just didn't care. It bothered her.

Towards the end of my interview with Aamenah, I had to
change the battery in the voice recorder. Aamenah sat quietly, lost
in her own thoughts, as I fiddled with the machine. And then, in a

tone both wistful and self-assured, she said: 'You know, knowledge is power. Your words are your only weapons at the end of the day.' There was something both remarkably mature and profoundly sad about Aamenah's statement. It's an indictment on the kind of society this generation are coming of age in that a young Muslim's orientation to her education – and the world – is one of battle and defence.

Adolescence is already a period when the pressure to conform, to tone down, to fit in and not stand out, is felt so intensely and acutely. Muslims have another burden to bear: juggling teachers' perceptions and the wider political debates and constraints, internalising social imaginaries, managing your self-presentation as a Muslim boy, a Muslim girl, as a teenager.

IDENTITY POLITICS

Jihan, the year 12 student we met in chapter 4, who came to Australia as a refugee from Iraq, contextualised the stifling of her voice, especially in her advocacy and activist work, to a wider agenda against so-called identity politics: 'People want to tone police us', she said,

> especially at this age when we can be shaped. I always get that. And I think it's most potent these days because you're dealing with a right-wing backdrop and a war on identity politics, and I'm scared of speaking from emotion, because emotion is so looked down on these days. You have to be rational. And it's this idea that these two qualities can't coexist. So it's really difficult growing up as a young person under that landscape.

Thinking through these stories, and Jihan's in particular, I was struck by how the containment and management of young people's voices in today's neoliberal climate is larger than simply zooming in on speech directly connected to the war on terror. The policing of 'emotion', the attempts to discredit vocal people of colour by dismissing their arguments as 'identity politics', accusing them of 'playing the race card', has become popular and mainstream. Canadian psychology professor, and author of the bestselling *12 Rules for Life*, Jordan B Peterson is probably the world's most outspoken and successful White male celebrity culture warrior, who dismisses 'the idea that women were oppressed throughout history' as 'an appalling theory', argues that Islamophobia is 'a word created by fascists and used by cowards to manipulate morons' and claims that 'White privilege is "a Marxist lie"'.

And students like Jihan have noticed. As Jihan put it,

> within our current landscape and the level of right-wing
> conservatives out there, it's very difficult to speak out because
> there's this attack on identity politics, and people don't see
> that there is that really close link between experience and
> identity. When you talk about the Middle East and the war
> on terror, or the refugee experience, they don't want to hear
> about identity, which means race, class, sexuality, these are
> the experiences that young people go through.

No less than Australia's Prime Minister, Scott Morrison, has weaponised the phrase 'identity politics' against people who bring up race and power in public debates. In fact, he used his address to the Australia–Israel Chamber of Commerce after the Christchurch attacks to declare,

If we allow a culture of 'us and them', of tribalism, to take hold; if we surrender an individual to be defined not by their own unique worth and contribution but by the tribe they are assigned to; if we yield to the compulsion to pick sides rather than happy coexistence, we will lose what makes diversity work in Australia.

Here, religion, ethnicity, gender, class, sexuality, disability are all 'tribal allegiances', manipulatively used as a powerplay of 'trading off against one another'.

Michael (17, Anglo-Australian Catholic, Blacktown) seemed to agree. He submitted a written reflection in a writing workshop. Verbose and overstated, it still gives an important insight into young people who are interpreting debates on White privilege, intersectionality and activism as an attack on Western values, particularly liberalism's veneration of 'the individual'. His views also resonate with a few other anonymous pieces submitted by students.

Michael believes that 'the war on terror is the West's war on its own inadequacies, fears, self-consciousness and fear of a paradigm shift away from the Western perception of individual freedoms'. Michael condemns the 'constant and frivolous dynamic of oppressed and privileged'. He's against 'a social and political climate' in which people are 'divided into so many groups.' For Michael, 'the barriers of class, race, and prejudice will destroy the western societal construct of the individual' for 'collectivism'.

This reads like an ode to the likes of Jordan Peterson, like the first draft of what will probably become a polished narrative of Western decline if Michael takes in the steady tide of books, blogs, columns and tweets by angry White men. There are notable similarities between Michael's sentiments and the arguments mounted by no less than Prime Minister Scott Morrison: intersectionality equals tribalism, attention to oppression and privilege is divisive and so on.

Mark alluded to these debates in my interview with him and offers an interesting perspective on how he responds to peers who share Michael's views. Frustrated by the level of 'political discussion', he told me he found it 'kind of disconcerting sometimes how difficult it is to just talk to someone about something these days'. Although he didn't use the language of 'identity politics', he attributed a lot of the problem among his white friends and peers to fear:

> I feel like the issue is a lot of people are scared, and they don't have the sort of security in themselves to go like, 'I have had a leg up in life'. But they don't want to hear that because it makes them feel like they didn't earn anything. And it scares them, so they say, 'Oh, feminism and racism and all that, that's just a joke. That doesn't exist anymore.' And they try to belittle those causes and say the people who propagate them are just complaining because they don't want to hear the facts that they have had some privilege in life.

Mark referred to 'our politicians', Trump and the internet as all implicated in a culture of 'silencing people who don't have power but who want to talk about the causes that actually mean something to them'.

My interviews and encounters with reflections like Michael's made me think about how young white people struggle to talk about White privilege without defensively feeling that these conversations foreclose their own identities, aspirations and self-worth. I don't just mean that 'equality feels like oppression' for students 'accustomed to privilege', as the adage goes. I'm thinking more about how critical reflection on one's privilege can be experienced as a threat to one's emerging sense of self and place in the world, to one's 'good intentions', 'hard work', agency. Like Jihan described, being confronted with her anger, not just her suffering, was sometimes perceived by refugee advocates around her as a threat and attack on their work and intentions. Acknowledging privilege can feel like a guilty confession of having enjoyed the proceeds of somebody else's theft. As Mark notes, it can be scary. Young people need to be in schools that consciously teach students how to speak about race, Whiteness, privilege and oppression. This means white students need to be introduced to their racial identities. For many, this will come as a surprise, given that Whiteness has always floated above 'diversity' and 'multicultural groups', constructed as a taken-for-granted, normalised universal. Students need an education system that gives them the intellectual tools to understand Whiteness not as skin colour or biology, but as a political identity, a location of structural advantage and privilege. They need to understand its material histories of violence that underlie present systems of power and knowledge, and the kind of societies it has created. And then they need to understand what this means for them in relation to the original and continuing owners of this land and non-white minorities.

As anthropologist Ghassan Hage cleverly wrote in response to Pauline Hanson's 2018 motion 'It's OK to be white':

It's ok to be white and be the descendant of people who have plundered, exterminated, enslaved and subjugated other peoples and their lands across this planet, if you recognise it and deal with its consequences. It's not ok to be a White who is aspiring to perpetuate what your ancestors have done in this regard … it's not ok to be White and demand a better life because you think you deserve more because you are White.

In my doctoral research interviewing 'Islamophobes', I came to various conclusions, one of which is that there is nothing natural or innate about encountering others from a White subject position of entitlement; it's not inevitable that white people will automatically claim what Hage calls 'governmental belonging', the feeling that one has a right to the nation and to manage others in the nation. Media, political and legal and policy narratives socialise White people into acquiring and claiming a certain orientation towards the nation, Indigenous people and non-white minorities. Discourses and emotional responses are learnt – and in this climate, learnt quite quickly.

There's a lot of work to do. For over 500 years, Whiteness has been normalised, humanised and celebrated. It's consumed ethnic, racial and religious others in the name of multiculturalism, compelled them to do the confessing and giving and, as we've seen by the testimonies of the young people above, censored and tone-policed their speech and political agency. It's time white students are taught to understand how to resist these socialisation processes, to understand the easy slippage between white (white-skinned, Anglo-Saxon heritage etc.) and White (a posture of entitlement, supremacy). Maybe Harmony Day ceremonies and multicultural education programs at school need to focus less on kebabs, laksa and saris, and offer posters, stalls and presentations on White Australia instead: how this political project of White majority nationhood emerged, whom and what it sought to destroy and control to maintain its majority, what White nationalism does to sustain its dominant position, and how white students and students of colour can work in solidarity to dismantle White supremacy and reimagine and work towards building a different kind of nation.

CHAPTER 13

TEACHERS AND CURRICULAR JUSTICE

Our capacity to generate excitement is deeply affected by our interest in one another, in hearing one another's voices, in recognizing one another's presence ... any radical pedagogy must insist that everyone's presence is acknowledged. That insistence cannot be simply stated. It has to be demonstrated through pedagogical practices. To begin, the professor must genuinely value everyone's presence. There must be an ongoing recognition that everyone influences the classroom dynamic, that everyone contributes. These contributions are resources.

—*bell hooks*

In Australia, schools have been found to be the most common setting in which children and adolescents experience racism. But speaking to high school students made it clear to me that focusing on racist incidents alone allows the deeper problem of *race* in the very structures of our education system to be ignored. And so, this is a chapter about race in the classroom. It's about how Islamophobia and wider discourses creep into classroom dynamics, curriculum structure, content and delivery and teacher–student relationships.

But before we get to the students' curriculum stories and experiences with the education system, we need to talk about teachers. Because when it comes to schools, there is probably nobody as enduring as the figure of the teacher as hero. Everybody loves the story of the teacher who defies the system, confronts the barriers of race/class/gender/sexuality and works against all odds to transform the life of a student, a classroom or a community. *To Sir with Love*, *Lean on Me*, *Dangerous Minds* and so many other films in this genre have indulged in romanticised stories of redemption and hope, often based on a White saviour narrative.

I grew up on this film genre. Working in schools for 15 years now, and coming from a family of teachers (that's why I know these films intimately!), I also anecdotally and through observation understand the emotional and physical toll the 'teacher as hero' expectation can have on teachers, who are often expected to work miracles (as well as record those miracles in never-ending documentation, metrics and rubrics). But as my interviews and workshops were with students, I explored teacher–student interactions only from the perspective of students, and so how teachers feel about the 'teacher as hero' is not something I addressed. What I found overwhelming in the responses of students was how much they relied on teachers to set the conditions of school as a safe space, how much they valued and wanted teachers to creatively deviate from the constraints of curriculum, opening up new and critical routes of learning and discovery, and how much they needed teachers to initiate relations of trust without indulging in the patronising and ignorant role of White saviour.

Jihan, whom we heard from in the previous chapter, felt that her capacity to speak critically depends on what subject and teachers I have. Working within the constraints of the educational syllabus, particularly legal studies, it's very difficult to have a radical opinion, especially when talking about immigration. You have to take a side that is very unbiased and you have to look at both sides, and when it comes to putting that human aspect into your argument, like, it's very difficult because you go down a Marxist path, for example, or an opinion that speaks from lived experience, they're not going to take that and you might get marked for it. Sometimes you have to play it safe.

Jihan found 'Society and Culture, and my particular teacher [a Lebanese Maronite woman], was very different'. Jihan felt her 'opinions, my voice, were not just tolerated, but she really pushed me to extend my thinking and take risks with my PIP' ('personal interest project', a major assessment in that). For Jihan, that kind of active encouragement and investment by her teacher made all the difference to the work she produced. 'It was all about identity politics and how lived, like, personal experience, delineates your identity politics. I'm so proud of my personal interest project.'

When Rokaya (whom we met in chapters 1 and 4) was in year 11, she was trying to think of a topic for her 'personal interest project'. She said she didn't realise

how passionately I felt about the representation of Muslim women and 'saving Muslim women' until I was in a non-Muslim environment and I had those ideas projected onto me. Like I remember this one guy ... this white guy. He was a friend of mine. But he always just had this underlying assumption that I'm hiding something from him. That there was something going on at home, like the angry bearded dad and oppressed mum kind of thing. It was just little microaggressions.

Rokaya initially reconsidered her topic on Muslim women because 'I thought maybe it's too political'. So she chose representations of women during the period Julia Gillard became Australia's first female Prime Minister. Except Rokaya 'wasn't feeling it'. It was only when another teacher (Lebanese Christian) approached Rokaya that Rokaya decided to stick with her topic: 'She gave me shivers so much when she was talking to me', Rokaya said happily. I could see how much this teacher had impacted Rokaya, as her face lit up in a way that it hadn't since we started the interview. It was the face of somebody who had experienced a teacher's validation and faith: 'She told me, "You have to write about your Muslim women topic. You'll do that more justice. Trust me, you'll get the award in the end for that. Don't pick the safer topic."'

As Rokaya researched her project, she started 'looking into the war on terror because those representations came in so much stronger'. One of her white male teachers, among others, advised her: 'don't think about the war on terror, just think about Muslim women here'. This is a classic case of the failure to understand what bell hooks, in her book *The Will to Change: Men, Masculinity, and Love*, describes as 'imperialist white-supremacist capitalist patriarchy'. Political systems and injustices are interlocking, none more so than imperial feminism. The way in which Muslim women have been used, abused, exploited – killed – in the name of the war on terror, in the name of 'rescuing' them, civilising them, undressing them and so on, is at the heart of what Rokaya sought to research and cannot be dismissed as two separate issues.

'I ended up getting full marks for my PIP', Rokaya continued, 'and I won an award, so everyone had to sit there and listen to an introduction to my topic, like, 1000 students at a presentation!

And it was that project that put me on the academic path I'm on now at uni.'

I came across countless such stories during my interviews: teachers who actively supported Muslim students and encouraged them to resist 'playing it safe'. In all such cases, the students were able to trust their instincts only because they trusted that a teacher would have their back.

Salim, whom we first met in chapter 9, spoke to me about a teacher he was able to open up to following the prayer group controversy at Epping Boys High School. Salim felt he could 'build a relationship with' that one teacher because she had experienced racism growing up.

> She was white but Jewish and she had some issues at my age as well, like people making fun of her background. She talked to me about how she used to defend herself as well and I was like, okay, I see how it is, you're having the same problems as I am. Yeah. I feel like because she had the same problems she was sympathetic and empathetic with me, so it turned out well.

Abear is the student who was verbally abused by the boys on a school bus as she walked to school. She told me that after it happened a few times, she worked up the courage to approach her year coordinator. That was 'the hardest part for me, because I didn't think I was going to be as emotional as I was'. She said, 'at first I put on a really brave front ... I just wanted it to be addressed'. But Abear found herself starting to explain what happened and then suddenly 'sobbing uncontrollably'. The outpour of emotion 'surprised me. It wasn't for show, I didn't realise how much it affected me until someone said, "Well, are you okay?" and "I can't believe that's happened to you", and you just break down at that point.' I asked Abear why her reaction surprised her. She didn't hesitate: 'He took me seriously'. The teacher arranged a meeting with the deputy principal the following day. Abear couldn't believe what happened next. The deputy 'actually went onto the bus, pretty much gave them all a huge lecture, and then had a conversation with their principal as well so they could find out which students were involved. It was taken seriously. I didn't have to worry about it from that point.'

The Psychology student we first met in chapter 11, Rania, said her most trusted teacher was her Legal Studies teacher in year 11 and 12, 'because he asked questions, he was genuinely interested in my culture, my beliefs'. If Rania was called on to answer a question, she didn't feel like 'he was treating me as the token Muslim. He was genuinely interested in me as an individual.' Rania's words reminded me of bell hooks's beautiful description of a 'classroom community' quoted at the beginning of this chapter. A safe space offers students community, and this requires transformative practices in what to teach and how to teach.

Tiyana, 17, is a brilliant, self-motivated, socially conscious student at Grammar College, who is so deeply interested in 'talking about the news and politics and discussing opinions' that she started a lunchtime initiative with some like-minded friends, calling it 'Topic Tuesday'. Throughout the week, Tiyana and her friends share links to news items and articles about a topic they've chosen to 'learn more about'. The week I met Tiyana, the topic was drugs. Other weeks it's 'something like gun laws in America, or it can be Indigenous rights'. Tiyana was inspired to 'shape my own view of the world' after a history class on the war on terror and terrorism.

I learnt that terrorism wasn't just about 9/11. I discovered there was so much more to the topic. I felt like I needed

to go and get my own information just so that I could
consolidate my own opinion about it, because I don't want to
be influenced by just one source. I didn't want to be ignorant
to the wider community, because I'm in a bubble, I'm in a
private school and stuff like that.

Tiyana approached some other girls in her year level and asked
them if they were 'okay' with her 'talking politics'. They were keen:
'So we just kind of collaborated'.

Tiyana's 'Topic Tuesday' idea was directly inspired by her
Geography teacher exposing her class to a broader and historical
understanding of terrorism. The lesson fired up Tiyana's political
awakening. Tiyana told me she started to 'look at the world and
politics differently'. Her teacher

spoke about the [Lindt Café] siege and she told us to look
at both sides. Don't make your opinion based off this one
article. She made me reflect about the effects of my, like,
immediate thoughts being like, 'Terrorist attack: Muslim'
and what that does to other people. I started to think about
Muslim girls at school. They're worried about wearing the
veil, and they're worried about showing their culture and stuff
like that, because they're afraid of being attacked.

For Tiyana, those reflections 'started' in that class, 'because my
teacher opened up that discussion'.

In these narratives, students credit their teachers with actively
creating conditions which engender their sense of trust, safety
and experiences of empowerment. But like any workplace, teachers will reflect the full human spectrum of political orientations,
dispositions, personalities and motivations. On entering a classroom, they will simultaneously be faced with multiple cases of

vulnerability and need. To be the hero to every student at once is an impossible demand. The embodied and emotional aspect of teachers' labour, what sociologist Raewynn Connell describes as 'emotion work', is demonstrated in these above accounts. So too, in the case of Rokaya's, Rania's and Tiyana's teachers, is teaching as intellectual work, which is the main point I will take up later on in this chapter. I'm less interested in charismatic and empathetic individual teachers than I am in looking at what kind of education system we should be offering students so that their experiences of growth, justice and equality aren't left to chance. After all, these students' positive experiences arose because they were lucky enough to encounter such teachers. In the stories below, we meet students who encountered the opposite kind of teacher. Teachers who contributed to feelings of insecurity, shame and vulnerability in the context of students' visibility as Muslims in a climate of Islamophobia. Was this just bad luck? Or can we try to think about this in structural terms? Let's first meet these teachers and then find out.

ISLAMOPHOBIA IN THE CLASSROOM

During my interview with Rania, she said, 'I want to tell you about this incident that happened in year 8 with my Geography teacher'. She sat up, animated.

> The teacher asked the class, 'Who here is Muslim?' So I raised my hand. I was writing at the time and kept writing. I wasn't really paying attention. Then she asks the class, 'Who's Pakistani?' I raised my hand again. That's when I started to notice people kind of around me were glancing at me.

Rania stood up at the desk between us, and placed her hands on the desk, leaning close to me. 'I still remember her two hands were on my desk, like I'm doing now, and she came up to me, close, and she said, "How do you feel about the Malala Yousafzai case?"' Rania sat down again. 'It was the day after the Malala Yousafzai incident', she explained.

Rania is referring to Pakistani education advocate Malala Yousafzai, who, while campaigning for girls' education after the Taliban took control of her home in the Swat Valley in Pakistan, was shot in the head by a member of the Taliban in 2012. To understand Rania's experience in the classroom, and the way in which her teacher was using Malala to attack Rania, means understanding how the figure of Malala has been coopted in the West to reinforce gendered Islamophobic narratives. Malala is portrayed as an activist *in spite of* her religion and culture, never *because* of her Islamic faith or her culture. She is the exception that proves the backwardness and ignorance of Muslims and Pakistanis.

Five years on, Rania was still visibly angered by her experience with her teacher. 'Randa, I was very shaken! I came home and told my mum and she was outraged!' Rania's mother complained to the school principal the next day and 'grilled' the teacher at parent–teacher interviews. After Rania's mother intervened, the teacher 'was very nice and it was fine'. Rania paused. 'But since that Malala moment, it was more of an emphasis in class ... that I belonged to a backward religion.' Rania said, after the incident, 'If I spoke about feminism, I wasn't taken seriously because I was Muslim, Pakistani'. Rania had a 'friend' who was 'very outspoken and very feminist, and I think my religion scared her off. We just found ourselves frequently disagreeing on topics ... she'd attack my religion as sexist, and I didn't feel that teacher was, like, a moderator.' Rania said that in years 9 and 10, she lacked 'the knowledge of how to defend my religion', so this friend 'got away with a lot in class. She looked down, kind of, it wasn't a genuine debate.' Importantly, Rania remembered 'feeling that it could have played out differently if the teacher had helped. But after that Malala incident it was, like, pretty obvious she looked down on my religion too.'

Aamenah, whom we met in chapter 11, had a very similar view. When reflecting on how she challenged teachers and voiced her opinion in class, only to be met with students telling her to stop, Aamenah was clear about why she thought other students felt free to shut her down:

> What a teacher feels, students feel. If the teacher gives off that they don't like a student, then the other students are going to gang up on that student. Unless you're ridiculously brave and whatnot. That's what's going to happen. If a teacher is irritated by your opinions, other kids will be annoyed. So, as ... older people are going to do it, then the younger people are going to do it.

For Rokaya too, teachers set the tone of a classroom, they send signals about the unspoken rules, which students are quick to pick up on. Rokaya vividly recalled an incident in class in year 11. Her teacher, 'she liked me a lot', she

> gave me this, like, safe-sex birth kit thing in front of the whole class. And she was like, 'Haha', you know, 'because you're going to be the first to get married'. She was joking about it, but I was traumatised! ... I tried to play it off, but I also tried to show the class that, 'No, that's wrong'. But yeah, she was laughing and, 'come on, it's a joke!' I said something, and the class kind of got defensive of *her* rather than of *me*. Like, *Oh, come on, like, it's just a joke!*

We can see here that Rokaya's classmates were mimicking the teacher's reaction and defensiveness, subjecting Rokaya to a double indignity: being presented with the birth kit, offensive in how it reduced Rokaya to the stereotype of the Muslim girl married off young and endlessly having babies, and then being gaslighted for taking offence.

Abear felt that 'generally within the school I wouldn't want to just broadcast my views about politics, Muslims, because my principal and the very senior people at my school, they weren't necessarily the most understanding when it came to that stuff'. Abear's sister and her sister's friend, in year 11 at the time, published an article in the *Sydney Morning Herald* about Australia's policies towards refugees and 'stopping the boats', signing off with their names and the name of their school. Abear's sister and friend were called into the principal's office and 'pretty much berated: "You can't do this. Why have you associated our school with this? If you have these opinions, you shouldn't really be sharing them and broadcasting them in this way." She was yelled at, essentially.' Abear pinpoints this incident as signalling to her the potential consequences of being outspoken, and how her school had failed to support her peers in what should have been a matter that instilled pride and encouragement. 'So from that point, I felt like maybe I would lessen my chances of maybe doing well in other subjects where I had more prejudiced teachers if I was as outspoken as she had been.' Abear was extremely studious and 'ambitious with my studies' and decided 'I would have to suck it up until I get my HSC [Higher School Certificate] and the results I want, then I'd go on and live my life in the world the way that I want to live it'.

In these vignettes, we see examples of teachers who have created conditions of insecurity and stigmatisation. We see an example of school leadership stifling and reprimanding certain political expression, and the ripple effect this has on another student's choice to self-censor, so that she can mitigate any risk of being marked down for speaking out. These are more examples of destructive and damaging teacher–student encounters based in what can only be described as Islamophobic and racist contempt for Muslims and Islam. The teachers here were clearly not cultivating any kind of relationship of trust and respect, and were in clear breach of their responsibilities as educators under departmental policies.

In year 12, Jeena, whom we first met in chapter 3, recalled the freedom she had to 'talk about gender' but not 'race, religion or politics': 'Whenever we would say something, the teachers would be like, "Oh, we're not allowed to get too deep into this"'. When Jeena and her peers wanted to talk about the Lindt Café siege, she said 'they shut it down under the guise of, "We're not allowed to share our political opinions as teachers"'. Jeena remembers vividly that when it came to 'terrorism and ISIS and what was happening', any discussion was 'shut down'. I started to ask Jeena a question, but she cut me off.

> Sorry, but I just find it very interesting how in White spaces, we're allowed to discuss gender, but we're not allowed to discuss things like race and religion. So, in Advanced English and English Extension one and English Extension two, I was very, very freely allowed to explore discussions on gender but not race.

The problem Jeena identifies here is typical of mainstream White feminism's historical and ongoing failure to comprehend how racism and sexism are experienced simultaneously, and how dismissing race in a feminist/gender analytical framework results in White feminism colluding with patriarchy *against* women of colour.

It's essential that we think about these encounters not as individual cases, but as symptoms of a social and political culture that has educated and trained bodies and minds to approach Muslims and Islam through certain frames (the Muslim woman as oppressed, the Muslim student as at-risk, the Muslim student as too political), which translate into paranoia or contempt. These stories underline my point that Islamophobia and external discourses infiltrate classrooms and teacher–student encounters.

It may be tempting to point to the NSW Department of Education's anti-racism policies as a means of 'solving' this problem (although the ambiguity and exclusion of detail in these policies, undermining their practical interpretation and implementation, has been written about by experts in the field). While schools must have complaints processes and a designated officer to deal with complaints, uneven power dynamics are likely to restrain students from complaining about teachers (in Abear's case, she would have been complaining about a principal!).

Recent studies about the implementation and impact of anti-racist policies, and the gap between policy and practice, also don't inspire much confidence. In a large-scale research project of 14 NSW public schools, which included 5128 responses to a survey of teachers, classroom teachers were found most likely to agree that racism is an issue in schools but had less knowledge of anti-racism and multicultural education policies and their implementation in schools. Teachers' acknowledgment of racism was also found to be much lower than that of the communities surrounding their schools. Staff in executive roles were least likely to acknowledge racism in schools, and society more broadly, but had greater awareness of policies and overestimated the effects of these policies. Teachers in schools in parts of Sydney with a high Asian presence showed the greatest awareness of the implementation of both multicultural education and anti-racism policies, but those in areas with a significant Muslim presence were rather less aware of these.

In Australia, schools have been found to be the most common setting in which children and adolescents experience racism. And since 9/11, there has been no shortage of studies showing that Muslims are the most negatively viewed minority group in Australia, subjected to hate crimes, verbal and physical abuse, property damage and discrimination, as the Islamophobia Register Australia reports of 2017 and 2019 have documented. Annual surveys by the Scanlon Foundation's *Mapping Social Cohesion* project report over 40 per cent of Australians who answer surveys anonymously online hold negative attitudes towards Muslims (compared to 25 per cent who will admit so to an interviewer).

Given the global circulation of ideas, fears, moral panics and stereotypes of the 'Muslim Other', it's a massive leap of faith to think that anti-racism policies will mitigate the harmful effects of a war-on-terror political climate, which maintains attention on Muslim youth and Islam as problems.

But even still, there is more at stake here.

What is at stake is not simply dealing with one racist teacher. The 'bad apple model' of racism, as Sara Ahmed puts it, ends up eliminating racist individuals so that 'institutions can keep their racism'. Focusing on racist individual teachers reproduces race, because it avoids addressing race as systemic and institutional.

Anti-racism policies address racism. Not race. There's a difference. Addressing racism would mean, for example, Rokaya's or Rania's teachers would face some kind of consequences for their conduct. We can see that addressing racism as perpetrator-based is rather like applying a bandaid or administering anaesthesia: it's an absolutely essential, but temporary, fix. Addressing *race* means confronting schools as educational institutions in a society structured around Whiteness. When it comes to teaching, the 'individual' and 'institution' is a false binary. Classroom teachers aren't tutors or consultants hired for the day. Their labour is exerted within, and accountable to, a school community: the local staff; the curriculum they teach, as well as the 'hidden curriculum' of the school's organisation, internal policies, environment, total culture and ethos; and external accountability bodies, such as the Department of Education for public schools or the Association of Independent Schools for private and non-government schools. Abear is a perfect example of the way the hidden curriculum in a school can injure students, even when there is a strong response to individual acts of racism. Abear's deputy principal immediately took action when she complained about what was happening on her way to school. But the protective benefits of this anti-racism response were limited when it came to Abear's capacity to speak freely in class. She was in a space of self-censorship and compliance, muted when it came to her political expression, because of the school ethos on political commentary. Anti-racism policies don't mean that race is being disrupted and challenged, a point made by education experts Dalal and Hussein Oubani, who argue that the exclusive reliance on anti-racism policies by the NSW education department has 'generated limited benefits because their protective capacities have been undermined by a lack of support from curriculum documents'.

Because my project is interested first and foremost in the point of view of students, I am thinking about what their stories tell us: when, how and why they've felt let down by the system; in which conditions they've experienced the liberating and transformative power of knowledge. When and why they have felt included, respected, intellectually challenged; and when and why they have felt excluded, tokenised or marginalised. The common thread I found was teaching as intellectual work. And this means talking about curriculum.

THE WHITENESS FRAME

My 11-year-old son has always loved jigsaw puzzles. He was one of those kids who automatically approached a puzzle by sorting all the pieces into two piles: the middle pieces and the edge pieces. First, he'd make the frame. And then he'd assemble the middle pieces in reference to the frame. My youngest son, five, categorically refuses this approach. He throws the pieces onto the floor and tries to work from the inside out. Needless to say, it's a long-winded and rarely successful approach (which usually ends with a frustrated cry for help)!

I think about this analogy a lot when I think about how schools – as institutions that teach a curriculum – function. No matter how many 'diverse' and 'multicultural' pieces are thrown into the curriculum puzzle, the cohering frame around which those pieces are organised and bordered is Whiteness. The border of Whiteness is not just cosmetic. It has historically been the 'site of erasure' of Indigenous peoples, explicit in its intent to 'disappear' Indigenous peoples, as Aileen Moreton-Robinson and others have written. The White border maintains its entitlement to determine the content and value of the pieces allowed within the body of the puzzle; the shape, relative weight, size and positioning of those pieces; the value judgment placed on what counts as knowledge and what doesn't. No matter how 'diverse' the pieces, they are ultimately contained within a border that illegitimately claims sovereignty.

Adopting this 'critical race theory' approach to schools means placing race at the centre of analysis. It is crucial to see Whiteness as endemic in educational institutions, because of how these institutions have been historically, and still are, structured on the presumption that Whiteness is the default and universal standard, and the principal authority. Curriculum content reinforces and reproduces those structures by reproducing White ways of knowing and learning, White histories and stories, all the while disavowing race in our education systems. Race is entrenched in Australian education policy documents such as the *Australian Curriculum*, the *Melbourne Declaration on Educational Goals for Young Australians* and the *NSW Curriculum*. This is an obvious conclusion when you take Indigenous people and racial minorities as your authority on *what race means*. As Indigenous and black scholars have argued, the privileging of a White 'master script', the foregrounding of Eurocentric perspectives, counts as 'epistemic racism' in Western education. This is what has prompted university movements and campaigns such as Rhodes Must Fall, Dismantling the Master's House and Why Is My Curriculum White? (which includes an Australasian offshoot).

It's tempting to see the solution as simply adding more 'diversity' into curriculum. Indeed, Australian education policy and curriculum documents now establish 'Aboriginal and Torres Strait Islander Histories and Cultures' and 'Asia and Australia's Engagement with Asia' as cross-curricular priorities in curriculum. But when the White 'master script' remains unaffected, it is tokenistic to 'add native, stir and proceed as normal', as British sociologist Gurminder Bhambra, citing the late Haitian anthropologist Michel-Rolph Trouillot, reminds us.

The emphasis on Indigenous histories and cultures in the national and NSW curriculum is framed in terms of knowledge about and respect for 'cultural identity', 'the value of Indigenous cultures', 'reconciliation'. Australia's so-called 'national identity' and 'cultural heritage' includes 'recognis[ing] the significance of Aboriginal and Torres Strait Islander Histories and Cultures'. Students learn about Indigenous people's 'contribution to Australia' as well as the consequences of colonial settlement.

The border is defined as respect and knowledge of history, culture, identity. The White border of education is focused on redressing terra nullius by teaching students that this land was not empty. But the fact that sovereignty was never ceded, that schooling is taking place on stolen land, that race continues to legitimate theft of Indigenous land are the 'unspeakable things' that remain invisible in the very orientation of the education system.

I can think of a million reasons why challenging students to understand what it means to live on unceded land would reconfigure the way we approach some of the most pressing existential questions of our time: race relations, the nation state, national security, climate change, the rise of White supremacy, Islamophobia and rising anti-Semitism, racial discrimination, the globalised movements of peoples, wealth inequalities. When I say students, I don't just mean white students. Settler-colonialism means that non-Indigenous people of colour are also settlers, including those who have been denied their homelands because of other colonial projects. I say this from my standpoint as the daughter of a dispossessed Palestinian living on stolen land. The colonial project that created the state of Israel and dispossessed my father's family from their homeland brought my father to another stolen land, Australia.

But there's more to it than just respecting, valuing, recognising. Gawaian Bodkin-Andrews and Bronwyn Carlson, drawing on other Indigenous scholars, powerfully put it into words when they argue that 'Aboriginal and Torres Strait Islander people should not be considered as being "known", but rather recognised and respected as "knowers"'. To decentre Whiteness means an epistemological revolution away from 'the lens of Western ways of knowing'. This would transform how subjects such as the 'Movement of peoples' or 'Migration experiences' are taught. It would mean putting young people in dialogue with Indigenous knowledge production and methodological standpoints, about the environment and climate change, for example. It would challenge notions of ownership and possession at the root of White supremacist assumptions and claims over who belongs and who doesn't. It would mean understanding the historical roots of 'paranoid nationalism'. An education system underpinned by a social justice agenda, which self-consciously seeks to destabilise the centrality of Whiteness, benefits everybody. Our schools can no longer pretend that young people aren't growing up amid the rise of neo-Nazi, White supremacist movements in Western countries, and the normalisation of hate speech and hate crimes. As Daniella (the Grammar College student we first met in chapter 1) bluntly told me the week Blair Cottrell appeared on Sky News: 'Hearing that, it doesn't shock me, which it should. Seeing a neo-Nazi on TV should be horrific, but to me, it's like, "Oh, okay". This is my world now.'

The national curriculum contains many laudable goals, but it's difficult to accept their transformative potential given that curriculum still centres Whiteness and fails to understand and embrace methodologies and findings emanating from Indigenous knowledge systems, as Indigenous academics have argued.

Curriculum explicitly recognises that education today has shifted from the local to global, with global integration and international mobility resulting in the worldwide movement of people and ideas. It recognises that Australians need to be 'Asia literate', given that India, China and other Asian nations are growing and their influence on the world is increasing. It seeks to deliver an education that offers skills to 'contribute to the creation of a more productive, sustainable and just society'. These are lofty goals but because they don't decentre Whiteness, they can be seen, as scholars Eve Tuck and K Wayne Young brilliantly argue, as an 'attempt to reconcile settler guilt and complicity and rescue settler futurity'.

In the NSW History curriculum, for example, in the elective 'Progressive ideas and movements', the following 'time span' is given: 'The Enlightenment, the American War of Independence, the French Revolution and the Industrial Revolution'. This is the stock-standard Western narrative of secularism, liberty, equality, fraternity, citizenship and rights. It is grounded in the West constructing an image of itself as intellectually superior to the East, based on the myth of a linear, isolationist line of continuity from ancient Greece and Rome to the present, which conveniently excises the role and presence of Islam in Europe, as well as the intellectual work of the more advanced Muslim empires during Europe's Dark Ages, which laid the groundwork for Europe's Renaissance.

This timeline is also problematic for its exclusion of a notable major historical moment: the insurrections that were occurring across the French Caribbean at the same time as the French and American revolutions, and the Haitian Revolution, the most successful slave revolt in history. What is excluded from history is even more revealing than what is included. As Michel-Rolph Trouillot argued in his groundbreaking book *Silencing the Past*, the West's failure to acknowledge the Haitian Revolution 'shows us that history is not simply the recording of facts and events, but a process of actively enforced silences, some unconscious, others quite deliberate'. To exclude the Haitian Revolution is to reject the growing body of scholarship that problematises the 'European/ Western' prism of modernity and its refusal to engage with the colonial matrix of power. This triumphant narrative of the West as 'reason, science, freedom, liberty' and so on shapes a deep-seated emotional and cognitive posture of superiority towards non-White knowledge, experience, stories and ways of knowing and living.

It also ignores and discounts, as Edward Said writes in *Culture and Imperialism*, the overlapping experience of Westerners and 'Orientals' (colonised non-white populations), the 'interdependence of cultural terrains in which colonizer and colonized co-existed and battled each other through projections as well as rival geographies, narratives and histories'. To ignore this, or relegate it as an elective subject, is to 'miss what is essential about the world'.

In the *Australian Curriculum*, under 'Movements for change in the 20th century', 'women's movements' is an elective topic, and the description of the unit makes it clear that the focus is on 'the legal and political entitlements of women in Western societies'. Women of colour are left out. There is nothing in the unit description requiring students to reflect on questions of race in first- and second-wave feminist movements, requiring them to learn about the campaigns and movements for gender equality in the global south, including Muslim countries. This is a thoroughly Eurocentric perspective that entrenches the dominant narrative that feminist struggles are exclusive to the West, that White feminism is all that matters. It has long been part of the classic White supremacist agenda to ignore the historical achievements and feminist contributions by women of colour, as though feminism began only when white women took notice. Indeed, feminist movements around the world had kicked off well before white women's feminism, and in many cases, white women were fighting for rights that women of colour already had (including abortion rights, rights to divorce, retaining one's maiden name upon marriage, rights to property and so on).

It's not an outrageous proposition to expect curriculums to understand that systems of education, knowledge and power are built on violence, erasure and suppression. Postcolonialism, theories on decolonisation, subaltern studies, intersectionality, critical race and Whiteness theories, imperial feminism, third-wave feminism/intersectional feminism have all come to public consciousness, and our education systems should be working to reflect Indigenous histories and models of knowledge, non-White histories and models of knowledge. What is required is no less than knowledge production, theories and histories by people of colour.

INVISIBLE PERSPECTIVES

From a specifically Muslim standpoint, what is also at stake is how serious curriculum is about responding to the incessant circulation of racist and Islamophobic narratives, the divisive political discourse, the geopolitical conflicts Australia is involved in, and the local and domestic policies directed at Muslims. It stands to reason that we ask how we can achieve what Dalal and Hussein Oubani (following Raewyn Connell's seminal work) advocate as curricular justice. In other words, curriculum reform based on the principle of redistributive justice, where the 'standpoint of the least advantaged', as Connell puts it, is included. This means that we think about certain learning areas in curriculums from the standpoint of Muslims and people of colour, when we consider that schooling today is taking place in the context of 'the war on terror', escalating Islamophobia and White supremacist violence in society, and a surveillance culture creating Muslim youth as being viewed as 'at-risk' and part of a 'suspect' community.

Curriculum documents ought to be held accountable to the standards and criteria they set for themselves. Using these goals shows gaping holes. Australian academics Eeqbal Hassim and Jennet Cole-Adams point out that 'being "Asia literate" means being aware of Islam and Muslim cultures'. The majority of the world's Muslims live in Asia, in the three most populous Muslim-majority countries (Indonesia, Pakistan and Bangaldesh) and so, as Australian academic Gilbert Caluya notes, 'To talk about Muslims and Asians as distinct groups is at best misleading'. Islam is the fastest growing religion in the world, and Australia has critical trade and educational links with the Middle East and Asia more broadly.

In spite of the fact that one in four human beings on this planet are Muslim, or that according to national Census data, the number of Muslims in Australia has almost doubled in ten years, consider for a moment that out of 102 prescribed texts for the 2019–2023 NSW HSC Curriculum, a mere two are authored by Muslims: Algerian writer Kamel Daoud, and Pakistani gender-rights activist Malala Yousafzai (co-authored with Christina Lamb). Daoud's novel is a postcolonial retelling of Albert Camus's novel *The Stranger*. Yousafzai's book is a memoir, and it's a powerful and significant inclusion. But it's telling that the only Muslim female narrative HSC English students are exposed to reinforces the Muslim woman as the victim of male misogyny, etc. Of the 102 prescribed texts, the only additional texts which would appear to touch on the topic of Muslims is the SBS series *Go Back to Where You Came From*.

There are no texts set in a Muslim-majority country. No texts produced by Muslims in the past two decades. In the elective 'Worlds of upheaval', students study 'textual representations of the experiences of individuals and communities seeking unity, certainty, solace, justice or restoration in periods of significant social and political change and upheaval'. The set novels are Elizabeth Gaskell's *North and South*, Mary Shelley's *Frankenstein* (incidentally, I studied both these brilliant novels in my first-year English Literature class at university) and Madeleine Thien's *Do Not Say We Have Nothing*? It's not that these books shouldn't be studied. And it's not only that the themes which preoccupy and saturate tabloid media, popular culture and political discourse are rendered completely invisible to HSC students. It is the fact, too, that given how significant, in size and impact, the Muslim world has been in shaping human civilisation, so little value is given to Islam and Muslim histories, experiences and contributions in the classroom.

The English K–10 NSW syllabus provides a comprehensive list of suggested texts. There are three texts with 'Afghan' characters: two of them, *Soraya the Storyteller*, about an Afghan refugee, and *Taj and the Great Camel Trek*, an adventure story described as 'a tribute to the Afghan camel drivers who were instrumental in the exploration of Australia' are written by a white woman, Rosanne Hawke. The third text is *Parvana*, about a young girl growing up in Afghanistan under Taliban rule, written by another white author, Deborah Ellis. This represents another example of a curriculum that is out of touch with sophisticated debates and scholarly discussion over the question of authenticity in literature and whose voices take up space. This is a potent example of how 'diversity' is steered by, and accountable to, Whiteness. Rather than include Afghan writers and composers in the curriculum, Afghan stories are inserted via white writers. To add insult to injury is the fact that these texts are explicitly mapped onto the syllabus goals of 'Intercultural experiences/Insights about the peoples and cultures of Asia'.

Is it too much to ask that insights about the peoples and cultures of Asia be offered by *Asian writers*, who, after all, are more than capable of telling their own stories and who do not need their stories and experiences mediated through white writers? That non-Asian white writers are standing in for Asia creates an Orientalist agenda that privileges White voices while erasing and rendering invisible non-White writers, depriving marginalised communities of access to economic and cultural capital.

Of the hundreds of suggested texts from kindergarten to year 10, only two texts are composed by Muslims: *Tea with Arwa*, a memoir by Arwa El Masri, and my own novel set in occupied Palestine, *Where the Streets Had a Name*. There are no films, graphic novels or picture books either composed by Muslims or with a specifically Muslim-oriented story.

Text selection is left to the discretion of teachers and schools, who determine suitability considering the 'interests and abilities of their students as well as the ethos of the school and its local community'. There is scant research, if any, evaluating any corresponding link between the demographic make-up of schools and the texts students are exposed to. But some conclusions are, I believe, safe to make. And they are important to make because, as race scholar Alana Lentin writes, racism is 'more insidious in its motility, its ability to hide itself by consuming its traces'. It is crucial that we expose these traces, make it impossible for race to continue to hide.

This is a curriculum that offers *two* Muslim writers on a long list of texts (and as one of those writers, I can definitely say that my book set in Palestine is not being widely taken up by schools). The absence in curriculum documents of any explicit requirement for teachers to select texts addressing the Muslim world or Muslim-related topics makes it highly plausible that most schools, particularly those with predominantly non-Muslim student populations, would not consider that Muslim-related texts, written and produced by Muslims no less, suit the 'interests' of their students or ethos of their school and local community. In fact, the marginalisation and near erasure of Muslim voices in the English curriculum must be placed in the wider context of the intractable Whiteness of the literary canon taught by teachers of the Australian English curriculum. One recent study, conducted by academics Larissa McClean Davies, Susan K Martin and Lucy Buzacott, surveyed 700 English teachers around Australia, asking them what books they taught in class.

The majority of the works cited have been in the school literary canon for generations (I recognised 14 out of the 15 as books I studied in high school), and are 'written in the past, by male British or American writers'. The list of top 15 books included no texts by Australian women, migrant Australians or Indigenous writers. It's hardly a surprise that Muslim texts would be virtually absent.

As I noted in chapter 6, the *School Communities Working Together* fact sheet for students refers to students and their family and friends 'affected by conflict which is taking place overseas' or 'who live in parts of the world which are affected by the conflict reported through the media'. In the context of a document clearly responding to the war on terror and conflicts in the Middle East and Afghanistan, this is a clear acknowledgment that these conflicts are directly relevant to some students' lives – and are significant enough as 'grievances' to warrant departmental policies. And yet, learning about these conflicts is optional. The NSW History curriculum offers an *optional* in-depth study, 'The globalising world', which contains three *optional* studies, one of which is 'Migration experiences', which contains within it further *optional* in-depth studies: a choice between 'the response of Australians, including the Australian media, to the arrival of refugees from Indochina in the 1970s and 1980s OR refugees from Afghanistan and Iraq since 2001'.

The 2019 National History Challenge for Australian Students was on the theme of 'Australian wartime experiences', with a focus on the Anzacs or the Vietnam War. Australia's military contribution and involvement in the US-led war on terror – in Afghanistan, Iraq, around the Arabian Gulf, the Philippines – remains marginal and insignificant. This perpetuates ignorance about the extent to which Australia has been involved in conflicts since the Anzacs and the Vietnam War, conflicts which have caused and contributed to massive death tolls and destruction. It ignores the fact that Australia, like America, lied about Iraq possessing weapons of mass destruction to justify the war on terror, a fact exposed by whistleblower and Australian politician Andrew Wilkie. Oubani and Oubani make a crucial point: expanding history curriculum to include studies on 'the significant Muslim mortalities in the last century due to war, oppression and economic sanctions would enable a more inclusive account of human suffering to be presented and allow a greater understanding of the alienated and marginalised minority groups living amongst us'.

The 'heroic' teachers described in the opening of this chapter exemplify teachers who are attempting to compensate for this flawed system at an individual level. This sets them up for the challenges and risks of establishing a case for 'suitability' and relevance. It means they need to do more work and spend more time sourcing and then learning new texts and developing new resources. It means leaving Muslim and non-Muslim students' exposure to texts addressing issues of incredible relevance today to the discretion, judgment and political and moral orientation of their teachers. We can't ignore the fact that Australia's teaching profession is predominantly white Anglo in comparison to the Australian population as a whole – specifically white women. While 27 per cent of the Australian population were born overseas, this is only the case for 12 per cent of teachers in NSW. Teachers must be guided, supported and given the tools to decentre Whiteness, rather than leaving to luck whether students will have a teacher with the inclination, resources and time to adapt an existing curriculum.

I'm not saying this from an ivory tower. I personally know the time and effort it takes to work *around* and *through* curriculum. A few years ago, my daughter was learning Medieval History as a year 8 subject. It didn't surprise me that despite attending an Islamic school, she was learning about this period through the narrow prism of Europe, casually referring to this period as the 'Dark Ages'. I spent several weeks writing an alternative lesson plan, one that troubled the notion that the Middle Ages were 'dark' by turning the gaze *from* Europe, to Asia and Africa. I presented the lesson to my daughter's class, introducing them to the Axum Empire, the Kingdom of Ghana, the Mali Empire, the Songhai Empire, the Ethiopian Empire, the Mossi Kingdoms and the Benin Empire. I showed them Balkh, Samarqand, Baghdad and Cordoba. The class – whose backgrounds ranged from Afghanistan to India, Pakistan, Somalia, Jordan, Egypt, Iraq and Syria – were completely surprised. Surprised by the fact that while Europe was living in the Dark Ages, people of colour were enjoying enlightenments and renaissances, and that the intellectual work of the more advanced Muslim empires during the Middle Ages laid the groundwork for Europe's Renaissance.

This was new knowledge to *Muslim* students. Invisible and excluded histories deny racial minorities born, educated and socialised in Australia of *their own* heritage and histories too. They are the products of this education system and have therefore internalised their own invisibility and marginalisation. Recall Tahminah, whom we met in chapter 9, an Afghan Muslim girl born, raised and schooled in Australia, who grew up with a false and stereotypical imaginary of her parent's homeland. Schools owe students an education that validates and challenges their histories, experiences and aspirations. It's difficult for marginalised students to trust an education system that treats their histories, religion, culture and experiences as 'optional'.

STUDENTS FILLING THE GAPS

The emancipatory potential of culturally relevant curriculum is obvious. But there's another incentive made apparent to me from my interviews. A recurring narrative by many Muslim students was that they felt the need to compensate for gaps in curriculum, in the way a Muslim-related topic was discussed in class, in the way information was presented. This accords with other studies in the UK, US and Australia, which have similarly found that Muslim youth feel a responsibility to take on the role of educators on history, culture, faith and politics.

Rokaya, who attended an Islamic school from kindergarten to year 10, said,

> I knew zero about politics. It sounds awful but we went to
> our classes, we hung out and just spoke about non-political
> stuff in our free time. It was a total bubble. You get this
> impression outside that Muslims are all, like, politically
> charged but that's not my experience at my school all those
> years. It's embarrassing actually. It took me going to a non-
> Muslim school and being one of five Muslim kids in
> a school of about a thousand, to wake up. I had to.

The experience of 'a massive jump from no politics to being questioned about everything to do with politics and Islam' threw Rokaya into a period of manic self-education: 'I got to the point where I borrowed Edward Said, and I was 17 and trying to make sense – it was like a boot camp of reading, introductory readers on Islamophobia, and this is all just to survive classroom discussions, not for any subject!'

Abear felt this responsibility to educate others from year 7, when 9/11 was mentioned in a history class. She remembers feeling 'really, really stressed', because she

> didn't know about it. I was never really into non-fiction. I was always kind of into the fantasy books and things like that. That wasn't part of my world. I didn't want to think about anything like that. I was very much a child, and so when we spoke about that event in class, I wasn't wearing the hijab at the time. Not a lot of people knew I was Muslim.

When Abear got home that night, she said she

> did my own research and asked some questions. From then on, any time we spoke about it or someone mentioned it in conversation at lunchtime, I just felt really stressed, really, really stressed out. I was stressed that someone was going to ask me a question, because with time people did know. They knew that I was Muslim, and I wasn't going be able to answer it. I remember the feeling, this stress of, *Am I responsible with it? Do I need to have this knowledge? Am I a good Muslim? Am I a bad Muslim for not knowing about this and being able to defend my religion and my community?* I was like, *But I'm just a child. Why should I know? Why do I have to know about this stuff?* I was born here like anyone else, and I just remember feeling that pressure and that responsibility.

Simply because Abear is Muslim does not mean she had either the knowledge or inclination to seek knowledge about an event like 9/11. She was into fantasy books, but we see here how a classroom discussion confronts her with the script and role she is expected to recite and perform as a Muslim student in school. She understands that as a Muslim, she will be expected to perform the role of tutor, defender, ambassador. This goes back to my earlier discussion about *becoming Muslim*, about Muslimness as something young people learn to do, to enact through practices and actions, rather than something they are born into or just *are*. There is nothing 'natural' or innately 'Muslim' about feeling hailed to perform the role of tutor and educator. This is the subtle effect of wider discourses that circulate outside and inside classrooms, generating the force of their impact because they endure as taken-for-granted. Despite Tahminah, Rokaya and Abear narrating completely different circumstances, they all felt a responsibility to perform the same kind of role.

Almost 20 years on from 9/11, why should Muslim students need to be 'experts' on topics their teachers should have relative knowledge of? An education system should be responsive to the social and political climate in which students are being educated. Tahminah told me that she learnt about 9/11 in class 'as a recall of the event' and found it 'a bit problematic'. Whenever the teacher said, 'They were from Afghanistan', or referred to the Taliban regime or Islam, 'I felt like they didn't explain *Guys, this isn't the essence of Islam, by the way. This is the radical version of it.*' Tahminah felt 'disclaimers' were missing.

> They just teach it by the book, like, *this is what happened* and I think some students might walk away thinking, *Islam is a very violent religion. There are hundreds of thousands of extremists out there.* They'd say Islam, but I feel like they wouldn't explain it in great depth that there are radicals in each religion.

Tahminah felt compelled to try to offer more context but ultimately remained silent, 'because I didn't feel confident'.

Jeena, the university student we first met in chapter 3, had a similar experience in her Studies of Religion class, which was taught by two teachers, one of whom was Muslim. Jeena said that when they were learning about Islam, 'the textbook mentioned Holy War'. Jeena recalls: 'The Muslim teacher was more than happy to freely discuss that as, like, socio-politically, he was happy to discuss that, as well as fundamentally and what it means or whatever'. As for Jeena's second teacher:

> she wouldn't. Even though she knew our context, if she was talking about something like that, she would just very much be textbook, which I understand, but I feel like … As an educator, and you're looking at the context of your students … Our Studies of Religion class had one Christian and, like, 28 Muslims in it. We were all Muslims in that class, and it's weird to me that you would just be textbook about something like Holy War.

I return here to Raewynn Connell, who draws a distinction between 'teaching bodies of facts' versus teaching as intellectual work: 'What teachers do in schools is never just conveying a set of facts to pupils', she writes. 'Teachers necessarily interpret the world for, and with, their pupils'. This means teachers must know the facts they are presenting *and* understand 'how interpretation is done, of the cultural field in which it is done, and of the other possibilities of interpretation that surround one's own'. It seems to me this critical analysis is what Tahminah and Jeena were craving when learning about 'Holy War' or '9/11'. A 'recall of the event' is how Tahminah describes her teacher's approach. Her teacher presents as an uncritical conduit who isn't paying attention to how the facts she is presenting are burdened by so many floating meanings. Jeena and her class wanted a lesson that was culturally relevant, led by a teacher who could understand 'the context' of her students' lives.

To offer culturally relevant curriculum that responds to today's social and political climate requires extensive work. Sourcing new texts, mastering new material, learning about new authors and thinkers, keeping up to date with emerging research, scholarship and debates. Including Muslim experiences, histories and knowledge in curriculum content means fundamental and radical transformation and decolonisation of the curriculum. It requires a fundamental re-evaluation of the kind of education Australian students are receiving about a demonised community in the national population, and a sizable one at that when we take NSW as a case study. It's impossible to expect individual, motivated teachers to shoulder this burden. Impossible *and* unfair, to the teachers and students whose experiences then become left to chance. Students should be able to trust that the curriculum they are being taught safeguard against the possibility of a teacher who is biased or too invested in the status quo, as a member of the dominant population, to care to push for change.

One of my favourite moments in all my interviews was speaking to Shanad (17, Lebanese-Australian, Punchbowl) about her English classes in high school. Shanad was a self-described 'book nerd'. Her favourite subject was English, but she resented the fact that 'all the books forced upon me in high school were written by white people. I was a Shakespeare nerd. Obsessed. His plays were presented as white, interpreted and explained through white people. Where was the racial analysis? *Romeo and Juliet* is basically a story of two Arab kids!' I laughed so hard. Having grown up in an Arab Muslim community, where cross-cultural and cross-religious relationships were very often taboo, I understood exactly what she meant. But I had never thought of Shakespeare's famous play in that way. When I finished our interview, I jotted down a line in my field notes:

A different syllabus, a different teacher, Arab lens on Romeo and Juliet. Student with a sparkling mind.
What a missed opportunity.

REFERRED PAIN

In late 2017 the NSW Police Force conducted a police training exercise to test their response to a terrorist or high-risk incident. Two hundred police and emergency services personnel descended on Sydney's Central Station. Two officers, wearing chequered headscarves, boarded a train, acting as 'active armed offenders'. They displayed the Islamic State flag, simulated stabbing and shooting people and held train passengers as hostages at gunpoint. The NSW Civil and Administrative Tribunal found that the exercise racially vilified Palestinians and Arabs and portrayed them as potential terrorists, ordering NSW Police to publish an apology and implement racial-vilification training for senior officers. The crucial 'terrorist signifier' in the exercise was the chequered headscarves. The tribunal found that they would have been recognised by members of the public as keffiyehs, used by Palestinian and Arab communities, and would therefore have the capacity to encourage members of the public to believe that 'Palestinians and/or Arabs were to be feared, despised, hated, and/or held in serious contempt as possibly or probably being terrorists'.

It was NSW Police's defence argument about the scarves that stood out for me. Denying there was any racial vilification, the police argued that the scarves had been bought from an army disposal store years earlier and were part of a 'non-specific mix of criminal/terrorist style items' of clothing.

This brings me full circle, to how racism's efficiency is achieved specifically by being non-specific. A very specific and identifiable item of national clothing can be emptied of its specificity only if Palestinians/Arabs/Muslims/brown people are nothing more than synonyms for terrorist. The keffiyeh is quintessentially Palestinian and Arab, yet here we see it's sold in an army store and purchased by the police for a terrorist training exercise. What did the sign on the store shelf say, one wonders? 'Criminal/terrorist fashion: One size fits all'?

The defence that the keffiyeh forms part of a 'non-specific mix of criminal/terrorist style items' of clothing is a semiotic collapse of breath-taking proportions, because it so perfectly encapsulates how the war on terror sees Muslim bodies. The Muslim is made into a terrorist mannequin, whom law enforcement, government, CVE policymakers and the media have dressed up with the clothing, accessories, suburbs, accents, hijabs, hairstyles, languages, religious practices of 'Muslims,' of 'Arabs', of 'brown and black people'.

This is the inventory of terrorism. And as this book has shown, its traces mark the lives of young people, both Muslim and non-Muslim.

I didn't set out to write this book to simply offer a descriptive study of experiences of Islamophobia or youth identities. When I met Bilal, the student who told me what he said might be 'taken the wrong way', I wanted to understand the political and symbolic violence exercised obscurely against young Muslims by the state – and so-called neutral policies and political practices – in a war on terror context, and how this leaves its traces on both Muslim *and* non-Muslim youth. I've sought to mine deep into how this violence is experienced, enacted, resisted and subverted by young people in the everyday contexts of their schools, and to reflect on how years of countering violent extremism policies, political and media rhetoric and community partnerships have normalised a hypersensitivity and policing of young Muslims' bodies, speech and the spaces they move in, and what this means for the everyday lives of these young people.

It's clear that sustained media and political narratives about Muslims in the context of the war on terror have created pervasive, loose and mobile racial summaries that attach to and arrange bodies ('radical', 'suspicious', 'angry'), and spaces (Western Sydney 'ghetto', 'dangerous', 'radicalisation'). Young people are pinned with these predetermined, readily accessible scripts and stereotypes, which follow them into classroom interactions. Performing Muslimness can offer redemption, or it can be a burden, forcing a 'performance' of an essentialised Muslim identity that many students are often still trying to understand and make sense of themselves. Others, also attuned to the signifiers attached to their performances, embrace their performance, provoking, subverting and playing around with the meanings ascribed to them. And then there are those who withdraw to the safety of strategic anonymity and hiding.

What is clear about this generation is that the ideals of relational trust and 'open classroom climates' within schools sit in tension with the wider discursive and racialised construction of young Muslims as 'politically risky' subjects or 'would-be terrorists'. Exchanges between students and teachers, and mutual dependencies and vulnerabilities, therefore need to be understood against the background of the war on terror, the racialisation of Muslims, geopolitical fears and CVE policies and discourse. Despite the lofty goals of an education curriculum that seeks to produce 'global citizens' with 'intercultural understanding', the Whiteness of Australia's school system endures, policing the borders of the conversations we urgently need to be having in schools across curriculum: Indigenous sovereignty and what this means not only for what is taught, but how it is taught; the decentring of Whiteness; Islamophobia, racism and the normalisation and enabling of White supremacy. Muslim and non-Muslim students make it clear that they want classrooms and school environments that are self-consciously and unashamedly responding to the world they are growing up in, invested in social justice and transformational awareness. They narrate the dearth of exposure to Muslim stories, histories and narratives in their classrooms, but also in some cases reveal how teachers who pushed beyond the borders of Whiteness changed their lives, provoked them to think about the world in a completely different way. To offer students a safe space to work through their political and religious ideas and identities in dialogue with the world around them means rewriting the master script of education.

Two things happened as I started writing the conclusion to this book. The first was yet another ABC *Q&A* controversy, involving a feminist panel convened to coincide with the feminist ideas festival Broadside. Hosted by veteran journalist Fran Kelly, the panel featured Egyptian feminist journalist Mona Eltahawy, journalist and author Jess Hill, Indigenous writer Nayuka Gorrie, businesswoman Hana Assafiri and anti-ageism campaigner/author Ashton Applewhite. In a discussion about the efficacy of violence to effect change, and whether 'violence begets violence', as the audience member's question had posed, Eltahawy (who had until that point not held back on the 'fuck the patriarchy' attitude) responded, 'How long must we wait for men and boys to stop murdering us, to stop beating us and to stop raping us? How many rapists must we kill?'

Nayuka Gorrie joined in the discussion, adding 'when you

say violence begets violence, it's almost sounding like it's a level playing field which it's not. I wonder what our kind of tipping point in Australia's going to be when people will start burning stuff? I look forward to it'. Gorrie also attacked respectability politics, arguing that being articulate and polite in the face of oppression only gets you so far:

> We've tried for 230-plus years to appeal to the colonisers'
> morality which doesn't seem to exist. I think violence ...
> is OK because if someone is trying to kill you, there's no
> amount of, 'Oh, but I'm really clever'. You know, 'I'm really
> articulate'. No amount of that is going to save you. So, yeah,
> let's burn stuff.

Over 250 complaints – about coarse language, 'radical views', a perceived lack of impartiality, 'endorsing violence' – culminated in the extraordinary decision by the national broadcaster to pull the video of the 'offensive' episode from all of its platforms and cancel planned repeat broadcasts. An investigation by the ABC 'acknowledged that this episode offended some viewers who interpreted some panellist statements as advocating violence'. The episode remains unavailable to view online on ABC platforms.

There is perhaps no more obvious example of how angry, vocal and rebellious people of colour, particularly women, who refuse to 'play nice' when demanding justice expose the White patriarchal myth that all ideas are freely welcomed in the 'marketplace of ideas'. Gorrie's responses, in particular, were magnificent. They poked at the continued underbelly of settler-colonial violence, exposing the pretence that debate and polite discussion – the bastions of settler moves to innocence – will never address the fundamental question of justice for the owners of this land. As with all protests against injustice by people of colour, the manner in which they protest –

too angry, too crude, too loud, too violent, too extreme, not moderate enough, not civil enough, not reasonable enough – is used to distract from the justice of their demands, the substance of their causes. Naming the reality of patriarchy, violence against women, and state and police violence did not provoke the confected outrage. The word 'fuck' and rhetorical calls for violence did.

Again, young people notice. That is perhaps the point of the outrage machine. Indigenous people, people of colour and genuine white allies are demanding justice. As Chelsea Bond reminds us, because 'race is about power, and power is not readily relinquished ... we simply cannot outthink or outrun it. We must fight it head-on, and for that fight we need to be angry.'

When 'fighting head-on', expressing dissent, making demands and challenging the status quo attracts such intense backlash, it means White Australia is panicking. The more I spoke to young people about 'free speech' and public debates, the more these kinds of theatrical attempts to silence and punish people of colour seemed to share the characteristics of what doctors call 'referred pain'– what occurs when an injury to one part of the body results in the pain being felt in another part of the body, like when irritation of the diaphragm is signalled by the nerve as shoulder pain. Attacking vocal and loud women and people of colour refers so much of the pain to young women and people of colour. White elites and the outrage mob, manipulating sensory nerves, are able to attack one part of the body and hurt another. This is how young people experience these kinds of public rituals of punishment and repression. Eltahawy and Gorrie are attacked and injured, but the deepest pain is perceived by their young followers, admirers, observers. Speaking out in Australia is to provoke a White nervous system that will refer pain to those who dare to speak, and those who may, one day, want to speak. This is the context in which young people are coming of age.

The second thing that happened relates to the first. In December 2019, CIVICUS Monitor, which publishes an annual report assessing democratic freedoms of 196 countries, downgraded Australia's democracy from 'open' to 'narrowed'. The drop in status was 'partially due to increased restrictions on the freedom of expression and government surveillance', specifically raids on media outlets, 'the intimidation of journalists reporting on plans to expand state surveillance', the prosecution of whistleblowers and an increasing crackdown on peaceful protest. Between elected politicians who are openly contemptuous of democracy (consider, for example, home affairs minister Peter Dutton unabashedly stating that he has always seen 'parliament as a disadvantage for sitting governments') and the civil disobedience of Extinction Rebellion are a majority of Australians who have voted for, or consented by their silence to, dehumanising, destructive and anti-democratic policies. We are now – collectively and not just those 'problem' Muslims in the war on terror – bearing the fruits of two decades of the serious erosion of democratic rights in the name of national security.

I started this research project asking students what the war on terror means to them. Their narratives, poems and written reflections tell us something about how they interpret and navigate local and global life-worlds and politics, social institutions and hegemonic norms. They are caught up in the referred pain of the war on terror. It's clear that young people are growing up in, and shadowed by, more than just 'one' war. The war against 'terror', sure. But also: wars against free speech. Wars against Indigenous people. Wars against angry, vocal people of colour. Wars against tackling climate change. Wars against the planet and wars protecting ecological destruction and agribusiness. Wars against women. Wars against refugees. Wars inside borders and wars destroying borders. Wars on protests, people power and insurgent movements. Culture wars and Science wars. Wars for 'quiet

Australians' against noisy minorities and 'progressives'. Wars against those living in poverty, those with disabilities, those whom a savage neoliberal economy has left in a state of precarity, punished with the mantra 'have a go to get a go'. Wars against universities and wars against safe schools. The traces of the organising grammar of the 'war on terror' – security, insurgency, safety, borders, nationalism, social cohesion, values, identity politics and so on – are visible in the inventory of all the wars unleashed with such ferocity since 9/11.

And young people are wise enough to have noticed.

Maybe it's time we paid attention to what they have to say.

ACKNOWLEDGMENTS

I owe a debt of gratitude to the schools who opened their doors to me, the teachers who believed in my work and the young people who trusted me with their stories. It was a privilege to meet you all, listen to you, read your stories. Thank you.

I feel as though this book has been in the making for years, before I started my fieldwork, before I started writing. Working in community, reading, writing, researching, I've felt my head and heart stretch in ways I didn't think possible. I am so grateful to all the scholars, activists, artists, community members who have pushed my thinking, taken me on the wildest intellectual adventures and provoked me to think in new ways about how and why we fight race and injustice. Thank you especially to the Indigenous scholars and activists whose work has transformed my understanding of how to offer solidarity and reimagine what is possible in and for this country.

Thank you to NewSouth Publishing for believing in this book, for giving me an editorial experience that helped bring more clarity and focus to the text, for offering me such a wonderful team to work with: Phillipa McGuinness, Nikki Lusk (dream copyeditor), Sophia Oravecz, Elspeth Menzies, Joumana Awad.

The project on which this book was based was supported by an Australian Research Council Discovery Early Career Researcher Award. The award would not have been possible without the support of my sponsor, Professor Amanda Wise, and Macquarie University, especially the Sociology Department.

Acknowledgments

The biggest thanks is always due to my family, who remain a constant source of love and support.

Earlier versions of parts of chapters 4, 5 and 12 were first published in the following journal articles: Abdel-Fattah, Randa, 'Managing belief and speech as incipient violence: "I'm giving you the opportunity to say that you aren't"', *Journal of Policing, Intelligence and Counter Terrorism*, 14:1, 2019, pp. 20–38; and Abdel-Fattah, Randa, 'Countering violent extremism, governmentality and Australian Muslim youth as "becoming terrorist"', *Journal of Sociology*, 24 April 2019, <doi.org/10.1177/1440783319842666>.

NOTES

To improve readability, I have not included citation reference indicators in the text. Instead, citations are presented here in chapter order according to their relevant page number.

Introduction: Tracing race

2   Goldberg, David Theo, 'Militarizing race', *Social Text*, 34:4 (129), December 2016, pp. 19–40.

3   Hage, Ghassan, *Is Racism an Environmental Threat?*, Polity Press, Cambridge, MA, 2015.

6   'Full text: Senator Fraser Anning's maiden speech', SBS News, 15 August 2018, <www.sbs.com.au/news/full-text-senator-fraser-anning-s-maiden-speech>.

7   Cromb, Nat and Pearson, Luke, 'Dr Chelsea Bond delivers a masterclass in Indigenous Excellence', *IndigenousX*, 15 April 2019 <indigenousx.com.au/dr-chelsea-bond-delivers-a-masterclass-in-indigenous-excellence/>.

7   Moreton-Robinson, Aileen, 'Writing off Indigenous sovereignty: the discourse of security and patriarchal white sovereignty', in Moreton-Robinson, Aileen (ed.) *Sovereign Subjects: Indigenous Sovereignty Matters*, Allen & Unwin, Crows Nest, 2007, pp. 86–102.

9   Moreton-Robinson, Aileen, *The White Possessive: Property, Power, and Indigenous Sovereignty*, University of Minnesota Press, Minneapolis, 2015.

10   Morrison, Scott, 'Australia-Israel Chamber of Commerce speech', 19 March 2019, <www.pm.gov.au/media/australia-israel-chamber-commerce-speech>.

15   Koenig, Peter, 'The refugee crisis and the Mediterranean Sea – the largest graveyard in modern history', Global Research, 7 July 2018, <globalresearch.ca/the-refugee-crisis-and-the-mediterranean-sea-the-largest-graveyard-in-modern-history/5646765>.

15   Scahill, Jeremy, 'The assassination complex', *Intercept*, 15 October 2015, <theintercept.com/drone-papers/the-assassination-complex/>.

15   Coates, Ta-Nehisi, 'The first white president', *Atlantic*, October 2017, <www.theatlantic.com/magazine/archive/2017/10/the-first-white-president-ta-nehisi-coates/537909/>.

15   Mudde, Cas, 'Is Boris Johnson really Britain's Trump?' *Guardian*, 24 July 2019, <www.theguardian.com/commentisfree/2019/jul/24/is-boris-johnson-really-britains-trump>.

15   ABC Background Briefing, 'Haircuts and hate: The rise of Australia's alt-right', 14 October 2018, <https://www.abc.net.au/radionational/programs/backgroundbriefing/haircuts-and-hate:-inside-the-rise-of-australias-alt-right/10365948>.

16   Tyler, Imogen, 'The hieroglyphics of the border: racial stigma in neoliberal Europe', *Journal of Ethnic and Racial Studies*, 41:10, 2018, pp. 1783–1801.

16   'Tony Abbott calls for religious reformation of Islam', *Australian*, 9 December

2015, <www.theaustralian.com.au/nation/politics/tony-abbott-calls-for-religious-reformation-of-islam/news-story/de19d671a2dca24610db7fb32a0fef49>.

17   Bauman, Zygmunt, *Liquid Fear*, Polity Press, London, 2006.

17   Beck, Ulrich, *World Risk Society*, Polity Press, Cambridge, 1999.

17   Furedi, Frank, *Culture of Fear Revisited: Risk-Taking and the Morality of Low expectation*, Continuum, London, 2006.

17   Giddens, Anthony, *The Consequences of Modernity*, Polity Press, Cambridge, 1990.

17   Hörschelmann, Kathrin, 'Youth and the geopolitics of risk after 11th September 2001', in Pain, Rachel and Smith, Susan (eds), *Fear: Critical Geopolitics and Everyday Life*, Ashgate, Aldershot, 2008, pp. 139–156.

17   Demos, *Nothing to Fear but Fear Itself?* Demos, London, 2017.

19   Watkins, Megan, Lean, Garth and Noble, Greg, 'Multicultural education: the state of play from an Australian perspective', *Race Ethnicity and Education*, 19:1, 2016, pp. 46–66.

19   Hatchell, Helen, 'Privilege of whiteness: adolescent male students' resistance to racism in an Australian classroom', *Race Ethnicity and Education*, 7:2, 2004, pp. 99–114.

19   Forrest, James, Lean, Garth & Dunn Kevin, 'Challenging racism through schools: teacher attitudes to cultural diversity and multicultural education in Sydney', Australia, *Race Ethnicity and Education*, 19:3, 2016, pp. 618–638.

19   Ho, Christina, Vincent, Eve and Butler, Rose, 'Everyday and cosmo-multiculturalisms: doing diversity in gentrifying school communities', *Journal of Intercultural Studies*, 36:6, 2015, pp. 658–675.

19   Noble, Greg, 'Everyday cosmopolitanism and the labour of intercultural community', in Wise, Amanda and Velayutham, Selvaraj (eds), *Everyday Multiculturalism*, Palgrave Macmillan, London, 2009, pp. 46–65.

19   Ho, Christina, 'Respecting the presence of others: school micropublics and everyday multiculturalism', *Journal of Intercultural Studies*, 32:6, 2011, pp. 603–619.

20   Australian Bureau of Statistics, '2016 Census QuickStats: The Hills Shire', 12 July 2019, <quickstats.censusdata.abs.gov.au/census_services/getproduct/census/2016/quickstat/LGA17420>.

23   Hall, Stuart, Roberts, Brian, Clarke, John, Jefferson, Tony and Critcher, Chas, *Policing the Crisis*, Palgrave Macmillan, London, 1978, p. 170.

23   Sentas, Victoria, *Traces of Terror: Counter-terrorism Law, Policing, and Race*, Oxford University Press, Oxford, 2014.

Chapter 1: This is Australia

40   Harris, Anita, 'Shifting the boundaries of cultural spaces: young people and everyday Multiculturalism', Social Identities, 15:2, 2009, pp. 187–205.

40   Harris, Anita and Wyn, Johanna, 'Young people's politics and the micro-territories of the local', *Australian journal of political science*, 44, 2009, pp. 327–344.

40   Harris, Anita, 'Young people, politics and citizenship', in Furlong, Andy (ed.), *Handbook of Youth and Young Adulthood: New Perspectives and Agendas*, Routledge, Abingdon, Oxon, 2009, pp. 295–300.

42   Harris, Anita, Wyn, Johanna and Younes, Salem, 'Beyond apathetic or activist

youth: "ordinary" young people and contemporary forms of participation', *Young: Nordic journal of youth research*, 18:1 2010, pp. 9–32 at pp. 9–10, 24.

Chapter 2: Creating a suspect community
55 'Muslim boys', ABC *Q&A*, 3 November 2014, <www.abc.net.au/qanda/muslim-boys/10655822>.
56 Safi, Michael, 'Radicalisation in Australia: Muslim leaders work to dissipate "fixation" with Isis among youths', *Guardian*, 10 March 2015, <www.theguardian.com/world/2015/mar/10/radicalisation-in-australia-muslim-leaders-work-to-dissipate-fixation-with-isis-among-youths>.
56 Dabbagh, Omar, 'New Grand Mufti hopes to save young Muslims at risk of being radicalised', SBS News, 28 May 2018, <www.sbs.com.au/news/new-grand-mufti-hopes-to-save-young-muslims-at-risk-of-being-radicalised>.
57 Nayak, Anoop and Kehily, Mary Jane, *Gender, Youth and Culture: Young Masculinities and Femininities*, 2nd edition, Red Globe Press, London, 2013, p. 11.
58 Masquelier, Adeline and Soares, Benjamin, *Muslim Youth and the 9/11 Generation*, University of New Mexico Press, 2016.
58 Wyn, Johanna and Cahill, Helen (eds), *Thinking about Childhood and Youth, Handbook of Children and Youth Studies*, Springer, Singapore, 2015, pp. 3–4.
58 Maira, Sunaina Marr, *The 9/11 Generation: Youth, Rights, and Solidarity in the War on Terror*, Duke University Press, Durham, 2009, p. 17.
59 Tabbaa, Mohamad, 'Forget ISIS: what do Islamophobes really want?' *Daily Sabah*, 20 April 2015, <www.dailysabah.com/op-ed/2015/04/20/forget-isis-what-do-islamophobes-really-want>.
59 Tabbaa, Mohamad, 'The terror of responsibility: are terrorists criminals?', *Sajjeling*, 13 October 2015, <sajjeling.com/2015/10/13/the-terror-of-responsibility-are-terrorists-criminals/>.
59 Breen-Smyth, Marie, 'Theorising the "suspect community": counter-terrorism, security practices and the public imagination', *Critical Studies on Terrorism*, 7:2, 2014, pp. 223–240.
60 McGarrity, Nicola and Blackbourn, Jessie, 'Australia has enacted 82 anti-terror laws since 2001. But tough laws alone can't eliminate terrorism', *The Conversation*, <theconversation.com/australia-has-enacted-82-anti-terror-laws-since-2001-but-tough-laws-alone-cant-eliminate-terrorism-123521>.
61 Beydoun, Khaled A, 'Trump's Counterterror programme', *Al Jazeera*, 26 January 2017, <www.aljazeera.com/indepth/opinion/2017/01/trump-counterterror-programme-muslim-americans-170125103202700.html>.
61 Commonwealth of Australia, *Counter-Terrorism White Paper: Securing Australia, Protecting Our Community*, Department of Prime Minister and Cabinet, Canberra, 2010.
61 Commonwealth of Australia, *Australia's National Counter-Terrorism Plan*, Canberra: Australia New Zealand Counter Terrorism Committee, Canberra, 2017.
62 Aly, Anne, 'Countering violent extremism, social harmony, community resilience and the potential of counter-narratives in the Australian context', in Baker-Beall,

Christopher, Heath-Kelly, Charlotte and Jarvis, Lee (eds), *Counter-Radicalisation: Critical Perspectives*, Routledge, London, 2014, pp. 71–87.

62   Aly, Anne, 'Report on Australia's first Countering Violent Extremism Symposium', *Journal of Policing, Intelligence and Counter Terrorism*, 10:1, 2015, pp. 34–38.

62   Ali, Nadya, 'Mapping the Muslim community: The politics of counter-radicalisation in Britain', in Baker-Beall, Christopher, Heath-Kelly, Charlotte and Jarvis, Lee (eds), *Counter-Radicalisation: Critical Perspectives*, Routledge, London, 2014, pp. 139–155, p. 147.

63   Tyrer, David and Sayyid, Salman, 'Governing ghosts: race, incorporeality and difference in post-political times', *Current Sociology*, 60:3, 2012, pp. 353–367.

63   Mamdani, Mahmood, *Good Muslim Bad Muslim*, Permanent Black, Delhi, 2007.

64   Mahmood, Saba, 'Secularism, hermeneutics, and empire: the politics of Islamic reformation', *Public Culture*, 18:2, 2006, pp. 323–347 at 330.

64   Rabasa, Angel, Benard, Cheryl, Schwartz, Lowell H and Sickle, Peter, *Building Moderate Muslim Networks*, RAND Corporation, Santa Monica, 2007.

65   Melamed, Jodi, *Represent and Destroy: Rationalizing Violence in the New Racial Capitalism*, University of Minnesota Press, Minneapolis, 2011.

66   Commonwealth of Australia, *Protecting Australia Against Terrorism*, Department of Prime Minister and Cabinet, Canberra, 2004.

66   Commonwealth of Australia, *Transnational Terrorism White Paper: The Threat to Australia*, Department of Prime Minister and Cabinet, Canberra, 2004.

67   'No tiptoeing around Islam problem: Abbott', SBS News, 29 May 2017, <www.sbs.com.au/news/no-tiptoeing-around-islam-problem-abbott>.

68   Murphy, Katharine, 'ASIO chief says radical Sunni Islam creates terrorists not being a refugee', *Guardian*, 31 May 2017, <www.theguardian.com/australia-news/2017/may/31/asio-chief-says-radical-sunni-islam-creates-terrorists-not-being-a-refugee>.

68   Alberici, Emma, 'Interview: Andrew Hastie, Liberal MP', ABC *Lateline*, 31 May 2017, <www.abc.net.au/lateline/interview:-andrew-hastie,-liberal-mp/8577672>.

68   Alberici, Emma, 'Interview: George Brandis, Attorney-General', ABC *Lateline*, 31 May 2017, <www.abc.net.au/lateline/interview:-george-brandis,-attorney-general/8577680>.

68   Jamil, Uzma, 'How Muslims became corn', *ReOrient*, 2:2, 2017, p. 175.

69   Alberici, Emma, 'Interview: Richard Barrett, counterterrorism expert', ABC *Lateline*, 5 June 2017, <www.abc.net.au/lateline/interview:-richard-barrett,-counter-terrorism-expert/8591592>.

70   Tabbaa, Mohamad, 'Wither ISIS: what do islamophobes really want?', *Sajjeling*, 6 October 2018.

74   Tyrer, David and Sayyid, Salman, 'Governing ghosts: race, incorporeality and difference in post-political times', *Current Sociology*, 60:3, 2012, pp. 353–367, p. 354.

74   'Closer watch on schools, mosques', *Sydney Morning Herald*, 25 August 2005, <www.smh.com.au/national/closer-watch-on-schools-mosques-20050825-gdlxxl.html>.

75   'Minister tells Muslims: accept Aussie values or "clear off"', ABC News,

24 August 2005, <www.abc.net.au/news/2005-08-24/minister-tells-muslims-accept-aussie-values-or/2088062>.

76   Department of Immigration and Multicultural Affairs, *Muslim Community Reference Group*, 2006, <web.archive.org/web/20060918235700/http://www.immi.gov.au/living-in-australia/a-diverse-australia/communities/MCRG/index.htm>.

76   Commonwealth of Australia, *National Action Plan to Build Social Cohesion, Harmony and Security*, Department of Immigration and Citizenship, Canberra, 2006.

Chapter 3: Reinforcing a suspect community

79   Australian Government, *Living Safe Together: Building Community Resilience to Violent Extremism*, <www.livingsafetogether.gov.au>.

80   O'Donnell, Aislinn, 'Contagious ideas: vulnerability, epistemic injustice and counter-terrorism in education,' *Educational Philosophy and Theory*, 50:10, 2018, pp. 981–997, p. 986.

80   Middlemiss, Nicola, 'Education minister pushes for "Aussie values"', *Educator*, 2017, <www.theeducatoronline.com/au/news/education-minister-pushes-for-aussie-values/242074>.

80   'Revoke passport for anti-Australian behaviour', news.com.au, 27 May 2015, <www.news.com.au/national/breaking-news/revoke-passport-for-anti-aust-behaviour/news-story/c5904396f3a0f5439d831f72d85b2254>

80   Sommers, Marc, *Youth and the Field of Countering Violent Extremism*, Promundo-US, Washington, DC, 2019.

81   Sentas, Victoria, *Traces of Terror: Counter-Terrorism Law, Policing, and Race*, Oxford University Press, Oxford, 2014, p. 19.

81   Kundnani, Arun and Hayes, Ben, *The Globalisation of Countering Violent Extremism Policies: Undermining Human Rights, Instrumentalising Civil Society*, Transnational Institute, Amsterdam, 2018, p. 3.

81   Australian Government, *Living Safe Together: Building Community Resilience to Violent Extremism*, <www.livingsafetogether.gov.au>.

82   Commonwealth of Australia, *Counter-Terrorism White Paper: Securing Australia, Protecting Our Community*, Department of Prime Minister and Cabinet, Canberra, 2010.

82   Sayyid, Salman, 'Thinking through Islamophobia', in Sayyid, Salman and Abdoolkarim, Vakil (eds), *Thinking Through Islamophobia: Global Perspectives*, Columbia University Press, New York, 2010, pp. 15–17.

82   Australian Government, Strong and Resilient Communities, <www.dss.gov.au/our-responsibilities/communities-and-vulnerable-people/strong-and-resilient-communities>.

83   Hizb ut-Tahrir, *Government Intervention in the Muslim Community*, Hizb ut-Tahrir, 2013.

84   Gillborn, David, *Racism and Education: Coincidence or Conspiracy*, Routledge, London, 2008.

85   McClelland, Robert, 'Media release: 'Youth Mentoring Grants program to counter violent extremism', Parliament House, Canberra, 13 November

2010, <parlinfo.aph.gov.au/parlInfo/download/media/pressrel/366825/ upload_binary/366825.pdf;fileType=application%2Fpdf#search=%22media/ pressrel/366825%22>.

86 Johns, Amelia, Grossman, Michele and McDonald, Kevin, '"More Than a Game": the impact of sport-based youth mentoring schemes on developing resilience toward violent extremism', *Social Inclusion*, 2:2, 2014, pp. 57–70.

87 'Imams told to correct false Koran use,' *Sydney Morning Herald*, 16 September 2006, <www.smh.com.au/national/imams-told-to-correct-false-koran-use-20060916-gdoelw.html>.

87 Bishop, Julie, 'ABC 730, Interview with Leigh Sales', Minister for Foreign Affairs, 5 June 2017, <www.foreignminister.gov.au/minister/julie-bishop/ transcript-eoe/abc-730-interview-leigh-sales-1>.

88 Davey, Melissa, 'Bourke Street attack: Morrison accused of "scapegoating" Muslim community', *Guardian*, 12 November 2018, <www.theguardian.com/ australia-news/2018/nov/12/bourke-street-attack-morrison-accused-of-scapegoating-muslim-community>.

88 Goldberg, David Theo, 'Neoliberalizing Race', *Macalester Civic Forum*, 1:1, article 14, 2007.

89 Idriss, Sherene, *Young Migrant Identities: Creativity and Masculinity*, Routledge, London, 2017.

90 Ali, Nadya, 'Mapping the Muslim community: The politics of counter-radicalisation in Britain', in Baker-Beall, Christopher, Heath-Kelly, Charlotte and Jarvis, Lee (eds), *Counter-Radicalisation: Critical Perspectives*, Routledge, London, 2014, pp. 139–155, p. 153.

90 Beydoun, Khaled A, 'The Islamaphobia nobody talks or knows about', *TRT World*, 12 October 2018, <www.trtworld.com/opinion/the-islamaphobia-nobody-talks-or-knows-about-20840>.

91 Sentas, Victoria, *Traces of Terror: Counter-Terrorism Law, Policing, and Race*, Oxford University Press, Oxford, 2014.

92 Kundnani, Arun, 'Radicalisation: the journey of a concept', *Race & Class*, 54:2 2012, pp. 3–25.

92 Smith, Cameron, 'Race and the logic of radicalisation under neoliberalism', *Journal of Sociology*, 54:1, 2018, pp. 92–107.

92 O'Donnell, Aislinn, 'Contagious ideas: vulnerability, epistemic injustice and counter-terrorism in education', *Educational Philosophy and Theory*, 50:10, 2018, pp. 981–997.

Chapter 4: The 'science' of extremism

98 Qureshi, Asim, *The Science of 'Pre-Crime': The Secret Radicalisation Study Underpinning Prevent*, CAGE Advocacy UK Ltd, London, 2016.

98 Martin, Thomas, 'Governing an unknowable future: the politics of Britain's Prevent policy', *Critical Studies on Terrorism*, 7:1, 2014, pp. 62–78.

99 Latham, Susie, 'Countering Violent Extremism training is institutionalising Islamophobia', Power to Persuade, 27 July 2018, <www.powertopersuade.org.au/ blog/countering-violent-extremism-training>.

99 Yassine, Lobna and Briskman, Linda, 'Islamophobia and social work collusion',

in Baines, Donna, Bennett, Bindi, Goodwin, Susan and Rawsthorne, Margot (eds), *Working Across Difference: Social Work, Social Policy and Social Justice*, Macmillan, 2019, pp. 55–70.

100 Harris-Hogan, Shandon, Barrelleh, Kate and Smith, Debra, 'The role of schools and education in countering violent extremism (CVE): applying lessons from Western countries to Australian CVE policy', *Oxford Review of Education*, 45:6, 2019, pp. 731–748.

100 Kundnani, Arun, *A Decade Lost: Rethinking Radicalisation and Extremism*, Claystone, London, 2015, p. 7.

100 Sian, Katy, 'Born radicals? Prevent, positivism, and 'racethinking', *Palgrave Communications*, 3, 2017, pp. 1–8.

100 Home Office, *Revised Prevent Duty Guidance: for England and Wales*, UK Government, 2015, <www.gov.uk/government/publications/prevent-duty-guidance/revised-prevent-duty-guidance-for-england-and-wales>, p. 21.

101 Australian Multicultural Foundation, *Community Awareness Training Manual: Building Resilience in the Community*, Counter-Terrorism Coordination Unit, Victoria Police, Melbourne, 2015, pp. 5, 14, 18.

102 Ballantyne, Robert, 'Jihadi watch plan poses ethical issues – union', *The Educator*, 26 May 2015, <www.theeducatoronline.com/au/news/jihadi-watch-plan-poses-ethical-issues--union/200757>.

102 Dellal, B Hass, 'Australia's responses to the radicalisation of immigrant youth', UWA Public Policy Institute, 7 June 2019, <www.news.uwa.edu.au/2019060711431/uwa-public-policy-institute/radicalisation-blog-series-australia-s-responses-radicalis>.

103 Commonwealth of Australia, *Counter-Terrorism White Paper: Securing Australia, Protecting Our Community*, Department of Prime Minister and Cabinet, Canberra, 2010.

106 Burke, Liz and Vickery, Kara, 'Grand Mufti in damage control after criticism over not condemning Paris attacks', news.com.au, 18 November 2015, <www.news.com.au/finance/work/leaders/grand-mufti-in-damage-control-after-criticism-over-not-condemning-paris-attacks/newsstory/bdbb9d00ad573c99dd9bbc45c3d57d9b>.

106 Owens, Jared and Kelly, Joe, 'Mufti slammed for pushing victim mentality', *Australian*, 17 November 2015, <www.theaustralian.com.au/in-depth/paris-terror-attacks/paris-attacksmufti-slammed-for-pushing-victim-mentality/news story/82149c151467f6d0ac97b3705c7ea218>.

106 Peatling, Stephanie, 'Minister Josh Frydenberg accuses Grand Mufti of a failure of leadership', *Sydney Morning Herald*, 28 November 2015, <www.smh.com.au/federal-politics/politicalnews/government-minister-accuses-grand-mufti-of-a-failure-of-leadership-20151128-glan0h>.

106 Safi, Michael, 'Five things Australia's grand mufti may or may not have said about the Paris attacks', *Guardian*, 19 November 2015, <www.theguardian.com/world/2015/nov/19/five-things-australia-grand-mufti-paris-attacks>.

106 Norton-Taylor, Richard, 'Former MI5 chief delivers damning verdict on Iraq invasion,' *Guardian*, 20 July 2010, <www.theguardian.com/uk/2010/jul/20/chilcot-mi5-boss-iraq-war>.

106   Sedgwick, Mark, 'The concept of radicalisation as a source of confusion',
      Terrorism and Political Violence, 22:4, 2010, p. 481.

107   Alberici, Emma, 'IS a reaction to unjust occupation', ABC *Lateline*, 8 October
      2014, <www.abc.net.au/lateline/is-a-reaction-to-unjust-occupation/5800196>.

107   Bourke, Latika, 'Tony Abbott backs Lateline host Emma Alberici over fiery Hizb
      ut-Tahrir interview', *Sydney Morning Herald*, 9 October 2014, <www.smh.com.
      au/politics/federal/tony-abbott-backs-lateline-host-emma-alberici-over-fiery-
      hizb-uttahrir-interview-20141009-113fxd.html>.

107   'Be alert but not alarmed', ABC *Q&A*, 22 September 2014, <www.abc.net.au/
      qanda/be-alert-but-not-alarmed/10656152>.

107   Bourke, Latika, 'ABC's Q&A could be used as Islamic State propaganda: Liberal
      MP Craig Kelly', *Sydney Morning Herald*, 24 September 2014, <www.smh.com.
      au/politics/federal/abcs-qa-could-be-used-as-islamic-state-propaganda-liberal-
      mp-craig-kelly-20140924-10l9qy.html>.

111   Sentas, Victoria, *Traces of Terror: Counter-Terrorism Law, Policing, and Race*,
      Oxford University Press, Oxford, 201, p. 120.

112   Nasser-Eddine, Minerva, Garnham, Bridget, Agostino, Katerina, & Caluya,
      Gilbert, 'Countering violent extremism (CVE) literature review, Counter
      Terrorism and Security Technology Centre, 2011, DSTO-TR-2522.

114   Foucault, Michel, *Abnormal: Lectures at the Collège de France 1974–1975*,
      Marchetti, Valerio and Salomoni, Antonella (eds), Picador, New York, 2003,
      p. 19.

115   Tabbaa, Mohamad, 'The terror of responsibility: are terrorists criminals?',
      Sajjeling, 13 October 2015, <sajjeling.com/2015/10/13/the-terror-of-
      responsibility-are-terrorists-criminals/>.

115   'Muslim public schoolboys "excused" from shaking hands with women', National
      9 News, <www.facebook.com/watch/?v=427538397591862>.

116   'Muslim Schoolboys allowed to refuse women's handshakes', news.com.au,
      20 February 2017, <www.news.com.au/lifestyle/parenting/school-life/muslim-
      schoolboys-allowedto-refuse-womens-handshakes/news-story/4d8384afed9ff684
      c971d872b735b38b>.

116   Seymour, Bryan, 'Muslim Students at NSW public school allowed to refuse to
      shake hands with women', Yahoo News, 20 February 2017,.

Chapter 5: Free speech and angry youth

119–120 Bond, Chelsea, 'The audacity of anger', *Guardian*, <www.theguardian.com/
         commentisfree/2018/jan/31/the-audacity-of-anger>.

120   Harris, Anita, *Future Girl: Young Women in the Twenty-First Century*, Routledge,
      London, 2004.

121   Australian Government, *Preventing Violent Extremism and Radicalisation in
      Australia*, Attorney-General's Department, 2015 <www.livingsafetogether.gov.au/
      information/Documents/preventing-violent-extremism-and-radicalisation-in-
      australia.PDF>. The booklet was originally titled *Radicalisation Awareness Kit*.

123   Henebery, Brett, 'In schools, radical thought is not always a bad thing', *The

Educator, 23 July 2015, <www.theeducatoronline.com/au/news/in-schools-radical-thought-is-notalways-a-bad-thing/203010>.

124 'Teachers to enter war on teen radicalisation', *Daily Telegraph*, 21 September 2015.

124 Safi, Michael, 'Anti-radicalisation kit never meant for use in schools, says key author', *Guardian*, 25 September 2015, <www.theguardian.com/australia-news/2015/sep/25/anti-radicalisation-awareness-kit-never-meant-for-use-in-schools-says-key-author>.

124 Safi, Michael, 'Radicalisation Awareness Kit: schools warned not to jump to conclusions', *Guardian*, 22 September 2015, <www.theguardian.com/australia-news/2015/sep/22/radicalisation-awareness-kit-schools-warned-not-to-jump-to-conclusions>.

124 Triggs, Gillian, 'Laa Chol and racist fear', *Saturday Paper*, 28 July 2018, <www.thesaturdaypaper.com.au/opinion/topic/2018/07/28/laa-chol-and-racist-fear/15327000006610>.

124 NSW Ombudsman, *The Consorting Law: Report on the Operation of Part 3A, Division 7 of the* Crimes Act 1900, April 2016.

124 Police Accountability Project, 'Predictable, ineffective and dangerous: impacts of anti-association laws', 30 July 2018, <www.policeaccountability.org.au/racial-profiling/predictable-ineffective-and-dangerous-impacts-of-anti-association-laws/>.

125 'Australians' trust in government reaches new all-time low, study shows', SBS News, 11 December 2019, <www.sbs.com.au/news/australians-trust-in-government-reaches-new-all-time-low-study-shows>.

127 Faruqi, Osman, 'Australia is tearing down another woman of colour for daring to have an opinion', *Junkee*, 31 January 2018, <junkee.com/tarneen-onus-williams-media-target/144455>.

127 'Andrews troubled by Muslim rage areas', *Australian*, 8 June 2017, <www.theaustralian.com.au/nation/nation/muslim-leaders-want-taxpayerfunded-space-to-rage-for-young-men/news-story/bc7aff371df6c07b190a3bddb21bfa03>.

128 'Muslim youth "safe places" not "rage rooms": Islamic Council responds after Andrews, Hanson criticism', SBS News, 8 June 2017, <www.sbs.com.au/news/muslim-youth-safe-places-not-rage-rooms-islamic-council-responds-after-andrews-hanson-criticism>.

128 'Violent Salt artist Abdul Abdullah enrages RSL, George Christensen with depictions of soldiers', ABC News, 9 December 2019, <www.abc.net.au/news/2019-12-09/outrage-soldier-artwork-violent-salt-mackay/11746680>.

131 Moraro, Piero, 'Animal rights activists in Melbourne: green-collar criminals or civil "disobedients"?' *The Conversation*, 9 April 2019, <theconversation.com/animal-rights-activists-in-melbourne-green-collar-criminals-or-civil-disobedients-115119>.

131 Morrison, Scott, 'Address 2019 Queensland Resources Council Annual Lunch', Prime Minister of Australia, 1 November 2019, <www.pm.gov.au/media/address-2019-queensland-resources-council-annual-lunch>.

131 Karp, Paul, 'Scott Morrison threatens crackdown on protesters who would "deny liberty"', *Guardian*, 1 November 2019, <www.theguardian.com/australia-

news/2019/nov/01/scott-morrison-threatens-crackdown-on-secondary-boycotts-of-mining-companies>.

131 Scott Morrison tells students striking over climate change to be "less activist"', *Guardian*, 26 November 2018, <www.theguardian.com/environment/2018/nov/26/scott-morrison-tells-students-striking-over-climate-change-to-be-less-activist>.

132 'Education Minister Dan Tehan lashes orchestrated student climate strikes', SBS News, 18 February 2019, <www.sbs.com.au/news/education-minister-dan-tehan-lashes-orchestrated-student-climate-strikes>.

132 'Hundreds of thousands attend school climate strike rallies across Australia', *Guardian*, 20 September 2019, <www.theguardian.com/environment/2019/sep/20/hundreds-of-thousands-attend-school-climate-strike-rallies-across-australia>.

133 Thunberg, Greta, 'School strike for climate – save the world by changing the rules', TEDxStockholm, November 2018, <www.ted.com/talks/greta_thunberg_school_strike_for_climate_save_the_world_by_changing_the_rules/transcript?language=en>.

134 Editorial team, 'The BDS and Victoria Police', *Overland Literary Journal*, 16 August 2011, <overland.org.au/2011/08/the-bds-and-victoria-police/>.

134 Smith, Cameron, 'Race and the logic of radicalisation under neoliberalism', *Journal of Sociology*, 54:1, 2018, pp. 92–107 at p. 101.

135 De Genova, Nicholas, 'Antiterrorism, race, and the new frontier: American exceptionalism, imperial multiculturalism, and the global security state', *Identities: Global Studies in Culture and Power*, 17:6, 2010, pp. 613–640, p. 615.

Chapter 6: Profiling in schools

138 Australian Associated Press, 'NSW schools to be trained in countering student radicalisation', *Guardian*, 2 November 2015, <www.theguardian.com/australia-news/2015/nov/02/nsw-schools-to-be-trained-in-countering-student-radicalisation>.

138 NSW Government, 'Countering violent extremism', press release, 2 November 2015, <www.nsw.gov.au/your-government/the-premier/media-releases-from-the-premier/countering-violent-extremism/>.

138 Work Health and Safety, *School Communities Working Together*, NSW Department of Education and Communities, 2016.

138 Ballantyne, Robert, 'Govt beefs up anti-radicalisation support for schools', *The Educator*, 8 February 2016, <www.theeducatoronline.com/k12/news/govt-beefs-up-antiradicalisation-support-for-schools/211490>.

141 NSW Government, *Responding to Anti-Social and Extremist Behaviour*, Legal Issues Bulletin 57, <education.nsw.gov.au/about-us/rights-and-accountability/legal-issues-bulletins/bulletin-57-responding-to-anti-social-and-extremist-behaviour>.

142 Tyrer, David, & Sayyid, Salman, 'Governing ghosts: race, incorporeality and difference in post-political times', *Current Sociology*, 60:3, pp. 353–367 at p. 362.

143 NSW Government, 'School Communities Working Together: fact sheet for students', 8 September 2017, <www.education.nsw.gov.au/content/dam/main-

education/student-wellbeing/whole-school-approach/media/documents/School-Communities-working-together-fact-sheet_students.pdf>.

143 Alberici, Emma, 'Foreign Minister Julie Bishop talks about the London terror attacks', ABC *Lateline*, 5 June 2017, <www.abc.net.au/7.30/foreign-minister-julie-bishop-talks-about-the/8591460>.

145 Sentas, Victoria, *Traces of Terror: Counter-Terrorism Law, Policing, and Race*, Oxford University Press, Oxford, 2014, p. 8.

Chapter 7: Taming 'junior jihadis'

146 OnePath Network, *A Year in Review: Islam in the Media*, 2017, <www.onepathnetwork.com/islam-in-the-media-2017/>.

147 Balogh, Stefanie, 'Teachers 'must ID radical students,' *Australian*, 9 June 2017.

147 Dib, Jihad, 'School transformation – our students are worth it', TEDxSydney, 26 April 2014, <tedxsydney.com/talk/school-transformation-our-students-are-worth-it-jihad-dib/>.

147 'Principal Jihad Dib of Sydney's Punchbowl Boys High School is a study in success', *Sydney Morning Herald*, 15 August 2014, <www.smh.com.au/national/nsw/principal-jihad-dib-of-sydneys-punchbowl-boys-high-school-is-a-study-in-success-20140723-zw0nv.html>.

148 Urban, Rebecca, 'Exclusive: troubled Punchbowl Boys High School leadership team dumped', *Australian*, 3 March 2017, <www.theaustralian.com.au/nation/education/troubled-punchbowl-boys-high-school-leadership-team-dumped/news-story/d39b8b2dd42f19d770e15d4f6d16ef70>.

148 'Principal sacked for excluding women', *Daily Telegraph*, 3 March 2017, <www.dailytelegraph.com.au/news/nsw/school-leadership-sacked-for-excluding-female-staff-from-events/news-story/d9b0c0a060a799a8256c64b450c3b0b4>.

148 Bye, Clarissa, 'Cops feared boys being radicalised', *Daily Telegraph*, 4 March 2017.

148 Frost, Carleen, 'Hard-line principal's school is "off rails"', *Daily Telegraph*, 7 March 2017.

149 Urban, Rebecca, '19 schools in anti-extremist project', Australian, 10 March 2017, <www.theaustralian.com.au/nation/education/19-schools-in-nsw-antiextremist-project-as-principal-threatened/news-story/84123f7bbd2a30aa06bd3de4834a06df>.

150 Bolt, Andrew, 'Race on to surrender a culture', *Daily Telegraph*, 6 March 2017.

150 Magnay, Jacquelin, 'Scandals fail to hinder a minister's tour at Oxford', *Australian*, 9 March 2017.

150 'Editorial: A lesson on absent leadership: Who will stand up for fundamental Australian values?' *Australian*, 10 March 2017.

151 McDonough, Keely, 'A class war on terror threat', *Daily Telegraph*, 10 March 2017.

151 'Punchbowl parents vent their fury', *Daily Telegraph*, 10 March 2017; 'New evidence that terror training starts in high school', Ten News 5 pm, 10 March 2017.

151 Hennessy, Annabel and Clennell, Andrew, 'Shake it off', *Daily Telegraph*, 11 March 2017.

152 Maley, Paul and Khalik, Jennine, 'Inside Punchbowl Boys High School: a battle for hearts and minds', *Weekend Australian*, 11 March 2017.

153   Clennell, Andrew, 'Allah Allah Allah, Oi Oi Oi', *Daily Telegraph*, 13 March 2017.

153   Said, Edward W, *Covering Islam: How the Media and the Experts Determine How We See the Rest of the World*, Vintage Books, New York, 1997.

153   Urban, Rebecca, 'Schools' radical program "a stigma"', *Australian*, 13 March 2017.

153–154 McDonough, Keely, 'Behead of the class', *Daily Telegraph*, 16 Mar 2017.

154   McDonough, Keely, 'The unholy terrors', *Daily Telegraph*, 16 March 2017.

154   Deutrom, Rhian, 'Department told minister of move on school heads', *Australian*, 17 March 2017.

154   'Punchbowl's blind eye to violence', *Daily Telegraph*, 20 March 2017.

155   Hennessy, Annabel, 'School a radical swamp for years', *Daily Telegraph*, 14 March 2017.

155   'Lessons of hate', *60 Minutes*, 18 March 2017.

156   'Former prefect to *60 Minutes*: "This is what parents should fear at school"', Kidspot, 17 March 2017, <www.kidspot.com.au/parenting/real-life/in-the-news/former-prefect-to-60-minutes-this-is-what-parents-should-fear-at-school/news-story/7d9bfd2a676cf7b272a8ab19cf411f59>.

156   Hirsi Ali, Ayaan, 'A broad focus to tackle fundamentalism', *Daily Telegraph*, 27 March 2017.

158   Silmalis, Linda, 'Scandal-ridden school's radical change – Punchbowl Boys High', *Sunday Telegraph*, 11 March 2018.

Chapter 8: Velcro bodies

163   Abdel-Fattah, Randa, *Islamophobia and Everyday Multiculturalism*, Routledge, Abingdon, Oxon, 2018.

170   Ahmed, Sara, *The Cultural Politics of Emotion*, Edinburgh University Press, Edinburgh, 2004.

172   Aly, Ramy, *Becoming Arab in London*, Pluto Press, London, 2015, p. 1.

172   Idriss, Sherene, *Young Migrant Identities: Creativity and Masculinity*, Routledge, London, 2017.

174   Iner, Derya (ed.), *Islamophobia in Australia 2014–2016*, Charles Sturt University and ISRA, Sydney, 2017.

174   Iner, Derya (ed.), *Islamophobia in Australia Report II (2016–2017)*, Charles Sturt University and ISRA, Sydney, 2019.

174   Human Rights and Equal Opportunity Commission, *Isma*-listen: National Consultations on Eliminating Prejudice against Arab and Muslim Australians*, Australian Human Rights Commission, Sydney, 2003.

177   Mythen, Gabe, Walklate, Sandra and Khan, Fatima, 'I'm a Muslim But I'm Not a Terrorist: Victimization, Risky Identities and the Performance of Safety', *British Journal of Criminology*, 49:6, pp. 736–754.

178   Hussein, Shakira, *From Victims to Suspects: Muslim Women since 9/11*, NewSouth Publishing, Sydney, 2016.

Chapter 9: The Muslim performance

190   Hylton, Kevin, 'I'm not joking! The strategic use of humour in stories of racism', *Ethnicities*, 18:3, pp. 327–343, 2018, p. 327.

193   Sills, Liz, 'Hashtag comedy: from Muslim rage to #MuslimRage', *ReOrient*, 2:2, 2017, pp. 160–174 at p. 16.

193 Winkler Reid, Sarah, 'Making fun out of difference: ethnicity–race and humour in a London school', *Ethnos*, 80:1, 2015, pp. 23–44 at p. 23.

197 For a comprehensive overview of the body of scholarship regarding 'of Middle Eastern Appearance' see: Al-Natour, Ryan, '"Of Middle Eastern appearance" is a flawed racial profiling descriptor', *Current Issues in Criminal Justice*, 29:2, 2017, p. 107.

197 Ahmed, Sara, *The Cultural Politics of Emotion*, Edinburgh University Press, Edinburgh, 2004.

198 Said, Edward W, *Orientalism*, Penguin, London, 2007.

198 Said, Edward W, *Culture and Imperialism*, Vintage Books, New York, 1994.

198 Said, Edward W, *Covering Islam: How the Media and the Experts Determine How We See the Rest of the World*, Vintage Books, New York, 1997.

198 Shaheen, Jack G, *Reel Bad Arabs: How Hollywood Vilifies a People*, rev. edn, Olive Branch Press, Interlink Publishing Group, New York, 2012.

198 Shaheen, Jack G, *Guilty: Hollywood's Verdict on Arabs After 9/11*, Olive Branch Press, Interlink Publishing Group, Northampton, MA, 2012.

198 Krayem, Mehal, *Heroes, Villains and the Muslim Exception: Muslim and Arab Men in Australian Crime Drama*, Melbourne University Press, Carlton, Vic, 2017.

198 Hage, Ghassan, *White Nation: Fantasies of White Supremacy in a Multicultural Society*, Pluto Press, Annandale, NSW, 1999.

198 Breen-Smyth, Marie, Theorising the "suspect community": counter-terrorism, security practices and the public imagination, Critical Studies on Terrorism, 7:2, 2014, pp. 223–240.

198 Poynting, Scott, Noble, Greg, Tabar, Paul and Collins, Jack, *Bin Laden in the Suburbs: Criminalising the Arab Other*, Institute of Criminology, Sydney, 2004.

198 Poynting, Scott and Mason, Victoria, 'The resistible rise of Islamophobia: anti-Muslim racism in the UK and Australia before 11 September 2001', *Journal of Sociology*, 43:1, 2007, pp. 61–86.

198 Hussein, Shakira and Poynting, Scott, 'We're not multicultural, but …', *Journal of Intercultural Studies*, 38:3, 2017, pp. 333–348.

198 Abdel-Fattah, Randa, *Islamophobia and Everyday Multiculturalism*, Routledge, Abingdon, Oxon, 2018.

198 Poynting, Scott and Mason, Victoria, 'The new integrationism, the state and Islamophobia: retreat from multiculturalism in Australia', *International Journal of Law, Crime and Justice*, 36:4, 2008, pp. 230–246.

201 Aly, Ramy, *Becoming Arab in London*, Pluto Press, London, 2015.

202 Human Rights and Equal Opportunity Commission, *Isma*-listen: National Consultations on Eliminating Prejudice against Arab and Muslim Australians*, Australian Human Rights Commission, Sydney, 2003.

213 Bhabha, Homi K, *The Location of Culture*, Routledge, 1994, pp. 85–92.

213 For further reading on Australian national identity, see Flynn, Eugenia, 'Australian national identity: white patriarchy through the ANZAC legend, ACRAWSA, 27 April 2018, <acrawsa.org.au/2018/04/27/australian-national-identity-white-patriarchy-through-the-anzac-legend/>; Nicoll, Fiona, From Diggers to Drag Queens: Configurations of Australian National Identity, Pluto Press, Sydney, 2001.

Chapter 10: 'Gen Y jihadists'

216 Rice, Deborah, 'Epping Boys High School student investigated by counter-terrorism police over allegations radical Islam is preached in schoolyard', *Daily Telegraph*, 24 July 2015, <www.dailytelegraph.com.au/newslocal/counter-terrorism-police-investigate-epping-boys-high-student-over-preaching-in-the-playground/news-story/ca3b5cc42067a99a026a2d33f760e762>.

216 Olding, Rachel, 'Radicalisation of pupils: Epping Boys High not the only school investigated by police', *Sydney Morning Herald*, 24 July 2015.

218 Law, James and Wires, 'Police seeing extremism in kids "as young as 14",' news.com.au, 24 July 2015, <www.news.com.au/lifestyle/parenting/school-life/police-seeing-extremism-in-kids-as-young-as-14/news-story/e54266f50ee33b139171fdaa913c6b07>.

218 Rice, Deborah, Ryan, Brad, Santow, Simon, 'Epping Boys High School student investigated by counter-terrorism police over allegations radical Islam is preached in schoolyard', ABC News, 24 July 2015, <www.abc.net.au/news/2015-07-24/police-probe-claims-radical-islam-preached-at-sydney-school/6644696?height=467&ratio=3x2&width=700&pfm=ms>.

218 'Jihadi watch: schools plan to teach students and teachers how to spot terrorists', news.com.au, 24 May 2015, <www.news.com.au/lifestyle/parenting/school-life/jihadi-watch-schools-plan-to-teach-students-and-teachers-how-to-spot-terrorists/news-story/9d8d6a30ea5733908fcd860470259a83>.

219 Australian Government, *Review of Australia's Counter-Terrorism Machinery*, Commonwealth of Australia, January 2015, <www.homeaffairs.gov.au/nat-security/files/review-australia-ct-machinery.pdf>.

219 Jennings, Paul (ed.), *Gen Y Jihadists: Preventing Radicalisation in Australia*, Australian Strategic Policy Institute, Barton, ACT, June 2015.

219 NSW Government, 'Countering extremism in public schools', 29 July 2015, <www.nsw.gov.au/your-government/the-premier/media-releases-from-the-premier/2016/10/countering-extremism-in-public-schools/>.

219 Partridge, Emma and Olding, Rachel, 'Principals urged to report extremist behaviour to NSW Government hotline', *Sydney Morning Herald*, 28 July 2015, https://www.smh.com.au/education/principals-urged-to-report-extremist-behaviour-to-nsw-government-hotline-20150728-gim5nv.html

219 'NSW school prayer groups audited for extremist ideology', *BBC News*, 28 July 2015, <www.bbc.com/news/world-australia-33684960>.

220 'Probe into ISIS subversion of Aussie schools', *Straits Times*, 29 July 2015, <www.straitstimes.com/asia/australianz/probe-into-isis-subversion-at-aussie-schools>.

220 Olding, Rachel, 'Prayer group audit at NSW schools reveals guidelines not followed', *Sydney Morning Herald*, 2 September 2015, <www.smh.com.au/national/nsw/prayer-group-audit-at-nsw-schools-reveals-guidelines-not-followed-20150902-gjdht1.html>.

224 DiAngelo, Robin, *White Fragility: Why It's So Hard for White People to Talk about Racism*, Beacon Press, Boston, MA, 2018.

224 Hamad, Ruby, *White Tears, Brown Scars*, Melbourne University Press, Carlton, Vic, 2019.

Chapter 11: Narrating class

226 Itaoui, Rhonda, 'The geography of Islamophobia in Sydney: mapping the spatial imaginaries of young Muslims', *Australian Geographer*, 47:3, 2016, pp. 261–279.

227 Noble, Greg and Poynting, Scott, 'White lines: the intercultural politics of everyday movement in social spaces', *Journal of Intercultural Studies*, 31, 2010, pp. 489–505.

228 Abood, Paula, 'Seeing rape through race-coloured glasses: Sydney c: 2000', in Dreher, Tanja and Ho, Christina (eds), *Beyond the Hijab Debates: New Conversations on Gender, Race and Religion*, Cambridge Scholars Publishing, Newcastle, 2009, pp. 118–133.

228 Daglistanli, Selga, 'Like a pack of wild animals: moral panics around "ethnic" gang rape in Sydney', in Poynting, Scott and Morgan, George (eds), *Outrageous! Moral Panics in Australia*, ACYS Press, Hobart, 2007, pp. 180–195.

228 Dagistanli, Selga and Grewal, Kiran, 'Perverse Muslim masculinities in contemporary orientalist discourse: the vagaries of Muslim immigration in the West', in Morgan, George and Poynting, Scott (eds) *Global Islamophobia: Muslims and Moral Panic in the West*, Ashgate, Surrey, UK, 2012, pp. 119–142.

229 Collins, Jock, Noble, Greg, Poynting, Scott and Tabar, Paul, *Kebabs, Kids, Cops and Crime: Youth Ethnicity and Crime*, Pluto Press, Sydney, 2000. See also Poynting, Scott, Noble, Greg and Tabar, Paul, 'Middle Eastern appearances: 'ethnic gangs', moral panic and media framing', *Australian and New Zealand Journal of Criminology*, 34:1, 2001, pp. 67–90, 2001; Poynting, Scott, Noble, Greg and Tabar, Paul, 'Protest masculinity and Lebanese youth in western Sydney: an ethnographic study', in Tomsen, Stephen and Donaldson, Mike (eds), *Male Trouble: Looking at Australian Masculinities*, Pluto Press, North Melbourne, Vic, 2003, pp. 132–55; Poynting, Scott, Noble, Greg, Tabar, Paul and Collins, Jack, *Bin Laden in the Suburbs: Criminalising the Arab Other*, Institute of Criminology, Sydney, 2004; Tabar, Paul, '"Habibs' in Australia: language, identity and masculinity", *Journal of Intercultural Studies*, 28:2, 2007, pp. 157–172.

230 Al-Natour, Ryan, 'The constructions of Sydney's "Muslim ghettoes"', *Contemporary Islam*, 9:2, pp. 2015, pp. 131–147.

233 Amin, Ash, *Land of Strangers*, Polity Press, Cambridge, MA, 2012.

239 Ahmad, Michael Mohammed, 'The origin of Leb', in Abdel-Fattah, Randa and Saleh, Sara (eds), *Arab, Australian Other: Stories on Race and Identity*, Picador, Sydney, 2019, pp. 123–146 at p. 124.

239 Abdel-Fattah, Randa, *Ten Things I Hate About Me*, Pan Macmillan, Sydney, 2007.

241 Idriss, Sherene, *Young Migrant Identities: Creativity and Masculinity*, Routledge, London, 2017.

Chapter 12: Risky speech

247 'Blackouts, childcare and migration', ABC *Q&A*, 13 February 2017, <www.youtube.com/watch?v=8gINbYZFZoA>.

247 'Activist Yassmin Abdel-Magied "blind" to Islam's Treatment of Women', *Australian*, 17 February 2017, <www.theaustralian.com.au/nation/politics/activist-yassmin-abdelmagied-blind-to-islams-treatment-of-women/news-story/b9312e18fb0601744abdc86732c9351b>.

248 'More than 200000 words published about Yassmin Abdel-Magied since Last Anzac Day', *Crikey*, 27 April 2018, <www.crikey.com.au/2018/04/26/more-than-200000-words-published-about-yassmin-abdel-magied-since-last-anzac-day/>.

248 Abdel-Fattah, Randa and Krayem, Mehal, 'Off script and indefensible: The failure of the 'moderate Muslim', *Continuum*, 32(4), 429–443, 2018.

249 Flynn, Eugenia, 'Australian national identity: White patriarchy through the Anzac legend, Australian Critical Race and Whiteness Studies Association, 27 April 2018, <acrawsa.org.au/2018/04/27/australian-national-identity-white-patriarchy-through-the-anzac-legend/>.

249 Abood, Paula, 'One upon a time in the diaspora', in Abdel-Fattah, Randa and Saleh, Sara (eds), *Arab, Australian, Other: Stories on Race and Identity*, Picador, Sydney, 2019, pp. 71–81.

251 'Stranger than Fiction', ABC *Q&A*, 20 August 2018, <www.abc.net.au/qanda/stranger-than-fiction/10648460>.

256 Cook, Henrietta, 'What have I done wrong?': students falsely reported over terrorism', *Age*, 13 April 2019, <www.theage.com.au/national/victoria/what-have-i-done-wrong-students-falsely-reported-over-terrorism-20190412-p51dpe.html>.

257 Mythen, Gabe, Walklate, Sandra, and Khan, Fatima, '"Why should we have to prove we're alright?": Counter-terrorism, risk and partial securities', *Sociology*, 47:2, 2012, pp. 383–398.

257 Cherney, Adrian and Murphy, Kristina, 'Being a 'suspect community' in a post 9/11 world – The impact of the war on terror on Muslim communities in Australia', *Australian and New Zealand Journal of Criminology*, 49:4, 2015, pp. 480–496.

257 Maira, Sunaina Marr, *The 9/11 Generation: Youth, Rights, and Solidarity in the War on Terror*, Duke University Press, Durham, NC, 2009.

265 Morrison, Scott, 'Australia-Israel Chamber of Commerce speech', 19 March 2019, <www.pm.gov.au/media/australia-israel-chamber-commerce-speech>.

268 Hage, Ghassan, 'Dear White, It's OK to be white', *Cordite Poetry Review*, 2019, <cordite.org.au/essays/dear-white-its-ok-to-be-white/?fbclid=IwAR2Qob0Tpy MVpon2RtwL9XiX7bqRCD4xh3ehsmrHzEteYpfTMN2CiB-Xsc>.

269 Abdel-Fattah, Randa, *Islamophobia and Everyday Multiculturalism*, Routledge, Oxon, 2018.

Chapter 13: Teachers and curricular justice

270 hooks, bell, *Teaching to transgress: education as the practice of freedom*, Routledge, New York, 1994.

273 hooks, bell, *The Will to Change: Men, Masculinity, and Love*, Simon and Schuster, New York, 2004.

277 Connell, Raewynn, 'Good teachers on dangerous ground: towards a new view of teacher quality and professionalism', *Critical Studies in Education*, 50:3, 2009, pp. 213–229.

282 Dunn, Kevin, Lean, Garth, Watkins, Megan and Noble, Greg, 'The visibility of racism: perceptions of cultural diversity and multicultural education in state schools', *International Journal Of Organizational Diversity*, 15:1, 2014, pp. 17–29.

282 Watkins, Megan, Lean, Garth and Noble, Greg, 'Multicultural education: the state of play from an Australian perspective', *Race Ethnicity and Education*, 19:1, 2016, pp. 46–66.

283 Iner, Derya (ed.) *Islamophobia in Australia 2014–2106*, Charles Sturt University and ISRA, Sydney, 2017.

283 Iner, Derya (ed.) *Islamophobia in Australia II (2016–2018)*, Charles Sturt University and ISRA, Sydney, 2019.

283 Ahmed, Sara, *On Being Included: Racism and Diversity in Institutional Life*, Duke University Press, Durham, NC, 2014, p. 44.

283 Markus, Andrew, *Mapping Social Cohesion: The Scanlon Foundation Surveys*, Scanlon Foundation, Caulfield East, Vic, 2019, <scanlonfoundation.org.au/current-research/>.

284 Oubani, Dalal and Oubani, HM, 'Ensuring curricular justice in the NSW education system', *International Education Journal: Comparative Perspectives*, 13:1, 2014, pp. 30–45.

285 Moreton-Robinson, Aileen, 'The white man's burden: patriarchal white epistemic violence and Aboriginal women's knowledges within the academy'. *Australian Feminist Studies*, 26:70, 2011, pp. 413–431.

286 Ladson-Billings, Gloria, 'Just what is critical race theory and what's it doing in a nice field like education?', *International Journal of Qualitative Studies in Education*, 11:1, 1998, pp. 7–24 at p. 18.

286 Ladson-Billings, Gloria, 'Toward a theory of culturally relevant pedagogy', *American Educational Research Journal*, 32:3 Autumn, 1995, pp. 465–491.

286 Bhambra, Gurminder K, *Rethinking Modernity: Postcolonialism and the Sociological Imagination*, Palgrave Macmillan, London, 2007, p. 149.

287 Bodkin-Andrews, Gawaian and Carlson, Bronwyn, 'The legacy of racism and Indigenous Australian identity within education', *Race Ethnicity and Education*, 19:4, 2016, pp. 784–807, 2016, p. 789.

288 Tuck, Eve, and Yang, K Wayne, 'Decolonization is not a metaphor', *Decolonization: Indigeneity, Education & Society*, 1:1, 2012, pp. 1–40.

289 Trouillot, Michel-Rolph, *Silencing the Past: Power and the Production of History*, Beacon Press, Boston, MA, 1995.

289 Said, Edward W, *Culture and Imperialism*, Vintage Books, New York, 1993.

291 Hassim, Eeqbal and Cole-Adams, Jennet, *Learning from One Another: Bringing Muslim Perspectives into Australian Schools*, National Centre of Excellence for Islamic Studies, Melbourne, 2010, p. 1.

292 Caluya, Gilbert, 'Decolonising Asian Australia: towards a Critical Asian Australian Studies for the 21st century,' keynote lecture for the 7th Asian Australian Identities Conference, Genealogies of Identity Politics, Immigration Museum, 7 November 2019, Immigration Museum.

293 Kamp, A., & Mansouri, Fethi, 'Constructing inclusive education in a neo-liberal context: Promoting inclusion of Arab-Australian students in an Australian context', British Educational Research Journal, 36(5), 733-744, 2010.

294 Lentin, Alana, 'Racism in public or public racism: doing anti-racism in 'post-racial' times', *Ethnic and Racial Studies*, 2016, 39:1, 2016, pp. 33–48.

294 Davies, Larissa McLean, Martin, Susan K, and Buzacott, Lucy, 'Worldly reading:

teaching Australian literature in the twenty-first century', *English in Australia*, 52:3, 2017, pp. 21–30.

295 NSW Government, 'School Communities Working Together: fact sheet for students', 8 September 2017, <www.education.nsw.gov.au/content/dam/main-education/student-wellbeing/whole-school-approach/media/documents/School-Communities-working-together-fact-sheetstudents.pdf>.

295 Mansouri, Fethi and Jenkins, Louise, 'Schools as sites of race relations and intercultural tension', *Australian Journal of Teacher Education*, 35:7, 2010, pp. 93–108.

298 Harris, Anita and Hussein, Shakira, 'Conscripts or volunteers? Young Muslims as everyday explainers', *Journal of Ethnic and Migration Studies*, August 2018.

Conclusion: Referred pain

304 Mitchell, Georgina, 'NSW Police ordered to apologise for vilifying Arabs in terror exercise', *Sydney Morning Herald*, 2 May 2019, <www.smh.com.au/national/nsw/nsw-police-ordered-to-apologise-for-vilifying-arabs-in-terror-exercise-20190502-p51jfd.html>.

306 Coppock, Vicki, 'Can you spot a terrorist in your classroom?', *Global Studies of Childhood*, 4:2, 2014, pp. 1–18.

307 'Broadside', ABC *Q&A*, 4 November 2019, <www.abc.net.au/qanda/2019-04-11/11646878>.

310 Barreto, Marianna Belalba, Benedict, Josef, Perera, Dom, Leão, Débora, Mbataru, Sylvia and Severen, Ine Van, *CIVICUS: People Power Under Attack*, CIVICUS Monitor, December 2019, <civicus.contentfiles.net/media/assets/file/GlobalReport2019.pdf>.

INDEX

Index

Index